ANCIENT &
MEDIEVAL
Wargaming

ANCIENT & MEDIEVAL Wargaming

NEIL THOMAS

SUTTON PUBLISHING

First published in the United Kingdom in 2007 by
Sutton Publishing, an imprint of NPI Media Group Limited
Cirencester Road · Chalford · Stroud · Gloucestershire · GL6 8PE

British Library Cataloguing in Publication Data
A catalogue record for this book is available from the British Library.

ISBN 978-0-7509-4572-1

Typeset in 10.5/14pt Swis721.
Typesetting and origination by
NPI Media Group Limited.
Printed and bound in England.

Contents

Acknowledgements

I would like to start by thanking my father, Kaye Thomas, for typing the manuscript of this book. Also to everyone at Sutton Publishing for their efforts, especially Nick Reynolds, Julia Fenn and Jonathan Falconer.

This book has benefited greatly from the magnificent colour photographs that grace the plate section. The battle scenes were provided by *Miniature Wargames*® magazine, for which I would like to thank editor Iain Dickie and photographer Richard Ellis. I am also very fortunate to have been supplied some images by master figure painters Kevin Dallimore, Paul Baker (Brush Strokes) and Gerard Cronin (GJM Figurines).

Finally, any writers on Ancient and Medieval wargaming must record their debt to Phil Barker and other members of the Wargames Research Group. Without their pioneering work over the last forty years the hobby would be sorely diminished, both in size and in scope.

Key to Symbols

The illustrations of unit deployments in the army lists and battle reports, utilise various symbols to depict different troop types. They are defined below:

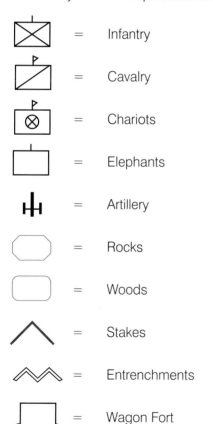

= Infantry

= Cavalry

= Chariots

= Elephants

= Artillery

= Rocks

= Woods

= Stakes

= Entrenchments

= Wagon Fort

Introduction

This book represents a sequel to and development of my earlier work, *Wargaming: An Introduction* (also published by Sutton). While my previous book covered all periods of wargaming by providing rules and an appropriate selection of army lists, this one specialises in the Ancient and Medieval periods. The aim is to provide a much more comprehensive examination of one of the most exciting epochs of wargaming, by greatly expanding the numbers of army lists, and providing some historical perspective.

One major change from my last book lies in the number of rulesets. I felt that the nuances of this epoch are best covered by four different sets of rules for each defined period: the Biblical age (3000 BC–500 BC); the Classical age (500 BC–AD 300); the Dark Ages (300–1100); and the Medieval age (1100–1485). However, the reader should rest assured that the rules systems for each period are essentially identical to that printed in *Wargaming: An Introduction*; all use the same core concepts, and are intended to be both simple and playable. However, the use of four different sets of rules allows for the subtle variations in each period to come to the fore (it also effectively prevents the contests between Ancient Egyptians and Wars of the Roses English armies, that are a lamentable feature of the many wargames competitions that use a generic ruleset covering the entire epoch from 3000 BC to AD 1485).

Each period is allocated five chapters. The first of these provides historical perspective; it outlines the major military (and occasionally political) developments. This should give any wargamer some useful contextual information, and hopefully give him or her the encouragement to pursue an interest by consulting the reading list provided. All wargamers should appreciate that there really is so much more to this hobby than playing games; the history of each individual period is absolutely fascinating, and an understanding of it will enrich the gaming experience immensely.

The second chapter in each section explains how I interpret the historical background in the wargaming context; in particular, I define the troop types that perform on the wargames table. The rules themselves form the third chapter.

The fourth chapter covers the army lists for the relevant epoch. Devoting an entire book to the Ancient and Medieval period allows me not only to cover a large number of armies, but also to greatly expand the format of each list. Every wargames force therefore contains far more than just the composition of each army and a brief interpretive paragraph. I am also able to include a set of special rules for each force; a diagrammatic representation of how armies can deploy on the wargames table; a guide to the availability of figures and their suitability for use in other wargames forces (with the best will in the world, no wargamer could possibly collect all the armies in this book: the opportunity of having units serve in more than one force does, however, allow for the rapid acquisition of extra wargames armies); a reading list; and finally some snippets of historical information and (where possible) a primary source quotation.

The final chapter of each section covers a wargames battle report. Each of these is based upon a famous historical battle. I start by stating what happened in the real life engagements, and then describe the events that ensued when the encounter was reproduced as a wargame. Hopefully, the reader will feel encouraged to follow suit; either by reproducing the battles described or (even better) research other momentous encounters and wargame them.

I end the book with some appendices covering wargames figures: the sizes and scales available; current prices (these are inevitably likely to change, and are only included as a general guide); and a list of useful addresses.

Having bought this book, the reader is about to sample the wargames period with the greatest variety of armies, and some of history's more fascinating personalities – now you too can be Alexander the Great, Julius Caesar, Queen Boudicca, King Arthur, William the Conqueror or Henry V. Who could possibly resist such a temptation?

Chapter 1

Biblical Warfare 3000 BC–500 BC

KEY EVENTS

Date	Event
2500–900 BC	Bronze Age.
2500–2100	Growth of Sumerian city states.
2100	Sargon of Akkad captures Sumerian cities.
1920	Fall of Akkadian Empire. Sumerian cities regain independence.
1793	Fall of Ur to Amorites. End of Sumerian city states.
1565	Hammurabi ascends Babylonian throne.
1400	Egypt invaded by Hyksos (Canaanite) armies.
1362	Babylon sacked by Hittites. End of Hammurabic Empire.
1185	Hyksos expelled from Egypt. New Kingdom created.
1115	Battle of Megiddo. Egypt defeats (Canaanite) King of Kadesh in history's first recorded battle.
1050	Rise of Hittite Empire.
1010–1000	Creation of Israelite kingdom as David defeats Philistines.
941	Battle of Kadesh. In the most famous encounter of the period, Egypt and the Hittite Empire fight in a bloody but inconclusive clash.
910–900	Mycenean Greek invaders besiege and take Troy.
900	Iron Age.
867–855	Sea Peoples invade Hittite Empire and Egypt.
858	Hittite Empire disintegrates as Hattusas falls to Sea Peoples. Replaced by confederation of minor kingdoms.
855	Battle of the Nile. Sea Peoples' invasion of Egypt repulsed.

850	Mycenean Greece falls to Sea Peoples.
810	Civil war in Egypt. New Kingdom divided in two.
745	Rise of New Assyrian Empire under Tiglath-Pileser III.
721	Samaria falls to Assyrians. New Assyrian Empire dominates Syria and Palestine.
720–700	Assyria dominates, but never entirely controls, Babylonian region.
675–650	Assyrians take Egypt, but are eventually expelled.
650–600	Scythian invasions of Middle East.
630–610	Babylonian revival under Nabopolassar.
612	Fall of Ninevah to Babylonians and Medes. Destruction of New Assyrian Empire.
587	Fall of Jerusalem to Babylonians. Downfall of Israelite kingdom.
550	Rise of Persia as Cyrus overthrows Median overlords.
539	Babylon falls to Persians.

A NOTE ON CHRONOLOGY

One of the greatest drawbacks in the study of this period is the lack of any reliable chronology until the year 763 BC (the latter date being identified thanks to the accurate modern backdating of a solar eclipse noted by Assyrian chroniclers). The last fifteen years have seen a challenge to the conventional dating, which has naturally enough been referred to as the New Chronology (which will doubtless become the Old Chronology over the next century or so). This new approach has been endorsed by Nigel Stillman in his *Chariot Wars* (Warhammer Historical Wargames, 1999), and has been followed by me.

To simplify the argument somewhat, the New Chronology rests upon archaeological evidence that the Egyptian 21st and 22nd Dynasties reigned concurrently in different parts of Egypt, rather than in succession as previously assumed. This actually helps matters greatly for any historian, since the new dating effectively abolishes the previous 350-year chronological gap from which no evidence has survived. With no fallacious gulf, there is no otherwise inexplicable 'dark age'. The New Chronology also provides support for the account provided in the history books of the Old Testament, and can in addition be confirmed by radiocarbon dating from Egyptian excavations (which previously tended to be ignored by scholars on the grounds that it rather inconveniently contradicted the conventional dating).

Readers who wish to examine the arguments supporting the New Chronology in greater detail might like to consult the following books:

James, Peter et al. *Centuries of Darkness*, Pimlico, 1991
Rohl, David. *A Test of Time*, Century, 1995

WHY WARFARE DEVELOPED

Warfare needs civilisation (although any decent civilisation neither wants nor needs warfare). This somewhat cryptic statement needs clarification. In essence, organised warfare can only occur between distinct political entities, be they formal states, an identifiable band of rebels, or a homogenous tribal grouping. It can therefore be seen that Stone Age hunter-gatherers may have fought between themselves, but such contests (even when involving different groups) were brief clashes that could not be dignified with the epithet of 'warfare'. Wars only started when humans settled in territories where greater food reserves could be garnered by cultivating land, rather than by following herds of wild animals around and killing beasts as required. One of the first environments where climatic conditions proved conducive to permanent settlement was what we now call the Middle East, especially the areas around the Rivers Tigris, Euphrates and Nile.

Once settlement occurred, civilisation could develop. Cities grew, and literacy arose; the latter being an aid to trade, a facilitator of good administration and a means of glorifying the local ruler and his favoured god(s). It is a somewhat depressing fact that the desirability of acquiring culture, poetry and philosophy provided little impulse for the development of literacy.

However, once small states arose, they began to find themselves at war with each other. By far the best explanation of why this state of affairs arose can be found from the great philosopher Thomas Hobbes:

> So that in the nature of man, we find three principal courses of quarrel. First, competition: secondly, diffidence; thirdly, glory. The first maketh men invade for gain; the second, for safety; and the third, for reputation.
>
> Thomas Hobbes, *Leviathan* (1651), quoted in Dawson, Doyne, *The First Armies*, Cassell, 2001, p. 14.

Although I would argue that man has no natural predisposition towards strife, unlike Hobbes (his rather gloomy thesis takes no account of the equally powerful human impulses of compassion for the plight of the helpless and disabled), his account does provide a good summary of the possible causes of strife. All three occurred in the first real civilisations, namely the Sumerian city states that grew in what is now Iraq. The original impulse was to seek safety and security, which explains the early development of fortified cities. However, a run of bad harvests would create a scarcity of resources, resulting in competition between neighbouring cities, and the consequent growth of aggressive campaigning and pitched battles. Finally, kings found it necessary to assert their political primacy, both over proximate political entities and their own nobility. As a result, such monarchs would engage in warfare, commemorating their victories in court propaganda extolling both the king and his god(s).

The Sumerian states did moreover have new and potent weaponry at their disposal. Whereas the flints and wooden clubs of Stone Age man could prove lethal, the invention of bronze allowed for the development of infinitely more dangerous pointed weapons (such as spears, swords and arrows). Moreover, the domestication of asses and eventually (albeit not by the Sumerians) horses resulted in the invention of the war chariot.

BIBLICAL INFANTRY

Although forming a large proportion of all Biblical armies, infantry was not highly regarded. This was principally due to the fact that the nobility fought from chariots, and spent little time with their foot soldiers. As a consequence of this neglect, many early Biblical armies only provided the most basic equipment for their infantry. They tended to be given a wooden shield and metal helmet for protection, but no body armour. Their chief weapon was the spear, either a long version used to thrust, or a shorter type that could be thrown at very close range (up to 10 or 20m). Provided that the infantry remained in the close formation that is clearly depicted on existing pictorial evidence, they could both engage their enemy counterparts with reasonable effectiveness, and ward off any frontal assaults from chariots.

Other foot soldiers were even less comprehensively equipped. These were unprotected by any armour or shield, but were given javelins (which could be thrown between 30 and 50m). Such skirmishers operated in dispersed formation; their role was to avoid hand-to-hand combat, and protect the flanks of close-order infantry. Nevertheless, the chief role of foot soldiers did not lie in pitched battle. Their major functions were to besiege and garrison fortresses (in which sphere chariots were utterly useless) and to protect friendly chariots from surprise attack, both by guarding the latter on the march and by providing sentry duty at night.

To generalise somewhat, infantry were regarded as the poor relations of chariots – a fact of which they were all too aware. Consisting as they did of conscripted men, neglected by the noble elite, and given limited protective equipment, morale and performance tended to be low. The one great exception to this was the army of New Kingdom Egypt, whose infantry eventually acquired body armour (albeit not metallic) in addition to their shields, as well as a degree of training which served them well. As a rule however, all foot (including the Egyptians) was far from highly disciplined, and as a result proved vulnerable to archery and chariot attack.

ARCHERY

Although simple bows had been around ever since the Stone Age, their effectiveness was limited by their short range (no more than 100m at best). All this changed by the time of the Akkadian Empire, which saw some foot soldiers (operating at close order) equipped with a new weapon, the so-called composite bow. This used a combination of wood, horn and sinew. It worked on the basis that when drawn, the ends of the bow would be pulled back to a much greater extent than the centre (the old bows, being made solely of wood, effectively had even pressure exerted all the way along the weapon). This allowed for much greater velocity for the arrow, and hence an increase both in range (up to 250m) and penetrative power. All this had major implications. Close-order Biblical Infantry was now vulnerable to long-range archery; the spearmen's limited discipline and enthusiasm made them especially vulnerable to effective bowfire.

As a consequence, foot archers equipped with composite bows proved to be important auxiliaries to spearmen. The Babylonian armies followed the Akkadians in equipping some troops with bows, and the Egyptian archers eventually replaced their simple wooden weapons with the composite version, after being subjected to its ill effects at the hands of the Hyksos invaders.

However effective it may have been in the hands of foot soldiers operating in close-order formation, the composite bow really came into its own as the weapon of choice for chariot warriors, to whom we must now turn.

CHARIOT WARFARE

As soon as asses became domesticated, the Sumerians hit upon the idea of using them as draught animals for battle wagons, and the chariot was born. It was however rather primitive at this stage. Of somewhat ramshackle construction, with four heavy solid wheels, and drawn by asses (onagers) noted chiefly for their foul temperament and contrary disposition, Sumerian chariots were not at first glance an especially formidable weapon – especially as the fighting crewman (as opposed to the unarmed driver) was equipped with javelins rather than a composite bow. Moreover, the onagers could only be controlled by having the chariot driver's reins attached to a nose ring, as the bit had not yet been devised. Some writers have therefore assumed that such limited performance meant that Sumerian chariots were little more than personnel carriers, being used to transport the warrior to the decisive point of the battlefield, at which time he would dismount and fight on foot.

Such a conclusion may appear plausible, but it would be mistaken. For one thing, modern tests with replicas of Sumerian chariots have shown them to be surprisingly manoeuvrable. Accordingly, it is possible to envisage their being used to drive up to javelin range, discharge a few missiles, and either retire or charge the enemy. For although it is true that the aforementioned modern tests showed that nothing would induce asses to charge a solid obstacle, bodies of men only form a rigid wall for as long as their morale holds. It is certainly possible to envisage a unit of Sumerian chariots head towards a body of enemy infantry with apparently murderous intent, which would have the effect of seeing the latter waver and run from the (socially superior) noble charioteers.

It is therefore clear that chariots could either engage their enemy equivalents with missilry; or fire at enemy infantry in order to create panic, prior to charging at their victims and thereby inducing a rout. The potential of the chariot was greatly increased once horses were introduced into the region, originally by Aryan invaders crossing the Caucasus Mountains into what is now Turkey. Although too small to ride, the early horses were easily domesticated (unlike the onagers), and provided excellent draught animals for chariots, whose construction was now greatly improved. New craftsmanship had by now created a much lighter vehicle than the Sumerian battle cart, and the new chariot only needed two light spoked wheels, as opposed to the four heavy and solid ones of the Sumerian version. The development of the composite bow, and the eventual use of quilted protection for horses and bronze armour for the crew served to create a formidable war machine. The chariot could advance with great speed, pepper the enemy with arrows, and retire or charge home as appropriate. Provided that clashes occurred on open terrain rather than in uneven rocky areas, the chariot dominated the Biblical battlefield.

Other developments followed. Many armies took to having a force of light infantry skirmishers accompany the chariots, either on foot or (I would maintain the more likely scenario) on the vehicles themselves prior to dismounting and engaging the enemy with javelin fire. Later chariots, especially in the Hittite and Assyrian armies, had a tendency to become heavier, carrying extra crew and being far more prepared to charge enemy units and engage them at close-quarters, rather than indulge in long-range skirmishing.

Chariots were undoubtedly the rulers of the Biblical battlefield. However, they were potentially vulnerable. The first problem was one of logistics. Any chariot force required a veritable army of carpenters, and a large supply of wood to keep it in the field. Consequently, a support network of cities was necessary – and if one of these fell to the enemy, the army would either be forced to retreat, or suffer unacceptable chariot losses owing to attrition. Of equal importance, chariotry could only dominate the arena for as long as enemy infantry proved vulnerable to archery. This would only be the case while foot soldiers remained poor relations; once they acquired discipline and *esprit de corps*, the ascendancy of chariots could be challenged – and with the invasions of the Sea Peoples, the gauntlet was well and truly thrown down.

THE SEA PEOPLES

The civilised parts of the Ancient world were always prone to mass migrations, and occasionally mass invasions. That of the Sea Peoples did, however, prove particularly destructive, causing as it did the end of the Hittite and Mycenean Greek empires, and the survival of the Egyptian New Kingdom only after a particularly bitter struggle.

The term 'Sea Peoples' is a convenient shorthand for groups of invaders from the Balkans, Sardinia, Sicily and Italy. They had originally served as mercenary infantry in the great kingdoms of the Middle East, and had carried news of wealth back to their homelands. As a consequence, the invasions started just after the Iron Age had begun.

The Sea Peoples were largely infantry armies operating in loose formation. This was essentially a compromise between the close order of Biblical infantry, and the dispersed formations of skirmishers. They could therefore move faster than close-formation foot, were not disordered by rocky or other potentially disruptive terrain, and could outclass skirmishers in hand-to-hand combat. They should have been defeated habitually by close-order foot in open terrain, but this does not seem to have happened. The fact was that the Sea Peoples were well led and highly motivated, in some contrast to the conscripts they opposed. With their nobles fighting in the ranks of the infantry, the Sea Peoples foot were able to dominate most of their foes. In essence, enemy bowfire did not demoralise them, and they could in any event move into close combat quite quickly – thereby reducing the time they were to be subjected to enemy bowshot.

The Sea Peoples were equipped with javelins, giving them a missile capability. However, they also had a long sword which, once penetrating beyond enemy spearpoints, could inflict great execution at close quarters. Moreover, the Sea Peoples tended to be equipped with superior iron weaponry, and also iron breastplates. Their round shields were large enough to be used for protection, but small enough to allow unimpeded use of the sword in close combat. All in all, the Sea Peoples presented a major challenge to the old empires, and demonstrated just how important it was to have an effective and well-equipped infantry force (one reason the Egyptians were able to resist the invasions was because their foot soldiers had body armour as well as a shield). The lesson was not lost upon the rising power of Assyria.

THE NEW ASSYRIAN ARMY

The kingdom of Assyria had always been surrounded by potential enemies, and its rulers appreciated that a high-quality army was essential if it was to survive. The creation of the New Assyrian Empire saw the arrival of the most formidable military machine yet devised.

The key to Assyrian success lay in the widespread use of iron weaponry, and the institution of a regular disciplined army. Mixed divisions of infantry, cavalry and chariots were created, which trained and campaigned together during spring and summer; the troops only returned to the fields to collect the harvest each autumn.

The most decisive Assyrian weapon was its Heavy Infantry arm. This was essentially close-order infantry operating in the Biblical tradition, but with the training and discipline more usually associated with the Sea Peoples. Half the men in each unit had thrusting spears, the rest being equipped with a composite bow. All had iron body armour; the spearmen had round shields too. The combination of disruptive archery and aggressive infantry whose close-order formation rendered it formidable in hand-to-hand combat, made for a terrifying instrument of war.

Other infantrymen formed auxiliary units. They had similar weaponry to the Heavy Infantry, but lacked body armour. They fought in a similar manner to the Sea Peoples, adopting a loose-order formation that was particularly effective in difficult terrain. As such, the auxiliary infantry provided useful and valued support for their heavier counterparts.

As already mentioned, the Assyrians were great advocates of heavy chariots. With a crew of three armoured fighting men equipped with thrusting spears (in addition to the unarmed driver), and pulled by four horses protected by quilted armour, the Assyrian chariot was a distinctly frightening weapon. It proved that the old king of the battlefield was still a vital weapon.

However, chariots eventually found themselves largely replaced by cavalry in the Assyrian battle order. Once horses became strong enough to bear the weight of riders it became inevitable that they would be ridden into battle. Despite not reaching their full potential owing to the lack of stirrups, cavalry could still be very useful on the battlefield. Indeed, the Scythian invaders who wrought such havoc in the seventh century BC consisted largely of light horse archers. Nevertheless, the Assyrians had a formidable cavalry arm of their own. They were equipped along the lines of Heavy Infantry units, with half the men having spears, and the rest composite bows. All had iron body armour, but were unshielded; horsemanship had not yet reached the stage where riders could both carry a shield and control their mounts. The Assyrian cavalry nevertheless proved very useful on the battlefield, although probably not as effective as chariots. The reason the latter were eventually replaced by the former was due to sound logistical factors: chariots needed a huge support network of carpenters and a ready supply of wood in order to function; cavalry required none of these, and military mathematics soon dictated that four separate horsemen would prove more useful in the long run than a single chariot drawn by four animals. Chariots were defeated by economic rather than tactical considerations; cavalry were only slightly less effective, but were much cheaper.

With such a magnificent army, the Assyrians acquired a huge empire. Few other states dared to resist them on the battlefield, and those who defended fortresses were dealt with ruthlessly. The Assyrians would butcher the garrison of any city that opposed them, and would not only deport surviving civilians, but would scatter them throughout the empire. This served to prevent any reassertion of ethnic identity; the unfortunate victims were separated from their compatriots, and also merely existing as a source of forced labour for their Assyrian overlords. The Assyrian empire may have been great in terms of its conquests; its art also has a certain grandeur, but does in a sense encapsulate the Assyrian dilemma. For the empire's art was devoted entirely to depiction of military accomplishments; the more refined aspects of life were not illustrated. The New Assyrian regime may have been a great empire; it was emphatically not a great civilisation.

As a consequence of their cruelty, the Assyrians only aroused hatred. Eventually, all the surrounding states allied themselves against their great oppressor, leading to the collapse of the Assyrian Empire when Ninevah fell to the Babylonians and Medians in 612 BC. Their appalling political legacy notwithstanding, the Assyrians' military system provided a template that was far ahead of its time. Although the concept of a regular army was not fully embraced for centuries, the example of disciplined Heavy Infantry was the key troop type whose potential was to be realised in the Classical age.

PRIMARY SOURCES

The Holy Bible: a modern translation is probably best, owing to its greater clarity and up-to-date scholarship. The Old Testament books from *Joshua* up to and including *2 Chronicles* (except *Ruth*) detail the Israelite invasion, conquest and consolidation over what is now referred to as the Holy Land.

SECONDARY SOURCES

Anglim, Simon et al. *Fighting Techniques of the Ancient World*, Greenhill, 2002
Carey, Brian Todd et al. *Warfare in the Ancient World*, Pen & Sword, 2005
Drews, Robert. *The End of the Bronze Age*, Princeton, 1993
Dawson, Doyne. *The First Armies*, Cassell, 2001
Montgomery, Field Marshal Viscount. *A Concise History of Warfare*, Wordsworth, 2000 (originally 1968)
Stillman, Nigel. *Chariot Wars*, Warhammer Historical Wargames, 1999
Stillman, Nigel, and Tallis, Nigel. *Armies of the Ancient Near East*, Wargames Research Group, 1984
Wise, Terence. *Ancient Armies of the Middle East*, Osprey, 1981

JOURNAL ARTICLES

Barker, Phil. 'Some Trust in Chariots' in *Slingshot* no. 203 (May 1999), 59–60
Charlesworth, Martin. 'The Tactical Use of Chariots in the Ancient Near East' in *Slingshot* no. 201 (January 1999), 15–19
Charlesworth, Martin. 'On Horses, Chariots, Bows and Scythes' in *Slingshot* no. 210 (July 2000), 21–5
Griffiths, Gareth. 'Some Practical Considerations on Chariot Warfare' in *Slingshot* no. 219 (January 2002), 46–8
Kinnear, Chris. 'Belshazzar's Feast' in *Slingshot* no. 205 (September 1999), 53–4
O'Steen, Stuart. 'Late Bronze Age Warfare: A Plausible Scenario' in *Slingshot* no. 212 (November 2000), 21–9

Chapter 2

Biblical Wargaming

W hen wargaming the Biblical period, any set of rules must account for the primitive level of infantry development and the vulnerability of many troops to archery. The problem was essentially one of discipline; relatively untrained units were prone to suffer far greater trauma from missilry, than the very capable troops featuring in the Sea Peoples and Assyrian armies among others.

This problem is best approached by increasing the varieties of infantry. The old Heavy Infantry and Warband categories from *Wargaming: An Introduction* remain (although the latter type is renamed Auxiliary Infantry), but a special category of Biblical Infantry has been added. This essentially represents a much less potent variety of Heavy Infantry.

Unlike my old rules, shooting now has an effect upon morale. Whereas all units have to assess their morale when a base is removed in hand-to-hand combat, the loss of a base from missile fire also mandates a morale test – except for Heavy Infantry and Auxiliary Infantry (who had sufficient training not to panic from the disruptive effects of arrows and javelins).

As was my practice in *Wargaming: An Introduction*, I have listed the main categories of troops used in these rules below.

HEAVY INFANTRY
Any army fortunate enough to enjoy the services of these troops is likely to be very effective. Being well-drilled, often quite heavily armoured, and extremely formidable in hand-to-hand combat, Heavy Infantry are best avoided by any enemy in open terrain. However, retaining their close-order formation necessitates slow movement, and they can be disordered (and hence rendered less effective in combat) in difficult terrain such as woods.

BIBLICAL INFANTRY

Essentially a much less effective variety of Heavy Infantry, these troops are not only less capable in combat but are vulnerable to missile fire. However, they are still competent troops in hand-to-hand combat in open terrain, since they are only inferior to Heavy Infantry, and superior to all archers and javelinmen.

AUXILIARY INFANTRY

These are disciplined troops who adopt a looser formation than the similarly well-drilled Heavy Infantry (which is why they are represented with three figures per base, rather than the four of close-order foot). They are accordingly less capable than Heavy Infantry when fighting in open terrain, although their training makes them fully the equal of Biblical Infantry. However, their loose-order formation makes them deadly in woods or rocky terrain (which has identical effects to wooded areas), where close-order troops are disrupted. Auxiliary Infantry also move faster than foot in tight formation, and can therefore spend less time assailed by missile fire before engaging archers and javelinmen in hand-to-hand combat.

HEAVY ARCHERS

These are close-order infantry that rely upon bows rather than close combat weapons. They are much less effective in hand-to-hand combat than close- or loose-order infantry, but the demoralising effects of their archery can wreak a heavy toll on all troops except Heavy Infantry and Auxiliary Infantry.

LIGHT INFANTRY

These troops skirmish at long range using javelins or bows. This sniping can be very effective, and their dispersed formation makes them extremely mobile. However, they are utterly ineffective in hand-to-hand combat in open terrain. As a consequence, Light Infantry were always expected to withdraw from mêlée, which they are allowed to do under these rules.

HEAVY CAVALRY

As already discussed, these only appeared at the end of the Biblical period. Although outclassed by Heavy Infantry, heavy horse are quite effective against other troops in the open, and are particularly useful if using their increased mobility to attack enemy flanks.

LIGHT CAVALRY

Although not a feature of many armies in this period, these very mobile troops can literally run rings round their opponents. They can withdraw from hand-to-hand combat when desired, and by using javelins or bows in a hit-and-run role, can be extremely useful.

HEAVY CHARIOTS

Being a more effective variety of Heavy Cavalry, these chariots can be exceptionally dangerous to enemy troops (this is reflected by Heavy Chariots being awarded a combat bonus in the initial round of hand-to-hand combat). The crewmen of these vehicles were usually equipped with long spears, although some were armed with bows. The latter are however assumed to be used in a close support role, rather than long-range firing. Accordingly, Heavy Chariots do not have a shooting capability in these rules.

LIGHT CHARIOTS

This more effective brand of Light Cavalry represented the defining troop type of the Biblical age. The nobility of the Ancient Near East were invariably light charioteers, and frequently played a decisive role in combat. Incidentally, the combat bonus enjoyed by Light Chariots in the first round of hand-to-hand combat, reflects deadly close-range bowfire rather than extensive engagement in close-quarter fighting.

A reading of the rules will reveal how the qualities of the various troop types are simulated. However, some other aspects of the wargame need to be explained. As far as movement is concerned, close-order units inevitably move more slowly than those in dispersed or open order. Light troops may also move and fire, although it will be apparent that men equipped with javelins have a greater fire and movement capacity than those equipped with bows. This is primarily because javelins were a very short-range weapon, and also because the soldier inevitably carried fewer of them than would be the case with the much lighter and smaller arrows. As a result, the light javelinman would hurl his weapon, and then make for the rear as quickly as possible. In contrast, the bowman would take the time to fire several shots at longer range before withdrawing from an advancing enemy.

You may wonder why cavalry with bows has a shorter firing range than its infantry counterpart. This stems from the fact that a mobile horse is inevitably not as stable a firing platform as the earth on which the footman stood. As a consequence, the effective range of the horse archer is reduced.

The role of armour is very important, for when a soldier is hit, he is not necessarily killed. It is quite possible that armour can turn away what would otherwise be a lethal blow. Accordingly, armoured troops always roll one dice for every potential casualty. If the dice score achieves the saving roll required for the relevant type of armour, the casualty point loss does not occur. In case the reader is wondering, armour classification is evaluated according to the following rough criteria. If a soldier is equipped with a breastplate *or* a shield, he counts as having light armour; if he has a breastplate *and* a shield, he has medium armour. These ratings can be augmented if the man has extra armour, horse armour, or an unusually large shield. Note that cavalry armour is often downgraded in effectiveness compared with its infantry counterpart. This is principally because it is harder to protect such a large target, and that horses can panic when wounds are inflicted upon them, unseating their riders as a result. This tendency is most easily simulated by conferring a lower saving roll upon cavalry than troops on foot with equivalent armour.

Hand-to-hand combat usually takes the form of a fight to the finish. However, light units and cavalry can engage in delaying actions by withdrawing from combat, provided that their movement factor exceeds that of their antagonists. Note that units can only withdraw in their own move; this means that they must suffer at least one round of hand-to-hand combat before retreating. Note that withdrawal from combat is not mandatory (although it is usually a very good idea for light troops), and there may indeed be occasions on which the wargames general demands the supreme sacrifice from his or her miniature warriors.

To win the wargames battle, the enemy force must be reduced to 25 per cent of its original force (that is to say, when armies only have two units left on the battlefield, since they always start with eight units). Note that exiting the board on the enemy side of the battlefield has an effect, in the sense that the exiting unit is eliminated but so also are two enemy units. This is because the exiting unit is assumed to be looting the enemy rear areas. This pillaging expedition renders the unit in question out of the battle (which is why it counts as being eliminated); however, the demoralising effect of having one's baggage looted results in very serious loss of cohesion on the enemy side. This is why two enemy units are immediately removed from the table (the enemy player may choose which units). You may wonder why only Heavy Infantry, Auxiliary Infantry or Heavy Archers may exit the battlefield and loot the enemy baggage, especially as history is littered with examples of light and cavalry units indulging in pillage. The reason is simply that the raids of these units only had a nuisance value, since they were only capable of assaulting unfortified areas. In contrast, heavier units could take and hold fortified camps, and it was the looting of such militarily significant targets that triggered panic on the enemy side.

Hopefully, you will gain some insight as to why the rules (which are in the next chapter) took the form they did. Needless to say, these rules, like any other set, reflect the prejudices and historical understanding of their writer. If you feel, after your own research, that my rules are faulty, then you must feel free to alter them. Any set of wargames rules will always be a work in progress; my sole object has been to produce a historically valid, yet playable and exciting game; my only hope is that readers of this book think I have succeeded.

Chapter 3

Biblical Wargames Rules

UNITS

Each unit generally consists of four bases, each of which has dimensions of 40mm × 20mm. Each base has a variable number of figures on it, depending upon the troop type, as listed below. (Note: the standard base size is ideal for 15–20mm figures. However, 25mm miniatures may require larger dimensions: 60mm × 40mm is suitable for these larger size figures.) As noted, units usually have four bases, which are aligned in two ranks of two bases.

Troop Type	Figures/models per base
Heavy Infantry, Biblical Infantry, Heavy Archers	4
Auxiliary Infantry, Heavy Cavalry	3
Light Infantry, Light Cavalry	2
Heavy Chariots, Light Chariots	1

HOW TO WIN
Victory is achieved as soon as one side is reduced to a strength of two remaining units.

a) *Exiting the map*. For every infantry unit (other than Light Infantry) exiting the mapboard on the enemy side, the enemy immediately withdraws *two* of his units. All three count as eliminated.

SEQUENCE OF PLAY
Each side follows the sequence listed below in each of its turns:

1) Charge sequence.
2) Movement.
3) Shooting.
4) Hand-to-hand combat.
5) Morale tests.

1) The Charge Sequence
Every time a general wishes a unit to enter into hand-to-hand combat with an enemy unit, the procedure is as follows:

1a) *Charge Declaration*. Declare the charge. Measure the distance between the units. If the charging unit can reach the enemy, move it into physical contact (bases touching).

1b) *Defensive fire*. If the defender is equipped with javelins, and if the attacker launched its charge from further than 8cm away, the defender may fire at its assailant.

1c) *Initiate hand-to-hand combat*. After removing any losses caused by defensive fire, the two antagonists will fight in the hand-to-hand phase.

2) Movement

2a) *Movement allowances*. In general, units move the distance listed below during each turn. They do not have to use up all their movement allowance, but may not carry over any unused movement to the next turn.

Troop Type	Movement per turn
Light Cavalry, Light Chariots	24cm
Heavy Cavalry, Heavy Chariots	20cm
Auxiliary Infantry, Light Infantry	12cm
Heavy Infantry, Biblical Infantry, Heavy Archers	8cm

2b) *Turning*. If an Auxiliary Infantry, Heavy Infantry, Biblical Infantry, Heavy Archer, Heavy Chariot, or Heavy Cavalry unit wishes to deviate more than 30° from a straight line, it must use up half its movement allowance to do so.

i) Light Infantry, Light Chariots and Light Cavalry may turn without penalty.

2c)   *Difficult terrain.* Ancient battles generally involved no more than three types of terrain; specifically hills, rivers and woods. They affect movement in varying ways.

   i)   Hills have no effect on movement (they were usually gentle slopes).
   ii)   All units take a complete turn to cross a river.
   iii) Cavalry and Chariots may not enter woods.
   iv)   Heavy Infantry, Biblical Infantry and Heavy Archers have their movement reduced to 4cm every turn they move in a wood.
   v)   Light Infantry and Auxiliary Infantry are unaffected by woods, and may move up to their full movement allowance if desired.

2d)   *Moving and firing.* Heavy troops may never move and fire. Light Infantry, Light Cavalry and Light Chariots may do so under certain circumstances.

   i)   Light Infantry may move and fire if equipped with javelins. The firing may either precede or follow movement.
   ii)   Light Cavalry and Light Chariots may move and fire if equipped with bows (firing must either precede or follow movement). However, Light Cavalry and Light Chariots equipped with javelins are allowed to split-move. That is to say, they may not only move and fire, but are allowed to fire at any point during their move (if the target is in range at the time of firing). They may for example move half their allowance, throw their javelins, turn around, and retire their remaining half-move away from the enemy they had just shot at.
   iii) No unit may ever fire if it is charging an enemy unit.

3)   Shooting

3a)   *Missile ranges.* When a unit wishes to shoot, it must first check to see if the enemy is in range.

Weapon	Range
Bow (on foot)	24cm
Javelin	8cm
Bow (on horseback), sling	16cm

3b) *Rolling to hit.* Infantry and cavalry units with bows, slings or javelin roll one die for each base currently remaining. A successful hit may possibly inflict a casualty point on the defending unit.

    i)   Bowmen, slingers and javelinmen hit on a throw of 4–6.

    ii)   Units in woods only suffer half the number of hits registered.

3c) *Saving rolls.* However, the defender is permitted what is known as a saving roll for each potential casualty. This is dependent upon armour thickness. For every hit scored, the defender rolls a die. If the score achieves the required saving roll, the casualty is not inflicted.

Type of armour	Saving roll required
Heavy armour, Heavy Chariot	4–6
Medium armour, Light Chariot	5–6
Light armour	6

3d) *Base removal.* For every four casualty points inflicted remove a base (denote the current number of casualties using markers).

4) Hand-to-Hand Combat

4a) *Procedure.* When units engage in hand-to-hand combat, the fight usually continues each turn until one side is eliminated (Cavalry, Light Chariots and Light Infantry may withdraw a full move after a round of combat, but only if their movement rate exceeds that of their assailants).

4b) *Order of striking.* Blows are always struck simultaneously.

4c) *Hand-to hand combat (open terrain).* Each base in a unit rolls a variable number of dice, depending upon the type of opponent it is engaging.

Own unit	Enemy unit			
	Heavy Infantry	Biblical Infantry, Auxiliary Infantry, Heavy Cavalry, Heavy Chariots	Heavy Archers	Light Cavalry, Light Infantry, Light Chariots
Heavy Infantry	1	2	3	4
Biblical Infantry	1	1	2	3
Auxiliary Infantry	1	1	2	3
Heavy Cavalry	1	1	2	3
Heavy Chariots	1	1	2	3
Heavy Archers	1	1	1	2
Light Cavalry	1	1	1	1
Light Infantry	1	1	1	1
Light Chariots	1	1	1	1

i)   Heavy and Light Chariots roll one extra die per base remaining in the first round of any combat.

ii)   Units uphill of their antagonists also roll one extra die per base remaining in the first round of any combat.

iii)   Units defending a river bank similarly roll one extra die per base remaining, if their assailants are crossing the river at the time. Again, this only applies during the first round.

iv)   Units attacking the flank or rear of an enemy always roll an additional die per base engaged.

v)   Units hit in their flanks may turn to face their enemy in the second or subsequent rounds of hand-to-hand combat, but only if they are not simultaneously being engaged to their front.

vi)   For every dice rolled, a 4–6 is needed to stand the chance of inflicting a casualty point loss on the enemy.

4d)   *Saving roll.* As with shooting, the defending unit is entitled to a saving roll for each potential casualty. Use the same chart provided in the shooting section of these rules (see 3c above).

4e)   *Combat in woods.* This uses a (very) different hand-to-hand combat table.

Own unit	Enemy unit	
	Auxiliary Infantry	Other Troops
Auxiliary Infantry	1	2
Other troops	1	1

5) Morale tests

5a) *When to test morale*. Units test morale when the following conditions apply:

    i) Whenever any unit loses a base in hand-to-hand combat.

    ii) Whenever any unit other than Heavy Infantry or Auxiliary Infantry loses a base as a result of missile fire.

5b) *How to test morale*. For every base removed, the victim must roll a die. For each failure to achieve the appropriate score, an additional base is removed.

Class of unit	Morale roll
Elite	3–6
Average	4–6
Levy	5–6

Chapter 4

Biblical Wargames Armies

The Biblical period will prove to be of great appeal to wargamers who enjoy the idea of chariot warfare. Given the limitations of Biblical Infantry, it is the battlewagons which usually prove decisive, and whose effective use requires bold and imaginative tactics.

As always, armies comprise eight units. The army lists provided below give the minimum and maximum numbers of each troop type permitted in each wargamer's force. As for terrain, I would suggest that the battlefield contain no more than three pieces, which can be made up of hills or rivers. The baseboard may be either green or sand; this is to account for the fact that although the common perception is that the Middle East consists mainly of sand dunes, there are also many fertile areas.

SUMERIAN ARMY
(2500 BC–1790 BC)

Unit type	Number per army
Chariots (Light Chariot (javelin), Elite)	1–3
Spearmen (Biblical Infantry, light armour, Levy)	2–5
Nim Skirmishers (Light Infantry (javelin), light armour, Levy)	2–4
Slingers (Light Infantry (slings), light armour, Levy)	0–2

Despite the unreliability of their steeds, the chariots inevitably form the core of this army. They should be at the forefront of any attack, with infantry assigned only to a support role. In the latter capacity, the javelinmen can both protect flanks and provide fire support for the chariotry. As for the spearmen, they can follow up a chariot-led assault, but their prime use lies in forming a defensive barrier by huddling behind their shields.

Incidentally, the epithet 'Nim' means 'flies'. This nickname was awarded to the javelinmen, owing to the fact that they operated in swarms, and could be extremely irritating!

SPECIAL RULES

1) *Onagers.* The Sumerian chariots were drawn by these barely domesticated ancestors of the modern ass. Unfortunately for the Sumerians, the onagers shared the rather contrary and frequently vicious disposition of their modern descendants. Whenever the Sumerian player wishes to move a chariot unit, he or she must roll a die and act according to the following table (if the player does not wish to move the chariot unit, it remains stationary: no die is rolled).

Die Roll Result

1   The onagers refuse to move. The chariot unit remains stationary.

2–3 The onagers are unenthusiastic, but are at least under control. The chariot unit moves at a rate of 12cm.

4–5 The onagers are keen to get stuck in. The chariot unit moves at a rate of 20cm, but must head towards the enemy (it does not have to engage any of its foes in hand-to-hand combat).

6   Blood lust! The onagers take out their foul mood upon the foe. The chariot unit moves 24cm towards the nearest enemy unit, and must engage it in hand-to-hand combat if possible.

2) *Interlocking shields.* Sumerian spearmen often bunched up behind their large shields, forming a strong defensive barrier but lacking mobility. Provided that a unit of spearmen does not move, it is treated as having medium armour (a saving roll of 5–6). It loses this benefit if it moves at any time (the Sumerians lacked the drill to change formation at will; once their units started advancing, they could no longer adopt a defensive formation).

SUGGESTED DEPLOYMENT

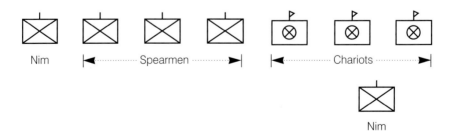

The chariots are concentrated on one wing in order to assault the enemy en masse (so far as the erratic nature of the onagers will permit any kind of concerted action). One unit of javelinmen provides fire support for the chariots, while the other protects the left flank. The spearmen can adopt a defensive posture (taking advantage of their enhanced saving role) until the chariot assault has weakened the enemy lines enough to permit a general advance.

CREATING THE ARMY IN MINIATURE
Sadly, no plastic figures are yet available for this army. As for metal figures, 15mm and 25mm ranges do exist, but are not provided by every manufacturer. Fortunately, the 6mm scale is covered by Irregular Miniatures.

ALTERNATIVE ARMIES
Sumerian figures can serve in Akkadian forces (naturally enough, since Akkad was in fact a Sumerian city). Since javelinmen and slingers tended to be equipped identically throughout the Biblical world, they may serve as skirmishers in any other army.

SECONDARY SOURCES
Stillman, Nigel. *Chariot Wars*, Warhammer Historical Wargames, 1999
Stillman, Nigel and Tallis, Nigel. *Armies of the Ancient Near East*, Wargames Research Group, 1984
Titensor, Mike. 'Do Ancients Stop at Qadesh?' in *Slingshot* no. 244 (January 2006), 37–44
Wise, Terence. *Ancient Armies of the Middle East*, Osprey, 1981
Woolley, C. Leonard. *The Sumerians*, Norton, 1965

THE STANDARD THAT WASN'T
The so-called 'Standard' of Ur was actually the soundbox of a stringed instrument, and not a battle banner. It is of great interest, as it depicts a Sumerian army in action; those who wish to see the original can find it in the British Museum.

AKKADIAN ARMY
(2100 BC–1790 BC)

Unit type	Number per army
Chariots (Light Chariot (javelin), Elite)	1–2
Spearmen (Biblical Infantry, light armour, Levy)	2–4
Archers (Heavy Archers, Light armour, Levy)	1–2
Nim Skirmishers (Light Infantry (javelin), light armour, Levy)	2–4
Slingers (Light Infantry (slings), light armour, Levy)	0–2

Although the chariots are still effective, they do not form such a high proportion of this army as the earlier Sumerian forces. Nevertheless, the presence of Heavy Archers actually makes this a very potent army in the Sumerian context: the composite bow can wreak havoc among enemy troops of indifferent morale, with its long range proving decisive. Provided that their opponents lack bows, Akkadian forces can adopt a defensive posture, with archery weakening the enemy, and spearmen standing firm to take advantage of the 'interlocking shields' special rule.

Readers may wonder why the Akkadian army list can be used for dates after the fall of the Akkadian Empire (in 1920 BC). This is simply in order to allow the deployment of armies from city states which, although not Akkadian themselves, fought according to the precepts of the latter.

SPECIAL RULES

1) *Onagers*. See Sumerian army list for details.
2) *Interlocking shields*. See Sumerian army list for details.

SUGGESTED DEPLOYMENT

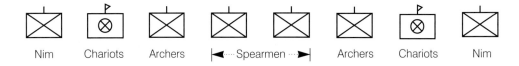

Nim   Chariots   Archers   ◄····Spearmen····►   Archers   Chariots   Nim

This layout is designed to maximise the potential of archery. The bowmen can fire to both their left and their right, thereby supporting all parts of the battle line. The spearmen are best used in a static role, taking advantage of their enhanced defensive capability. The chariots and Nim can either deal with any assault on the army's flanks, or may alternatively attack the enemy force once the latter has been weakened by bowfire.

CREATING THE ARMY IN MINIATURE

As already mentioned, this army is largely made up of Sumerian figures. Fortunately, those manufacturers who supply the latter army invariably provide suitable figures for Akkadian archers.

ALTERNATIVE ARMIES

As with the Sumerians, slingers and javelinmen may serve with almost any Biblical army. The Akkadian army can also (naturally enough) double up as a Sumerian force.

SECONDARY SOURCES

See Sumerian army list for details. For additional information, the following work may be consulted:

Leick, Gwendolyn. *Mesopotamia*, Penguin, 2001

DIVINE INSPIRATION

Naram-Sin, the mighty king of Akkad: when the four corners of the world opposed him with hostility, he remained victorious in nine battles because of the love of Ishtar [a favourite god] and even took the kings who had campaigned against him prisoner. Because he succeeded when heavily pressed in maintaining his city in strength, his city implored [various gods] . . . to have him as the god of their city Akkad and they built him a temple in the midst of Akkad.

Inscription on statue to Niram-Sin (reigned 2050–2010 BC), quoted in Leick, Gwendolyn, *Mesopotamia*, Penguin, 2001, p. 100.

Most Sumerian and Akkadian rulers tended to claim that they acted on behalf of a particular god. Naram-Sin was the first to declare himself divine. Such megalomaniacal tendencies were to recur with many powerful rulers of the Ancient world.

CONQUERING TO SURVIVE

Sargon originally found himself surrounded by enemies. However, this apparently unfavourable fact meant that each potential opponent was in range of his armies. By picking them off one by one, Sargon was able to establish the first significant empire in history. His approach has subsequently been referred to as the 'strategy of the central position', and has been adopted by all the great commanders – most notably Frederick the Great of Prussia.

MIDIANITE ARAB ARMY
(2000 BC–700 BC)

Unit type	Number per army
Camelry (Light Cavalry (bow), light armour, Average)	2–4
Skirmishers (Light Infantry (javelin), light armour, Levy)	2–4
Slingers (Light Infantry (slings), light armour, Levy)	2–4
Archers (Light Infantry (bow), Light armour, Levy)	0–2

With an army consisting entirely of light troops and possessing indifferent morale, the Arab commander must simply pepper the opposing lines with missiles. Note however that camels can be effective against chariots and cavalry on horseback, owing to the equine aversion for getting too close to the Arabs' mounts (see special rule below).

This army list represents the Arabian tribes who frequently made a great nuisance of themselves, inclined as they were to raid and plunder territories bordering their desert homeland (in what is now Saudi Arabia). The Midianites were eventually suppressed by the Assyrians, who used a combination of diplomacy (recruiting some Arab leaders as allies) and brutality (crushing any recalcitrant tribes) to reduce what had been a serious menace to an occasional minor irritation.

SPECIAL RULES

1) *Camels*. These rather contrary beasts were somewhat slower than horses, but had the advantage of repelling the latter owing to their rather unpleasant odour. Apply the following rules:

   a) *Movement*. Camelry moves at a rate of 16cm per turn.
   b) *Armour*. If attacked by horses in hand-to-hand combat (be they cavalry or chariots), camelry enjoys an armour saving roll of 4–6.

SUGGESTED DEPLOYMENT

|◀···· Camelry ····▶| Skirmishers |◀····· Slingers ·····▶| Skirmishers |◀···· Camelry ····▶|

Although the slingers can provide some useful missile fire, the camelry forms the chief threat from this army. It can engage enemy infantry with bowfire, and may be able to repel chariots and cavalry owing to its enhanced armour saving roll against horses. As for the javelinmen, they are deployed so that they can either protect the flanks of the slingers, or give active support to the camelry, as circumstances dictate.

CREATING THE ARMY IN MINIATURE

As with most other Biblical armies, there are not yet any plastic figures available. However, coverage in 6mm, 15mm and 25mm metal miniatures is very wide. Most companies produce generic javelinmen, slingers and light archers suitable for a wide selection of Biblical armies; more importantly, many figure designers seem to feel a compelling urge to produce Arab camel riders as part of their repertoire.

ALTERNATIVE ARMIES

As already stated, the light infantry figures can serve in most other Biblical armies.

PRIMARY SOURCES

Holy Bible (*Judges* Ch. 6–8 cover Gideon's campaign against the Midianites).

SECONDARY SOURCES

Healy, Mark. *Warriors of the Old Testament*, Firebird, 1989

Stillman, Nigel and Tallis, Nigel. *Armies of the Ancient Near East*, Wargames Research Group, 1984

Wise, Terence. *Ancient Armies of the Middle East*, Osprey, 1981

PLUNDER AND PILLAGE

Whenever the Israelites planted their crops, the Midianites, Amalekites and other eastern peoples invaded the country. They camped on the land and ruined the crops all the way to Gaza and did not spare a living thing for Israel, neither sheep nor cattle nor donkeys. They came up with their livestock and their tents like swarms of locusts. It was impossible to count the men and their camels; they invaded the land to ravage it.

Holy Bible (*Judges* 6: 2–5). (This and all subsequent Biblical quotes are taken from the New International Version translation.)

Like most nomads, the Midianite Arabs had little idea of the benefits of even the most rudimentary civilisation: their sole aim was to plunder resources, without leaving anything constructive in their wake.

CANAANITE AND PHILISTINE ARMIES
(1400 BC–1000 BC)

Unit type	Number per army
Chariots (Light Chariot (bow), Elite)	2–4
Spearmen (Biblical Infantry, light armour, Levy)	2–4
Skirmishers (Light Infantry (javelin), light armour, Levy)	2–4
Archers (Light Infantry (bow), light armour, Levy)	0–1

This is the quintessential Biblical army, with a striking force of horse-drawn light chariots supported (to no great effect) by rather poor-quality infantry. Accordingly, the number of chariot units should be maximised, since these can have a devastating effect upon enemy armies.

The list is designed to cover states operating in what is now Israel, Palestine, Lebanon and Syria. However, it can also be used for the armies of the Mitanni (operating in Northern and Western Iraq from 1250 BC to 990 BC) and even for the Hammurabic Babylonian empire (1565 BC to 1362 BC; see special rules below).

SPECIAL RULES

1) *Philistine armies*. These appear to have equipped some of their infantry with armour. Add the following entry to any Philistine army list:

Unit type	Number per army
Philistine Guards (Biblical Infantry, medium armour, Average)	0–1

2) *Hammurabic Babylonian armies*. These had close-order archers forming an integral part of their forces. Add the following item to any list applicable for Babylonian armies.

Unit type	Number per army
Heavy Archers (Heavy Archers, light armour, Levy)	1–2

SUGGESTED DEPLOYMENT

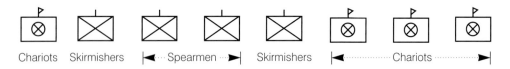

Chariots   Skirmishers |◀···Spearmen···▶| Skirmishers |◀·········Chariots·········▶|

The number of chariot units has been maximised, with most deployed on the right flank in order to overwhelm the enemy. The rather weak units of spearmen are bolstered by the skirmishers, while the single remaining chariot unit provides useful support for the left flank. The role of the infantry is largely defensive: it should only assault the enemy lines once these have been weakened by the massed ranks of chariots.

CREATING THE ARMY IN MINIATURE

As has been the case with earlier entries in this chapter, no suitable plastic figures are yet available. So far as 15mm and 25mm metal miniatures are concerned, a number of companies provide reasonable coverage. This is also true of the 6mm figures provided by Irregular Miniatures.

ALTERNATIVE ARMIES
The troops in this distinctly all-encompassing army roster cannot really be used for any other list in this chapter, apart from the skirmishers and archers. These can serve in most other armies.

PRIMARY SOURCES
Holy Bible (especially the books of *Joshua*, *Judges* and *1 Samuel*).

SECONDARY SOURCES
Derrick, Peter. 'A Fanfare for the Philistines' in *Slingshot* no. 221 (May 2002), 29–30
Healy, Mark. *Warriors of the Old Testament*, Firebird, 1989
Stillman, Nigel. *Chariot Wars*, Warhammer Historical Wargames, 1999
Stillman, Nigel and Tallis, Nigel. *Armies of the Ancient Near East*, Wargames Research Group, 1984
Wise, Terence. *Ancient Armies of the Middle East*, Osprey, 1981

DEATH OF A CHAMPION
As [Goliath] moved closer to attack him, David ran quickly towards the battle line to meet him. Reaching into his bag and taking out a stone, he slung it and struck the Philistine on the forehead. . . . Without a sword in his hand he struck down the Philistine and killed him . . .

When the Philistines saw that their hero was dead, they turned and ran. Then the men of Israel and Judah surged forward with a shout and pursued the Philistines to the entrance of Gath and to the gates of Ekron.

Holy Bible (*1 Samuel* 17: 48–52)

The rout of the Philistine army after Goliath's death shows just how fragile the morale of many Biblical armies could be. In this case, the entire army dissolved in panic once its leading warrior was killed by a mere Jewish slinger (albeit who was to become King David).

CULTURAL QUESTIONS
It would be fair to say that the Philistines have not enjoyed a great reputation down the centuries. Indeed, their name has entered our dictionary as the embodiment of uncultured materialism, and even boorishness. Such denigration is a common fate for those who end up on the losing side: the Philistines do not seem to have been any more or less artistically inclined than most people of their times. Their name does however live on in another respect; Palestine is a direct derivation from 'Philistine'.

NEW KINGDOM EGYPTIAN ARMY
(1200 BC–800 BC)

Unit type	Number per army
Chariots (Light Chariot (bow), Elite)	1–3
Spearmen (Biblical Infantry, light armour, Average)	2–4
Archers (Heavy Archers, Light armour, Average)	1–2
Sherden Guard (Auxiliary Infantry, medium armour, Elite)	0–1

The Chariots may be the most glamorous part of this army, but the infantry should not be neglected. The Sherden Guard are first-class troops, and the other foot enjoy higher morale than many of their rivals. The Egyptians were the first Biblical kingdom whose infantry had a genuine offensive capacity, which is something the wargamer should bear in mind.

SPECIAL RULES
1)   *Extra armour*. Some Egyptian infantry units enjoyed the benefits of extra body protection. One spearman unit may be equipped with medium armour.

SUGGESTED DEPLOYMENT

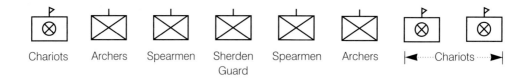

| Chariots | Archers | Spearmen | Sherden Guard | Spearmen | Archers | |◄┈┈┈┈Chariots┈┈┈┈►| |

Although the chariots are still the main strike force of this army, the infantry's assault capability is maximised by having the Sherden Guard at the centre of the line. The archers, deployed as they are between the infantry and the chariots, can support assaults (and defend against enemy attack) from all directions.

CREATING THE ARMY IN MINIATURE
As the Egyptians are one of the two truly famous Biblical armies (the other being the Assyrians), the wargamer is spoilt for choice. For the first time, one 20mm plastic manufacturer (Nexus) produces some figures for a Biblical force, and many 6mm, 15mm and 25mm metal companies have comprehensive ranges.

ALTERNATIVE ARMIES
Egyptian uniforms are rather distinctive, and figures cannot therefore serve in other forces. However, a case can be made for exempting the Sherden Guard

from this restriction; since they were armed and equipped as Sea Peoples, they may serve in the latter force – provided that the wargamer ignores the rather inconvenient fact that the sun-shaped disc featuring in the guardsmen's helmets was unique to the Egyptian army.

PRIMARY SOURCES

Herodotus (c. 450 BC). *The Histories* (tr. Aubrey de Sélincourt and rev. A.R. Burn), Penguin, 1972

SECONDARY SOURCES

Clark, S.J. 'The Egyptian Army in the New Kingdom' in *Slingshot* no. 182 (November 1995), 6–13
Healy, Mark. *Qadesh 1300 BC*, Osprey, 1993
Manley, Bill. *The Penguin Historical Atlas of Ancient Egypt*, Penguin, 1996
Shaw, Ian. *Egyptian Warfare and Weapons*, Shire, 1991
Stillman, Nigel and Tallis, Nigel. *Armies of the Ancient Near East*, Wargames Research Group, 1984

CHARIOT MAINTENANCE

You are brought into the armoury and workshops surround you. . . . They take care of your chariot so that it is no longer loose. Your pole is freshly trimmed and its attachments are fitted on. They put bindings on your collar piece . . . and they fix up your yoke. They apply your ensign, engraved with a chisel, and they put a handle on your whip and attach a lash to it.

Papyrus Anastasi I (c. 900 BC), quoted in Shaw, Ian, *Egyptian Warfare and Weapons*, Shire, 1991.

This extract encapsulates the problems of chariots. They may have ruled the battlefield, but they needed a great deal of logistical support in order to function.

THE REWARDS OF PIRACY

The Sherden were originally notorious pirates from Sardinia. Pharaoh Ramesses II was so impressed with the ferocity of these individuals, that he employed some as a royal bodyguard, where they enjoyed a privileged status as a result.

HITTITE KINGDOM ARMY
(1300 BC–710 BC)

Unit type	Number per army
Hittite Chariots (Heavy Chariots, Elite)	2–4
Syrian Allied Chariots (Light Chariots (bow), Average)	0–2
Spearmen (Biblical Infantry, light armour, Levy)	2–4
Skirmishers (Light Infantry (javelin), light armour, Levy)	1–2

For chariot lovers, this is undoubtedly the army of choice. The combination of shock action from the Hittites and effective missilry from the Syrian allies can have a devastating effect upon opposing armies. This is probably just as well, for the infantry cannot be relied upon to provide any effective support.

The equipment of Hittite chariotry has given rise to a good deal of discussion among historians, concerning its precise role on the battlefield. The chief pictorial sources (Egyptian illustrations of the Battle of Kadesh) show Hittite chariots as having only two horses, but three crewmen (a driver, a warrior and a shieldbearer). Moreover, the chariots are clearly shown as being equipped with long spears rather than bows. Some historians claim that all this is artistic licence designed to denigrate the Hittites by only showing them equipped with spears (always a weapon of commoners), rather than the traditionally aristocratic composite bow. I do not find these arguments convincing, for the Egyptian illustrations also clearly show that the Hittite chariots had their wheel axles in the middle, rather than at the rear of the cab (which was the usual arrangement for the Egyptian light chariots). Putting the axles in the middle of the cab allowed the Hittite chariots to accommodate the extra weight of an additional crewman, but did tend to reduce manoeuvrability. The combination of long spears, extra crew and less agility were all traits of heavy chariots, which explains why the Hittite vehicles have been so classified here.

Incidentally, this army list post-dates the fall of the Hittite Empire proper. This is so that the various successor kingdoms (which finally fell to the Assyrians) can be included within the parameters of this list.

SUGGESTED DEPLOYMENT

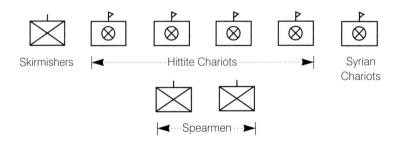

Skirmishers | Hittite Chariots | Syrian Chariots

Spearmen

This army has maximised the number of chariots, with its whole purpose being to get the Hittite vehicles into hand-to-hand combat as quickly as possible. The Light Chariot and skirmisher units simply have the role of protecting the Hittite vehicles' flanks. As for the spearmen, they have little effective role in this army, and are therefore assigned to the rear.

CREATING THE ARMY IN MINIATURE
Although there are no suitable plastic figures for the Hittites, metal figures in 6mm, 15mm and 25mm sizes are available from a range of manufacturers.

ALTERNATIVE ARMIES
Most units in this army are uniquely Hittite (due chiefly to the distinctive hairstyle favoured by the kingdoms). However, the Syrian chariots may serve in Canaanite and Israelite armies.

SECONDARY SOURCES
Gurney, O.R. *The Hittites*, Penguin, 1952
Healy, Mark. *Qadesh 1300 BC*, Osprey, 1993
Stillman, Nigel. *Chariot Wars*, Warhammer Historical Wargames, 1999
Stillman, Nigel and Tallis, Nigel. *Armies of the Ancient Near East*, Wargames Research Group, 1984
Wise, Terence. *Ancient Armies of the Middle East*, Osprey, 1981

A SUGGESTED STRATAGEM
And because [the enemy] had outposts, if I had tried to surround Pitaggatalis [the enemy general], the outposts would have seen me, and so would not have waited for me and would have slipped away before me. So I turned my face in the opposite direction towards Pittaparas. But when night fell, I turned about and advanced against Pitaggatalis. I marched the whole night through, and daybreak found me on the outskirts of Sapiddicura. And as soon as the sun rose I advanced to battle against him . . . and I destroyed the enemy.

The annals of Mursili II (c. 980 BC), quoted in Gurney, O.R., *The Hittites*, Penguin, 1952, p. 109.

Bringing an unwilling enemy to battle is an essential skill for any general to master. Mursili's use of feigned retreat worked brilliantly on this occasion, and demonstrates that Biblical warfare could be quite sophisticated.

HITTITE HIPPIES?
Egyptian Pharaoh Ramesses II ridiculed the Hittites in his propaganda, claiming that their long hair was evidence of effeminate degeneracy. However, the Hittites' battlefield performance showed that their army was far from effete.

ISRAELITE ARMY
(1220 BC–940 BC)

Unit type	Number per army
Simeonites and Ephraimites (Auxiliary Infantry, light armour, Elite)	1–2
Gadites and Issacher (Light Infantry (javelin), light armour, Average)	1–2
Benjaminites (Light Infantry (sling), light armour, Average)	1–2
Other Seven Tribes (Auxiliary Infantry, light armour, Average)	2–4

Israelite commanders are blessed with very reliable infantry, that is especially deadly in difficult terrain. Accordingly, the army should deploy as many units as possible in rocky areas, relying on its auxiliary infantry to absorb enemy assaults in the open.

Gamers who prefer to deploy chariots should note that Solomon's army (see special note below) allows these to be added to the Israelite roster, producing a distinctly formidable army.

SPECIAL RULES

1) *Guerrilla Warfare*. The Israelites specialised in luring the enemy into unfavourable terrain, where they could be ambushed. Apply the following rules to reflect this:

   a) *Extra terrain*. The Israelites may place two additional pieces of rocky terrain anywhere on the battlefield.

   b) *Ambush*. Up to two light infantry units may deploy anywhere on the battlefield. They may be placed after the enemy player has finished setting up his or her army.

2) *Solomon's Army* (980 BC–940 BC). King Solomon's force tended to fight on open terrain, and consequently acquired a large force of chariots. Apply the following rules:

   a) Disregard the Guerrilla Warfare rules. They no longer apply.

   b) Add the following entry to the Israelite army list:

Unit type	Number per army
Chariots (Light Chariots (bow), Elite)	1–3

3) *Benjaminites*. Some of these men appear to have been archers. To reflect this, up to one unit may swap their slings for bows if desired.

4) *Post-Solomonic armies* (740 BC–587 BC). Judging from the Biblical accounts of civil war and general decadence following the death of Solomon (see *1* and *2 Kings*), later armies seem to have lost their cutting edge. This can be accounted for by allowing for the increased prominence of the chariot arm, and decline in the quality of foot soldiers. Since this closely reflects Canaanite armies, use the Canaanite and Philistine list for any forces after Solomon's reign.

SUGGESTED DEPLOYMENT

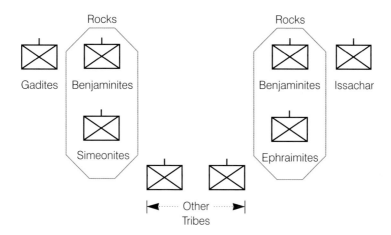

This is designed for a pre-Solomonic army, and uses rocks to best effect. The Benjaminites may snipe at the enemy while enjoying the benefits of cover, and any troops foolhardy enough to enter the rocky areas is likely to be destroyed by the Simeonites and Ephraimites. However, if the enemy aims for the other tribes, the fact that they are slightly to the rear (or refused, to use the correct military term), allows the Simeonites and Ephraimites to assail the flanks of any foe. The Gadites and Issachar should only fight delaying actions, withdrawing from any flank assault accordingly. If possible, other terrain pieces can be deployed to protect the retreating Israelite Light Infantry.

CREATING THE ARMY IN MINIATURE

Plastic figure ranges do not yet exist. As with other armies, 15mm and 25mm miniatures are produced by some companies – check advertisements and/or websites for details. As for 6mm metal figures, Irregular Miniatures provide a good selection.

ALTERNATIVE ARMIES

Light Infantry can serve in most armies. Remember that post-Solomonic forces can quite legitimately use Canaanite figures.

PRIMARY SOURCES

Holy Bible (especially the books of *Joshua*, *Judges*, *1 Samuel*, *2 Samuel*, *1 Kings* and *2 Kings*)

SECONDARY SOURCES

Healy, Mark. *Warriors of the Old Testament*, Firebird, 1989

Stillman, Nigel. *Chariot Wars*, Warhammer Historical Wargames, 1999

Stillman, Nigel and Tallis, Nigel. *Armies of the Ancient Near East*, Wargames Research Group, 1984

Wise, Terence. *Ancient Armies of the Middle East*, Osprey, 1981

OUTWITTING THE ENEMY

That night Joshua went into the valley. When the king of Ai saw this, he and all the men of the city hurried out early in the morning to meet Israel in battle . . . but he did not know that an ambush had been set against him behind the city. Joshua and all Israel let themselves be driven back before them, and they fled towards the desert. All the men of Ai were called to pursue them, and they pursued Joshua and were lured away from the city. . . . The [Israelite] men in the ambush rose quickly from their position and rushed forward. They entered the city and captured it and quickly set it on fire.

The men of Ai looked back and saw the smoke of the city rising against the sky, but had no chance to escape in any direction, for the Israelites who had been fleeing towards the desert had turned back against their pursuers. For when Joshua and all Israel saw that the ambush had taken the city, they turned round and attacked the men of Ai. The men of the ambush also came out of the city against them, so that they were caught in the middle, with Israelites on both sides. Israel cut them down, leaving them neither survivors nor fugitives.

Holy Bible (*Joshua* 8: 13–16; 19–22).

Although some historians have questioned whether or not Joshua really did capture the Canaanite city of Ai in his campaigns (c. 1220 BC), this account gives a very clear description of the sort of tactical ruses necessary for an infantry army to outwit and destroy a force equipped with chariots. The feigned retreat invariably led a rash or impetuous enemy to destruction.

MYCENEAN GREEK ARMY
(1120 BC–850 BC)

Unit type	Number per army
Chariots (Heavy Chariots, Elite)	2–4
Spearmen (Biblical Infantry, light armour, Average)	2–4
Archers (Light Infantry (bow), light armour, Levy)	1–2

Although the spearmen are more effective than most Biblical Infantry, this army inevitably relies upon its chariots for maximum impact. Other troops are there to provide support: the Elite chariotry will win the battle – and in the age of Homeric heroism, that is precisely how it should be.

SPECIAL RULES

1) *Large shields*. The spearmen were (like the Sumerians) were equipped with these, but could also (unlike the Sumerians) use them effectively. Provided that Mycenean Spearmen move no more than 4cm per turn, they are regarded as being equipped with medium armour.

2) *Integral archers*. The Spearmen seem to have had some bowmen serving within the ranks. To reflect this, one base of any Spearman unit may fire up to a range of 24cm provided that it does not move that turn.

3) *Achilles' Myrmidons*. These appear in *The Iliad*, and seem to have fought much as Sea Peoples did. If the wargamer believes that such troops really did appear in Mycenean armies, add the following item to the list:

Unit type	Number per army
Myrmidons (Auxiliary Infantry, medium armour, Average)	0–1

4) *Trojans*. To fight battles from *The Iliad*, the wargamer should use this list to depict the Trojan army. However, I would argue that historical accuracy dictates that Troy, being located as it is in Asia Minor, would be likely to have used the Hittite military system. If the wargamer agrees, then use the Hittite army list.

SUGGESTED DEPLOYMENT

Chariots   Archers |◄·········· Spearmen ··········►| |◄·········· Chariots ··········►|

Most of the chariots are concentrated on one flank, in order to engage the enemy in overwhelming strength. The opposite flank is protected not only by the remaining chariot unit, but also by bowfire from the archers (whose firing can also cover any attack against the Greek centre). As for the spearmen, their enhanced saving roll and supplementary missile capability makes them very useful in a defensive role; however, their reasonable morale allows them to support the chariot assault in addition.

CREATING THE ARMY IN MINIATURE
No plastic figures yet exist for this army, but there is now fairly extensive coverage in 6mm, 15mm and 25mm metal miniatures.

ALTERNATIVE ARMIES
The archers may serve in most other Biblical armies. The same cannot unfortunately be said for the spearmen and charioteers, whose dress was rather distinctive.

PRIMARY SOURCES
Homer (c. 700 BC). *The Iliad* (tr. E.V. Rieu), Penguin, 1950

SECONDARY SOURCES
Burn, A.R. *The Pelican History of Greece*, Pelican, 1982
Hanson, Victor Davis. *The Wars of the Ancient Greeks*, Cassell, 1999
Stillman, Nigel. *Chariot Wars*, Warhammer Historical Wargames, 1999
Stillman, Nigel and Tallis, Nigel. *Armies of the Ancient Near East*, Wargames
    Research Group, 1984

THE PERILS OF RETREAT
Diomedes was certainly the first to kill a Trojan man-at-arms. His victim, Agelaus son of Phradmon, had swung his horse round for flight. He had no sooner wheeled than Diomedes caught him in the back with his spear, midway between the shoulders, and drove it through his breast. He crashed from his chariot and his armour rang about him.

Homer (c. 700 BC), *The Iliad* (tr. E.V. Rieu), Penguin, 1950, p. 152.

Many chariot mêlées must have happened like this, with two chariot forces facing each other, only for one to lose its nerve and attempt to flee from combat. As was the case here, any failure to stand firm tended to prove fatal.

HOMERIC HISTORY
The Iliad is certainly the first (and one of the greatest) historical novels ever written. For all its distinctly fictional characters and references to divine intervention,

however, it does record an undoubtedly historical war. More importantly, some of the descriptions do provide an excellent illustration of Ancient hand-to-hand combat.

SEA PEOPLES ARMY
(870 BC–840 BC)

Unit type	Number per army
Nobles (Auxiliary Infantry, medium armour, Elite)	1–2
Warriors (Auxiliary Infantry, medium armour, Average)	5–7
Archers (Light Infantry (bow), light armour, Levy)	0–1
Skirmishers (Light Infantry (bow), light armour, Levy)	0–1
Chariots (Heavy Chariots, Elite)	0–1

With large numbers of well-armoured, highly disciplined and fast-moving infantry, the Sea Peoples' historic tactic was to charge (and usually rout) the enemy. The wargamer should do the same; it may be true that the flanks are vulnerable to enemy chariots, but if the main body of the foe can be eliminated first, this is unlikely to prove too much of a problem.

SPECIAL RULES

1) *Chariots*. Although chariots seldom seem to have played much of a role in the Sea Peoples' armies, it is possible that light chariots may have been fielded in some campaigns. If the wargamer prefers, he or she may replace the heavy chariot unit with one of light chariots (equipped with a bow).

SUGGESTED DEPLOYMENT

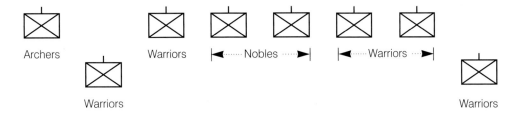

This wargaming general has proved immune to the appeal of the chariot, preferring instead to rely upon infantry. Note that the nobles are placed in the centre of the line, where they are best placed to target and destroy enemy infantry. Two of the warrior units have been refused; this is to provide some protection for the flanks of the front line, since any attacks there can themselves be outflanked by the refused units. Moreover, deploying the leftmost warrior unit to the rear allows the archers a wider field of fire to their right, thereby supporting the attack.

CREATING THE ARMY IN MINIATURE
Plastic figures for the Sea Peoples are now available, as are metal miniatures in 6mm, 15mm and 25mm. Chariots and light infantry are not so readily obtainable, but any figures from generic Biblical armies may be used if desired.

ALTERNATIVE ARMIES
Sea Peoples did serve as mercenaries in some armies, and their figures may be fielded accordingly. Obviously, any non-specific chariots and light infantry can fill the ranks of suitable Biblical forces.

SECONDARY SOURCES
Drews, Robert. *The End of the Bronze Age*, Princeton, 1993
Stillman, Nigel and Tallis, Nigel. *Armies of the Ancient Near East*, Wargames Research Group, 1984
Wise, Terence. *Ancient Armies of the Middle East*, Osprey, 1981

THE SEA PEOPLES WHO WEREN'T
The term 'Sea Peoples' is something of a misnomer, since although many invaders come from the Mediterranean islands, others resided in Asia Minor. The latter did not have to invade anywhere by sea, contenting themselves instead with land assaults upon the Hittite Empire.

NEW ASSYRIAN IMPERIAL ARMY
(750 BC–610 BC)

Unit type	Number per army
Chariots (Heavy Chariots, Elite)	1–2
Cavalry (Heavy Cavalry, light armour, Elite)	1–2
Line Infantry (Heavy Infantry, medium armour, Elite)	2–4
Auxiliary Infantry (Auxiliary Infantry, light armour, Average)	2–4
Archers (Light Infantry (bow), light armour, Levy)	0–2

Commanding an army that has the ability to annihilate most of its foes is not the greatest of challenges. It will nevertheless prove extremely satisfying. The array of different troop types, combined with distinctly colourful dress, is also likely to add to this army's appeal.

SPECIAL RULES

1) *Terror* (optional rule). The reputation of the Assyrians was such that many opponents often ran away before contact. Accordingly, any enemy troops in hand-to-hand combat with Assyrian chariots, cavalry, line infantry or auxiliary infantry, must test morale before the first round.

2) *Mixed units*. Half of every line infantry, auxiliary infantry and cavalry units were equipped with bows (and should be depicted as such by using the appropriate figures provided by all manufactures). These units fire bows with half their remaining bases every turn (even if they move).

3) *Babylonian armies*. Assyria's most doughty opponents seem to have worked on the principle that imitation was the sincerest form of flattery. They use the Assyrian army list, but with the following modifications:

   a) *Downgrade morale*. Downgrade cavalry, line infantry and auxiliary infantry one morale class (so that Elite troops become Average, and Average become Levy).

   b) *Disregard Terror rule*. Sadly for the Babylonians, they do not seem to have terrified anyone unduly.

4) *Median armies*. If the wargamer would like to confront the Assyrians with a Median army, use the Early Achaemenid Persian army list provided in Chapter 9.

SUGGESTED DEPLOYMENT

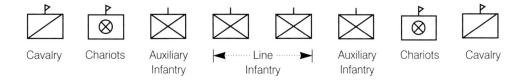

| Cavalry | Chariots | Auxiliary Infantry | ◄······ Line ······► Infantry | Auxiliary Infantry | Chariots | Cavalry |

The Cavalry are a good choice for protecting the army's flanks, since they are not only mobile but have a missile capability as well. The auxiliary infantry can, given their additional speed, provide an effective link between the line infantry and the chariots. The Heavy Infantry are positioned to smash the enemy centre.

CREATING THE ARMY IN MINIATURE

Figure designers have always been attracted to the Assyrian army, and wide ranges exist in 6mm, 15mm and 25mm metal miniatures. Some plastic figures are also available.

ALTERNATIVE ARMIES

Since Babylonians dressed the same as Assyrians, the latter figures can quite legitimately serve in the former army. However, Assyrian figures cannot be fielded in any other force; their dress was too distinctive.

SECONDARY SOURCES

Healy, Mark. *The Ancient Assyrians*, Osprey, 1991

Leick, Gwendolyn. *Mesopotamia*, Penguin, 2001

McLaughlin, D.M. 'Assyrian Infantry in Battlefield Formation' in *Slingshot* no. 179 (May 1995), 1–2

Stillman, Nigel and Tallis, Nigel. *Armies of the Ancient Near East*, Wargames Research Group, 1984

Stillman, Nigel. *Chariot Wars*, Warhammer Historical Wargames, 1999

Wise, Terence. *Ancient Armies of the Middle East*, Osprey, 1981

THE SACK OF BABYLON

As a hurricane proceeds, I attacked it [Babylon] and like a storm, I overthrew it. . . . Its inhabitants, young and old, I did not spare and with their corpses I filled the city. . . . The town itself and its houses, from their foundations to their roofs I devastated, I destroyed, by fire I overthrew. . . . In order that in future even the soil of its temples be forgotten, by water I ravaged it, I turned it into pastures.

The sack of Babylon (689 BC) recorded in the *Annals of Sennacherib*, quoted in Healy, Mark, *The Ancient Assyrians*, Osprey, 1991, p. 47.

This rather grisly account shows the extent to which the Assyrians revelled in brutality and conquest. These traits may have served to win them an empire; they were not calculated to inspire affection.

CIMMERIAN AND SCYTHIAN ARMIES
(750 BC–50 BC)

Unit type	Number per army
Nobles (Heavy Cavalry (bow), medium armour, Elite)	1–2
Warriors (Light Cavalry (bow), light armour, Average)	6–7

Although this army has the simplest list imaginable, it can be very effective. Massed ranks of mobile archers can whittle down enemy troops very rapidly. The Scythian wargamer would be well advised to target enemy archers (thereby negating any missile retaliation) and staying out of charge range. The nobles can of course enter hand-to-hand combat with some effect, but should avoid doing so until the enemy is gravely weakened by bowfire.

Incidentally, the Cimmerians and the Scythians were originally enemies, the former being driven out of the Asian steppes into the Middle East by the latter. However, once the Scythians saw the rich pickings enjoyed by the Cimmerian raiders, they too invaded what is now Iraq in order to join in the fun.

SPECIAL RULES

1) *Noble cavalry*. The Cimmerian and Scythian nobility was rather more mobile than most other heavy horse. They accordingly enjoy the following benefits:

    a)   Nobles may turn without restriction.

    b)   Nobles may fire their bows after they move (they may not fire before they move, unlike Light Cavalry).

2) *Classical crossover*. The Scythians made a great nuisance of themselves well into the Classical period, before finally being defeated and absorbed by the Sarmatians and Parthians. This army list may be used for Scythian troops fighting in the Classical period, with the following modification:

    a)   If fighting in Classical times, Scythian nobles now have heavy armour, but may no longer turn without restriction (they may still fire their bows after movement).

SUGGESTED DEPLOYMENT

Note how there is a gap left in the centre. This is so that massed horse archery can concentrate upon the enemy flanks, with the nobles positioned in reserve, ready to attack any weakened enemy. As for the centre, that can be outflanked once the wings have been routed.

CREATING THE ARMY IN MINIATURE

Although there are no plastic figures listed as Scythians, those listed as Persians can be pressed into service, since some have the appropriate dress (it would be advisable to check before purchase). However, metal miniatures in 6mm, 15mm and 25mm are widely available; do bear in mind that they are frequently catalogued under other periods such as 'Classical' or 'Greek and Persian Wars' ranges, rather than under entries for 'Scythians' or 'Cimmerians'.

ALTERNATIVE ARMIES

The horse archers listed in my Early Achaemenid Persian army list were often of Scythian origin: warriors may be fielded accordingly.

PRIMARY SOURCE

Herodotus (c. 450 BC). *The Histories* (tr. Aubrey de Sélincourt and rev. A.R. Burn), Penguin, 1972

SECONDARY SOURCES

Cernenko, E.V. *The Scythians*, Osprey, 1983
Hildinger, Erik. *Warriors of the Steppe*, Spellmount, 1997
Karasulus, Antony. *Mounted Archers of the Steppe*, Osprey, 2004
Stillman, Nigel and Tallis, Nigel. *Armies of the Ancient Near East*, Wargames Research Group, 1984

WASTE NOT, WANT NOT

As regards war, the Scythian custom is to drink the blood of the first man he kills. The heads of all enemies killed in battle are taken to the king; if he brings a head, a soldier is admitted to his share of the loot; no head, no loot. He strips the skin off the head by making a circular cut round the ears and shaking out the skull; he then scrapes the flesh off the skin with the rib of an ox, and when it is clean works it in his fingers until it is supple, and fit to be used as a sort of handkerchief. He hangs these handkerchiefs on the bridle of his horse, and is very proud of them. The finest fellow is the man who has the greatest number.

Herodotus (c. 450 BC), *The Histories* (tr. Aubrey de Sélincourt and rev. A.R. Burn), Penguin, 1972, p. 291.

This rather gruesome custom indicates how savage the Scythians were. Being essentially nomadic, civilisation meant nothing to them other than a source of plunder. They certainly made no useful contribution to human history, and the state of the world was greatly enhanced when the Scythians were finally conquered.

Chapter 5

Biblical Battle Report

Given the lack of comprehensive documentation of most Biblical campaigns, one may think that it would be difficult to select an appropriate engagement to wargame. Fortunately for all of us, the Battle of Kadesh (941 BC) is an exception to this rule – extensive records exist, and it is moreover a fascinating encounter.

THE BATTLE IN HISTORY

The tenth century BC saw a major intensification of tension between the neighbouring empires of the Hittites and the New Kingdom Egyptians. Accordingly, when the former saw fit to flex its muscles by exerting political influence over Syria, Pharaoh Ramesses II of Egypt felt compelled to respond to the Hittite challenge. Accordingly, the Egyptians landed an army in Syria in 942 BC, and advanced on the city of Kadesh (whose king was a Hittite ally) the following year.

The campaign appeared to start well for the Egyptians, when some Hittite deserters informed Ramesses that Kadesh was badly defended. Accordingly, the Egyptian Pharaoh ordered a rapid advance towards the city, so that it could be besieged and taken before any relieving army arrived. With the Egyptian force divided into its four divisions (Amun, together with Ramesses' Ne'arim bodyguard; Re; Ptah; and Set), this meant that four separate marching columns would proceed along the plain of Kadesh to the west of the River Orontes. A camp was to be set up to the northwest of Kadesh, from where the city could be besieged.

All went well at first. The Amun division headed past Kadesh as planned, and constructed a camp. Meanwhile, the Re division proceeded on its march, heading towards the camp in column formation. Ramesses was doubtless congratulating himself on a job well done.

Unfortunately for the Egyptians, things were not what they seemed. They had actually been outsmarted by the Hittite King Muwatallis II; for the so-called 'deserters' who informed Ramesses that Kadesh was undefended, were actually spies planted by the Hittites. Not for the first or the last time in history, misinformation had been spread successfully, because the story was one that the recipient wanted to hear. Ramesses believed himself to be an outstanding strategist; he therefore convinced himself that he had stolen a march on Muwatallis and since the 'deserters' confirmed the analysis, Ramesses subscribed to their account. In fact, the Hittite army, which was of a similar strength to the Egyptian force (approximately 20,000 men), was concealed behind Kadesh and the wooded area to the south of the city, to the east of the Orontes. Moreover, the Hittite chariots were poised to strike.

It will be recalled that the Re division, oblivious to all this, was marching towards the Egyptian encampment in columnar formation. This rather unfortunately presented the Egyptians right flank to the Hittites, whose massed chariots rapidly forded the Orontes, and then its Al-Mukadiyah tributary. They promptly assaulted the right flank of the Re division: the devastating effects of this assault were greatly exacerbated by the fact that the Hittites used heavy chariots. These were designed to engage in hand-to-hand combat, rather than skirmish in the manner of the Egyptian light chariotry. As a result, the Re division was destroyed, with only a few terrified remnants surviving to head towards the Egyptian Camp – with the Hittites in hot pursuit.

A thunderstruck Ramesses now had to respond. With his army in disorder, the Camp had to be protected. Accordingly, the remaining Egyptian chariots fought a delaying action, engaging the Hittites with archery. The latter meanwhile arrived at Ramesses' Camp, and proceeded to assault it. However, the Amun division was now in some sort of order, and managed to hang on long enough for the Ne'arim to take a hand. These Elite troops (including the Sherden Guard) were able to assail the Hittite chariotry's flanks, and in concert with the rest of the Egyptians were able to force a Hittite retreat.

The reader may wonder what the Hittite infantry had been up to while all this excitement was going on. There is certainly no description of their involvement in the battle; however, in an age that glorified the achievements of chariots to the exclusion of everything else, this is not surprising. What may have happened is that the Hittite foot soldiers took a long time to form up for battle, deploying to the east of the Orontes opposite the Egyptian Camp. They may have played a role in extricating their noble compatriots from their imbroglio, at the end of the battle.

In tactical terms, the Battle of Kadesh was a stalemate, with both armies breaking off the engagement in exhaustion. From the strategic point of view, the campaign was a victory for the Hittites; Ramesses was forced to withdraw not only from Kadesh, but to retreat all the way to Egypt as well. Ramesses II had to devote much energy to reasserting Egyptian authority in Canaan and southern Syria, following the failure of the Kadesh campaign. However, Ramesses was greatly assisted by a formidable propaganda operation. His somewhat tarnished authority was bolstered by his chroniclers, who stressed how heroically the Pharaoh had performed on the battlefield. They even went as far as to claim that Kadesh had been a great Egyptian victory. This was, as we have seen, somewhat at variance with the facts – any tactical victory was Pyrrhic at best (to use a Classical anachronism). Nevertheless, putting one's story across was a vital necessity – and veracity was not a precondition of any such propaganda.

RECREATING THE BATTLEFIELD

With most of the battlefield comprising a flat sandy plain, a 3ft × 4ft piece of unpainted hardboard sufficed for most of this terrain. The Rivers Orontes and Al-Mukadiyah were represented by an old pair of jeans cut into strips. Kadesh city was depicted by some card buildings (home made), and the surrounding woods by trees from S & A Scenics. As for the Camp, its walls were improvised using a farmyard stone wall bought from a toyshop.

ARMY COMPOSITION

Owing to the lack of comprehensive information concerning orders of battle (that luxury tends to be confined to the Classical period), armies had to be improvised from the lists provided in Chapter 4. In the Hittites' case, this meant that four Hittite chariots were deployed, given their prominence. The infantry contingent comprised three units of spearmen and one of skirmishers.

The Egyptian army consisted of the maximum number of chariots (three), but infantry played rather more of a role than in the Hittite force. Two units of spearmen, and two more of archers were seen as being essential to reflect this: moreover, the Elite Ne'arim also had to be represented. For this contingent, the Sherden Guard were the obvious choice to make up the remaining unit of the Egyptian army.

PLANS AND DEPLOYMENT

The special nature of the Battle of Kadesh meant that deployment was largely predetermined. The three units of the Re division (units 9, 10 and 11) were placed in a marching column on the left-hand edge of the board. The Hittite chariots (units 1, 2, 3 and 4) were deployed to their right flank, within a charge move (much to the delight of the Hittite general).

However, creating an adequate simulation of the battle meant that some special rules had to be provided. Chief among these was a plausible reinforcement schedule. Given the importance of the Egyptian arrivals, one unit per turn arrived from turn 2 onwards. It was felt that the two chariots would be first to arrive (from the top right-hand corner of the board), followed by the Amun division, represented as the latter was by the remaining units of archers and spearmen (one of each). These would appear within the Camp; they were assumed to depict how the latter

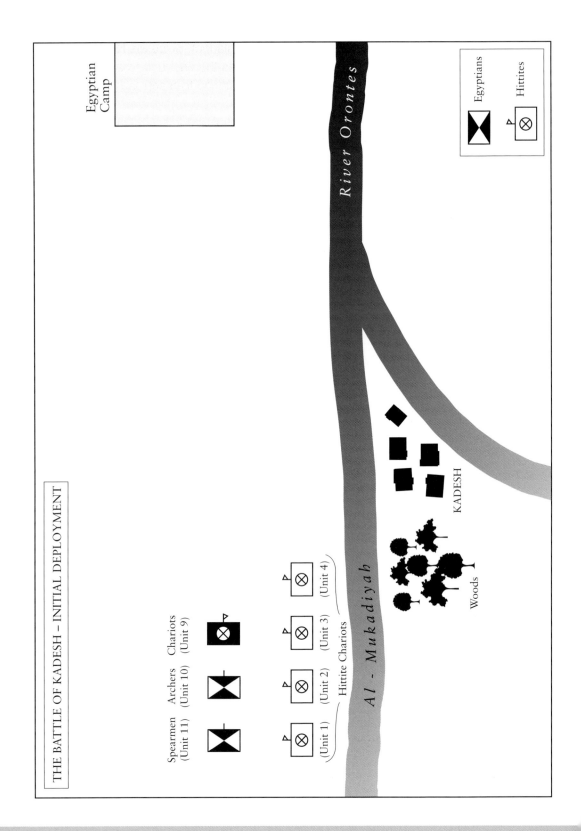

THE BATTLE OF KADESH – INITIAL DEPLOYMENT

Egyptian Camp

River Orontes

Al - Mukadiyah

KADESH

Woods

Spearmen (Unit 11)

Archers (Unit 10)

Chariots (Unit 9)

Hittite Chariots

(Unit 1)

(Unit 2)

(Unit 3)

(Unit 4)

Egyptians

Hittites

Egyptians

Hittites

got itself in some sort of order to resist the Hittite onslaught. Since the Ne'arim was the last contingent to arrive, the Sherden Guard was the final unit to appear; like the chariots, this seems to have marched some distance to reach the battle, and therefore entered the board from the top right edge.

As for the Hittite infantry, their rather tardy contribution to the historical battle was represented by a distinctly late arrival. One unit per turn arrived from turn 6 onwards (the latter being the same turn on which the Sherden turned up). The skirmishers were deemed to arrive first, since it was likely that light infantrymen would be more likely to put in an early appearance than the slow-moving spearmen.

Some special rules were also necessary to reflect the importance of the Egyptian Camp. Since this appeared to have been well defended in the historical battle, it was felt appropriate to allow any garrison to fight with one extra die, per base engaged in hand-to-hand combat. Moreover, Hittite units would take a complete turn to cross the Camp walls on order to assault the defenders behind them. However, the loss of their baggage was deemed to be likely to have a severe effect upon Egyptian morale. Accordingly, if the Hittites were ever to be the sole occupiers of the Camp, the Egyptians would immediately have to eliminate two of their units.

A final rule had to be applied with respect to exiting the board on the enemy side. It was felt that this aspect of the existing rules was inappropriate for Kadesh. With such a fluid battle, thanks to units appearing all over the place, there was no discernible point at which to exit. The Hittite focal point was Kadesh itself, which could only be taken by a formal siege: since this did not fall within the parameters of a tabletop engagement, the Egyptians literally had nowhere to pillage. As for the Hittites, their only objective was the Egyptian Camp (the rules concerning which have already been outlined); there was absolutely no benefit to be gained from exiting the battlefield.

With so few units deployed on the board, planning was relatively simple. The Hittite King Muwatallis II had to first destroy the Re division, and then launch his chariots in an assault on the Egyptian Camp. As for our wargaming Pharaoh Ramesses II, his task was to salvage whatever part of the Re division he could, fight a delaying action with his chariots (making the most of their archery), and defend the Camp with his infantry.

TURN-BY-TURN ANALYSIS
Since the battle proved to be something of a titanic struggle (taking fifteen turns to resolve), the main events will be summarised, rather than giving a detailed account of every turn.

The battle began with Muwatallis striking the flank of the Re division; units 1 and 2 engaged units 10 and 11, while 3 and 4 hit the Re's chariot unit (unit 9). This was designed to concentrate maximum strength against the most dangerous part of the Re division, and prevent unit 9 escaping (since units that are engaged on two sides cannot evade, which the Egyptian Light Chariot would normally have attempted to do). By the end of turn 2 all the Re division had been wiped out, although the Hittite advance on the Egyptian Camp had been delayed by the resistance of the spearmen (unit 11).

End of Turn 2	Eliminated Units
Hittites	None
Egyptians	Three units (9, 10 and 11)

Following this encouraging start, Muwatallis ordered his Hittite chariots to attack the Egyptian Camp as soon as possible. However, his somewhat disorderly assault came into difficulties. Not only were the leading Hittite chariots assailed by archery from Ramesses' chariots (units 12 and 13), but the Amun divisional infantry (units 14 and 15) arrived at the Camp. With the Hittite plan having thus misfired our wargaming Muwatallis was forced to revise his ideas somewhat. Accordingly, units 3 and 4 attempted to engage the Camp, but 1 and 2 turned to face the Egyptian chariots; their aim was to force the latter into the corner of the battlefield, from whence they would be unable to avoid protracted hand-to-hand combat (no unit is ever allowed to withdraw off the battlefield). Be that as it may, turn 6 saw the first Egyptian success of the battle. Although one of the Hittite chariots (unit 4) was now engaging the Egyptian archers defending the Camp (unit 14), the effect of sustained archery from both the archers and the Egyptian chariots had weakened the attackers. Moreover, the augmented combat power unit 14 enjoyed, thanks to the Camp, meant that the Hittites lost their first unit of the battle.

End of Turn 6	Eliminated Units
Hittites	One unit (4)
Egyptians	Three units (9, 10 and 11)

Turns 7 and 8 saw the Hittite infantry units begin to arrive, but they were not a factor as yet. However, the loss of unit 4 had forced Muwatallis to divert unit 1 from its attempts to pin down the Egyptian chariots (12 and 13), and assault the Camp instead. Accordingly, unit 12 was able to escape the Hittite net, and proceeded to move towards the rear of those units assailing the Amun division. However, Muwatallis was able to pin unit 13 in the corner of the board, and engage it with his Heavy Chariots (unit 2). A protracted tussle ensued.

As for our wargaming Ramesses, he had deployed the Sherden to good effect. While the remaining Hittite chariot (unit 3) was busy engaging the Camp, it had presented its flank to the Egyptian Guards. Nor was Ramesses slow to seize his opportunity; his Elite bodyguard (unit 16) was ordered to attack the charioteers' flanks. The situation at the end of turn 8 can be seen on the map provided.

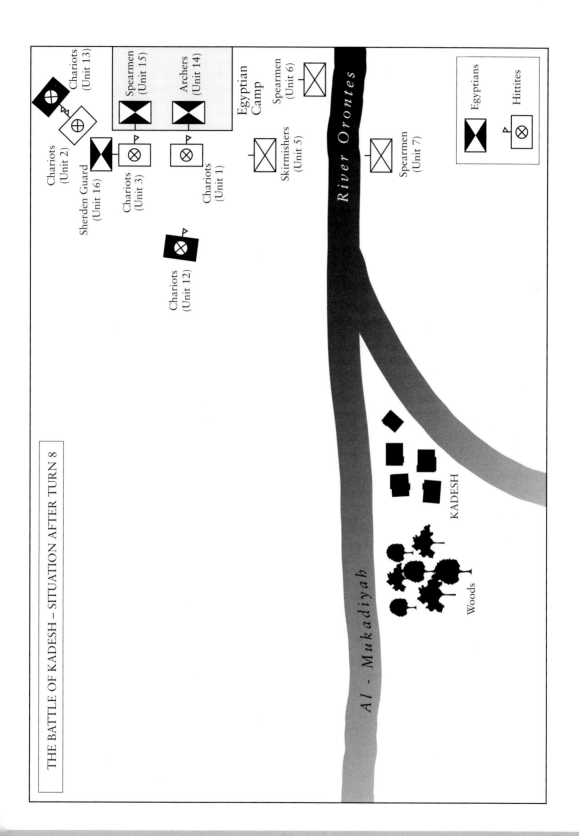

THE BATTLE OF KADESH – SITUATION AFTER TURN 8

Chariots (Unit 13)

Chariots (Unit 2)

Spearmen (Unit 15)

Archers (Unit 14)

Egyptian Camp

Spearmen (Unit 6)

Sherden Guard (Unit 16)

Chariots (Unit 3)

Chariots (Unit 1)

Skirmishers (Unit 5)

Spearmen (Unit 7)

Chariots (Unit 12)

River Orontes

Al - Mukadiyah

KADESH

Woods

Egyptians

Hittites

Turn 9 saw the elimination of the Hittite unit being attacked by the Sherden and the spearmen within the Camp (unit 15). This latter unit enjoyed the benefits of medium armour, and showed some endurance. Accordingly, with no immediate threat, our wargaming Ramesses diverted unit 15 to that part of the Camp facing the Hittite infantry. He also directed the Sherden Guard to continue rolling up the Hittite flank, by engaging the second Hittite chariot assaulting the Camp (unit 1). This move had succeeded in destroying the Hittite aggressors by turn 11, but not without serious consequences; the chariots may have died, but they took the Egyptian archers (unit 14) with them! Meanwhile, one of the Egyptian chariots (unit 12) was engaging the Hittite skirmishers (unit 5). Ramesses had hoped that the charge bonus enjoyed by his chariots would overcome the Hittite levies; however, this expectation proved somewhat optimistic. In a surprising turn of events, the skirmishers not only withstood the chariot onslaught, but fought back with great effect (more prosaically, both sides lost a base in combat, but the ensuing morale tests saw the Hittite Levy pass and the Egyptian Elite fail – thereby losing another base). Accordingly, the Egyptian chariots withdrew on turn 12, relying upon shooting rather than mêlée, in an attempt to cool the Hittite skirmishers' surprising ardour. Moreover, the Hittite chariots (unit 2) finally succeeded in overcoming their much lighter Egyptian opponents (unit 13). Things were looking good for Muwatallis.

End of Turn 12	**Eliminated Units**
Hittites	Three units (1, 3 and 4)
Egyptians	Five units (9, 10, 11, 13 and 14)

Turn 13 saw the Hittites seize the initiative. The final Hittite chariot (unit 2) headed towards the now undefended side of the Camp, while the Hittite spearmen finally played a part in the battle. Muwatallis evidently thought that his levies were possessed of surprising strength. Accordingly, two units of spearmen (units 6 and 8) were devoted to engaging the Egyptian Camp. This proved rash in the extreme; the defenders not only enjoyed the bonus of the Camp walls, but also the benefits of superior morale and armour. Accordingly, one of the aggressors (unit 6) found itself eliminated, only inflicting minimal losses on the Egyptian spearmen (unit 15). As a result, the other unit of Hittite infantry devoted to assaulting the Camp (unit 8) decided to wait until it could launch a simultaneous assault with the chariots (unit 2).

Ramesses had meanwhile attacked the final unit of Hittite spearmen (unit 7) with his Sherden Guard (unit 16). Muwatallis had responded by attacking the Guard's flanks with his skirmishers (unit 5). Ramesses replied in turn by engaging the Levy Light Infantry's rear with his remaining chariot unit (unit 12). The situation at the end of turn 14 is illustrated on the map provided.

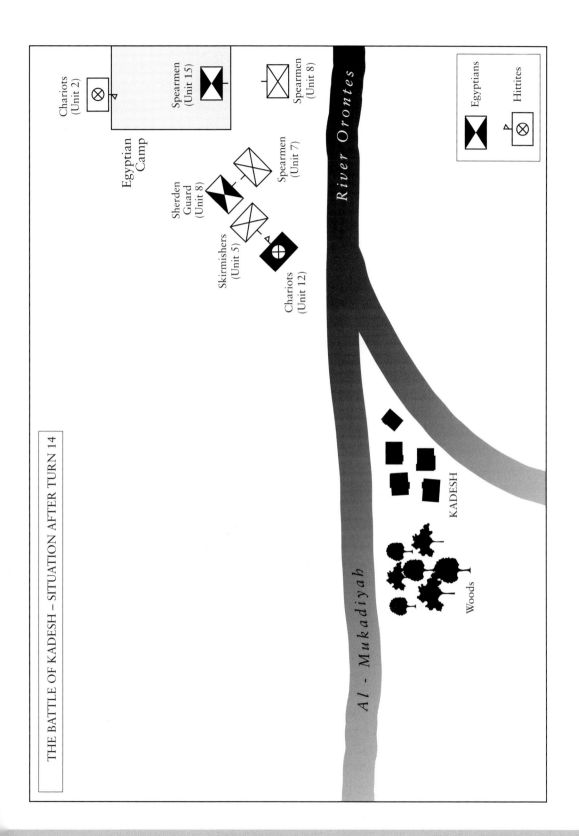

THE BATTLE OF KADESH – SITUATION AFTER TURN 14

Chariots (Unit 2)

Egyptian Camp

Spearmen (Unit 15)

Spearmen (Unit 8)

Sherden Guard (Unit 8)

Spearmen (Unit 7)

Skirmishers (Unit 5)

Chariots (Unit 12)

River Orontes

Al - Mukadiyab

KADESH

Woods

Egyptians

Hittites

Turn 15 saw the final resolution of the battle. The Sherden Guard finally succumbed to the pressure of being engaged both in front and on the flank. Despite the fact that the Egyptian chariots were simultaneously able to destroy the Hittite skirmishers, Ramesses now had only two units remaining. The battle was accordingly lost; however, since Muwatallis only had three units of his own left on the battlefield, the Hittite victory proved to be distinctly narrow. Ramesses was forced to withdraw; his propagandists would once again have to write up a defeat as a victory.

End of Turn 15	**Eliminated Units**
Hittites	Five units (1, 3, 4, 5 and 6)
Egyptians	Six units (9, 10, 11, 13, 14 and 16)

CONCLUSIONS AND SUMMARY

Muwatallis had won his battle, but his wargames generalship was not of the highest order. Despite his efficient destruction of the Re division, his obsession with assaulting the Egyptian Camp led to the destruction of two chariot units and an infantry element. The Hittite Chariots would have been better deployed in rounding up their Egyptian counterparts. As it was, one Egyptian chariot, together with the Sherden Guard, wrought much havoc. Although Muwatallis improvised effectively (with his aggressive use of his skirmishers, allowing the front and flank attack combination upon the Sherden Guard, being especially noteworthy) his obsession with an eye-catching objective rather than the destruction of the Egyptian army nearly proved his undoing.

Conversely, our wargaming Ramesses played a poor hand rather well. His chariots were given an effective skirmishing role, the Amun division defended the Camp with some success, and the Sherden Guard's attacks nearly won the battle. Unfortunately, when any wargamer is fighting against the odds (thanks to the historical Ramesses believing the Hittite spies, and thereby condemning the wargamer's three units representing the Re division to destruction), the deleterious effects of any errors are greatly magnified. Accordingly, our wargaming Pharaoh had much cause to regret his faulty manoeuvring, which exposed one of his chariots (unit 13) to destruction; similarly, allowing the Sherden to engage in frontal combat without flank protection from the second chariot (unit 12) was another error. These would not normally have proved serious; however, given the appalling situation Ramesses found himself in, they proved decisive.

SECONDARY SOURCES

Drews, Robert. *The End of the Bronze Age*, Princeton, 1993

Healy, Mark. *Qadesh 1300 BC*, Osprey, 1993

Montgomery, Field Marshal Viscount. *A Concise History of Warfare*, Wordsworth, 2000 (originally 1968)

Chapter 6

Classical Warfare
500 BC–AD 300

KEY EVENTS

Date	Event
490 BC	Battle of Marathon. Athenians defeat Persian invasion.
480–479	Persian Emperor Xerses invades Greece with massive army. Greeks win decisive victories at Battles of Salamis (on sea) and Plataea (on land).
430–404	Peloponnesian War. Athenian Empire crushed by Sparta and her allies.
371	Battle of Leuctra. Epaminondas of Thebes defeats Spartans. Thebans dominate Greece.
362	Battle of Mantinea. Stalemate between Thebes, and their Spartan and Athenian foes, but Epaminondas killed. Theban ascendancy ends.
359–355	Rise of Macedonia.
350–300	Consolidation of Roman Republic.
338	Battle of Chaeronea. Macedonian defeat of Thebans and Athenians secures hegemony over Greece.
334–329	Alexander the Great invades Persia.
331	Battle of Gaugemela. Alexander defeats and destroys last Achaemenid Persian army. Takes control of Persia following subsequent assassination of Darius III.
323	Death of Alexander the Great.
320–280	Division of Alexander's Empire between Seleucid, Antigonid and Ptolemaic Empires.
260–200	Seleucid Kingdom loses control of Asia Minor and Persia. Territories reduced to Holy Land and Mesopotamia (now Iraq).
250–200	Rise of Parthian Kingdom. Old Persian heartland (now Iran) under their control.

265–240	First Punic War. Rome defeats Carthage and seizes Sicily.
219–202	Second Punic War. Despite Hannibal's brilliance, Carthage is decisively defeated by Rome.
216	Battle of Cannae. Hannibal's most outstanding victory over Rome.
202	Battle of Zama. Scipio Africanus' Roman army crushes Hannibal's Carthaginians.
190	Battle of Magnesia. Rome defeats Antiochus III, effectively destroying Seleucid kingdom.
168	Battle of Pydna. Romans defeat Macedonians, ending Antigonid dynasty, and controlling Greece as a result.
146	Rome sacks Carthage and enslaves its inhabitants; the city is razed to the ground.
73–70	Slave revolt under Spartacus. Italy devastated, but Rome eventually regains control. Spartacus killed in battle.
58–51	Julius Caesar's Gallic War. Gaul falls under control of Rome.
53	Battle of Carrhae. Parthians destroy invading Roman army. Independence of Parthia secured.
49–45	Caesar establishes Roman Empire with victory in civil war over Pompey and Republicans.
44	Assassination of Caesar. Power struggle ensues.
31–30	Octavian (soon to become Emperor Augustus) secures power with defeat of Antony and Cleopatra in Egypt. Ptolemaic kingdom destroyed.
AD 9	Germans defeat Romans in Battle of Teutoburg Forest. Rome abandons attempts to seize Germany.
43–60	Roman conquest of Britain (except Scotland).
61	Boudiccan Revolt. Britons under Boudicca sack Londinium (now London), but are brought to battle and annihilated by Romans.
101–106	Emperor Trajan defeats and annexes Dacia, marking final territorial seizure by Roman Empire.
113–117	Despite tactical successes, Trajan fails to annex Parthia.
122	Hadrian's Wall built.
220–250	Rise of Sassanid Persia.
225	Parthian kingdom falls to Sassanids.
250–285	Germanic and Gothic tribes attack Rome's northern frontier.
271	Dacia surrendered to Goths.
285–305	Reign of Emperor Diocletian. Order restored, at cost of punitive taxation.

THE PHALANX

Classical civilisation was, as is well known, dominated by Greece and Rome. The Western European identity was founded by the Ancient Greeks, and consolidated by the Romans. This remarkable success was not due solely to the undoubted merits of Greek culture and philosophy, but was achieved chiefly by the superiority of the respective military systems of Greece and Rome. Both were founded upon the Heavy Infantry.

It was the Greeks who first developed the concept of armies based almost exclusively upon Heavy Infantry, with little if any support from archers (unlike the Assyrian foot). This stemmed largely as a result of political and economic developments. For the geography of Greece, forming as it did small areas of cultivated land divided from each other by mountainous terrain, tended to dictate the development of city states with surrounding farmland. Although the more powerful of these (such as Athens and Sparta) could bring their smaller neighbours under their control, no single power could dominate the Greek mainland.

These cities were originally dominated by an aristocratic culture, which tended to favour mounted warfare as a badge of status (the invading Sea Peoples soon seem to have fallen into such habits where they succeeded in gaining control). However, all that was to change from 700 BC onwards. For the Greek cities appear to have experienced a degree of prosperity, and traded widely. As a consequence, farmers who were not of the aristocracy became quite wealthy; moreover, they soon decided that they wanted a say in the government of their city state (or 'polis', to give it its Greek term – from whence the word 'politics' derives). This desire became a distinct possibility once iron became readily available. The farmers soon equipped themselves with body armour, shields and spears: as a result, they were able to challenge the authority of kings. The only major exceptions to this rule were Thessaly and Macedonia, which retained both their aristocratic government and their cavalry; other states underwent an evolution towards more participation that was especially well described by the great philosopher Aristotle, in the fourth century BC:

> The earliest form of government among the Greeks after monarchy was composed of those who actually fought. In the beginning that meant cavalry, since without cohesive arrangement, heavy armament is useless; and experience and tactical knowledge of these systems did not exist in ancient times, and so power again lay with mounted horsemen. But once the polis grew and those with hoplite armour became stronger, more people shared in government.
>
> Aristotle, *The Politics* (c. 330 BC), quoted in Hanson, Victor Davis, *The Wars of the Ancient Greeks*, Cassell, 1999, p. 56.

The hoplite referred to by Aristotle was the generic term for Greek Heavy Infantry. Armament took the form of a thrusting spear approximately 12ft in length – the weapon was designed for close combat, being far too heavy to be thrown. The hoplite also had a short sword, to be used if his spear either broke or became embedded in a victim. It was, however, armour, rather than weaponry, that made the hoplite so formidable. The average Greek Heavy Infantry soldier sported an iron helmet (often enclosing most of the face), breast and back plates, leg armour known as greaves, and carried a large shield in addition.

Nevertheless, it should never be forgotten that the hoplite was essentially a civilian with no great enthusiasm for warfare (except in Sparta, which was essentially a military state whose citizens revelled in deeds of valour accordingly). Training was accordingly limited; Greek hoplites simply formed up in a tightly packed column known as a phalanx, presenting a hedge of spears and a wall of shields. The average phalanx was intended to march towards its enemy counterpart, indulge in a vicious mêlée, and break it. The Greeks simply believed in marching through, rather than around, the enemy. With this steamroller tactic to the fore, subtlety was conspicuous largely by its absence, as were cavalry and light infantry. Most armies had a force of the city's poor equipped as javelin-armed skirmishers; they seldom did anything more than guard the flanks of however many phalanxes were on the battlefield.

In many ways, the hoplite phalanx was little more than a superior version of the Biblical Infantry we met in Chapter 1. Both were equipped with long spears, and fought in closely packed columns. However, the armour of the hoplite made him a far more formidable adversary than his unsophisticated Biblical counterpart; moreover, the Greek infantryman's social status gave him pride and confidence. For the mass participation in government had allowed for the development of either an accountable monarch (as in Sparta, which had two kings in order to avoid a singular dictatorship), an oligarchy (as at Thebes) or an outright democracy (most famously at Athens). The Biblical infantryman was an unwilling conscript with no reason to feel any affection towards his overlord; the Greek was a free citizen with pride in his city and confidence in his comrades. This mindset represented a combination that the Persian Empire found impossible to confront.

THE ROUT OF ARCHERY

The Achaemenid Persian Empire represented the culmination of all that was most effective in Biblical practice. Based as it was upon a monarchy, an aristocratic culture developed that may have lacked the creativity of Greek civilisation, but nevertheless produced an effective administration of a truly vast territory (stretching from the borders of India up to and including Egypt and Asia Minor). With such a stratified society, cavalry remained significant, whereas infantry had a rather lesser status.

Given these developments, it was unlikely that Persian foot would develop into a phalanx: they lacked both the armour (although some at least appear to have been equipped with breast and back plates) and the *esprit de corps*. As a result, they relied upon archery; the composite bow was a tried and trusted weapon that could both keep enemy horsemen at bay and – eventually – whittle down opposing infantry. It is true that some Persian infantry appear to have been equipped with spears, either instead of or in addition to their bows, but archery was always the prevailing tactic of Persian foot.

Persian cavalry also tended to rely upon bowfire, at least in the earlier Achaemenid armies; heavy horsemen were, however, equipped with spears, and were willing to enter close combat, especially when engaging enemy flanks. This latter trend developed to the extent that later Achaemenid heavy cavalry dispensed with their bows, relying upon swords, and spears designed for throwing (up to a range of 20m).

Unfortunately for the Persians, their military system proved woefully unable to cope with the Greek approach. With heavy armour protecting the hoplites from the effects of archery, the Greeks operated in their preferred fashion and marched straight through the Persian lines. Following the catastrophic invasions of Greece in 490 BC and 480 BC, the Achaemenids were forced to admit defeat. By the end of the fifth century BC, Persian rulers confronted the inevitable, and started hiring Greek hoplites as mercenaries.

However, Greek warfare had not stood still. King Philip II of Macedon had appreciated that the best way to succeed lay in combining Heavy Infantry (which he had developed into pikemen equipped with a weapon 24ft long) with effective cavalry and Light Infantry support. It was here that the aristocratic culture of the Macedonians proved useful; for heavy cavalry had always played a significant role in their armies – indeed, it could even be argued that producing effective Heavy Infantry was more of a challenge for Philip than producing horsemen.

Philip II had already dominated Greece when he was assassinated in 336 BC (the Greek armies could simply not cope with the potent new combined-arms approach). His son had rather more grandiose ambitions, which led to his becoming Alexander the Great following his army's annihilation of the Achaemenid Persians. This was a graphic testament to the inability of the Biblical system to cope with Classical Greek warfare; despite the almost inevitable division of Alexander's empire between his generals following his early demise, there appeared to be no reason why the Greek military system should not continue to dominate the Ancient world.

THE BARBARIAN CHALLENGE

The phalanx may have shown itself infinitely superior to armies based upon infantry archers, but was not without its drawbacks. In particular, the Greek system was only strong for as long as the phalanxes maintained an unbroken front of spearpoints or pikes. If the formation became disrupted for any reason, it was horribly vulnerable to a determined attack from enemy foot willing to enter close combat. Such a threat was presented by the Gallic raiders who plagued Alexander's successors in Macedonia, and especially Asia Minor (where they settled in an area known as 'Galatia', whose name is derived from 'Gauls').

It is not altogether surprising that the phalanx found the Gauls (a constituent part of the Celtic people) so difficult to cope with. For just as the Greeks were effectively Biblical Infantry with greatly enhanced capabilities, the Gallic tribes were essentially a more powerful version of the Sea Peoples. They combined the virtues of the latter – rapid movement, effectiveness in disruptive terrain owing to their loose-order formation, and high motivation – with the crucial addition of an impetuous charge. Barbarian warriors such as the Gauls may have lacked formal military organisation, but exploited this deficiency by engaging the enemy at running pace, rather than a walk or a jog. Meeting the foe at the charge certainly served to disorder such formation as the Gauls possessed, but the shock of impact could crush the stoutest of enemies. Once a phalanx had been disrupted in this manner, the barbarians could wreak execution with their swords, which were longer and more effective than the Greek version (it should be remembered that the hoplites and Macedonian phalangites only used their swords as a secondary weapon, if their spears or pikes could no longer engage the enemy).

It must be stressed that the phalanx could and did win many battles against barbarians – particularly when supported by the superb heavy cavalry that was such a feature of Macedonian and Successor armies. However, the barbarians did provide a serious challenge to the Greek military system, and it became obvious that any effective innovations in warfare would have to deal both with disciplined phalanxes and ferocious Celtic tribesmen.

THE ROMAN LEGIONARY

The response to both phalanx and barbarians came from a rather unlikely source. The originally tiny Italian city state of Rome found itself engaged in a battle for survival from its foundation (which, according to Roman legend, occurred in 753 BC) until 300 BC, by which time it was the dominant power in Italy.

The Roman Republic was originally ruled by the northern Italian Etruscan kingdom. This borrowed many elements from Greek culture, including its military system. Accordingly, Rome followed suit, and was able to expel its overlords when it became apparent that the Etruscans lacked the determination to hang on to their territories (Roman historians frequently express their contempt for Etruscan cowardice). However, the Greek system may have been able to overcome a similar army of inferior morale, but soon ran into difficulties when facing the Samnite tribes. These were based in the mountains of central Italy, and fought according to the barbarian pattern outlined above, which as we have seen could be extremely effective in disruptive terrain. Accordingly, it was obvious that the Romans needed to create foot soldiers able to cope with both Etruscan and Samnite systems. Their response came in the form of the legionary – probably the most formidable infantryman in history.

The military problem was simple enough. Any effective close-order infantry had to maintain its formation while disordering and demoralising that of the enemy. Whereas a phalanx was irresistible if it contacted the enemy in good order, it was vulnerable if its formation was disrupted. Conversely, a barbarian charge may have met the enemy in a somewhat disorderly state, but Celtic warriors could wreak fearful execution in close combat. It was therefore necessary to devise an infantry system that could retain close-order formation under the most extreme stress, and both render a phalanx disordered, and blunt the impact of a barbarian charge.

Defensive equipment was fairly straightforward. With close-order formation being essential, a large shield and a metal helmet provided good protection. This combination was augmented when some, and eventually all, legionaries acquired iron body armour. It was with offensive weaponry that the Romans displayed their genius. They devised a heavy throwing spear known as the pilum. This was weighted so that the butt end was heavier than the point, which meant that the pilum only had a range of 15–20m. However, the heaviness of the weapon gave it the ability to penetrate armour; and if the point embedded itself in an enemy's shield, the weight of the butt would drag the latter to the ground, rendering it useless. The shock effect of a volley of pila (plural of pilum) would serve to disrupt a phalanx, and substantially blunt the impetus of a barbarian charge. The Romans would meanwhile maintain their formation and enter hand-to-hand combat, where their other weapon played its part. This was a short thrusting sword known as the gladius. At first sight, this seemed a fairly innocuous weapon compared with the longer and rather impressive barbarian swords – and it will be recalled that the Greek short sword was no match for the Celtic version. However, both the above were cutting swords, whereas the gladius was designed to thrust. As such, any legionary equipped with a gladius only needed a small area in which to operate, in some contrast to swords which required their users to have a wide swinging arc. This allowed for a tightly packed formation protected by a wall of shields, which served the Romans well. With more men operating in a given area than the Gauls or a disordered Greek phalanx could manage, the legionary was far more effective. Moreover, a thrusting weapon had other advantages. First, using it required far less energy than a cutting weapon – readers should consider the difference between an upward thrust involving the motion of the forearm alone, and the effort required in swinging one's entire arm. Second and crucially, the impact of a cutting weapon tends to be dissipated along the entire length of the blade (and can therefore be deflected by armour); whereas any thrusting weapon concentrates its force on a particular point, and was far more likely to penetrate armour (not that many Celts enjoyed such protection) and inflict a lethal or incapacitating wound.

This is not to say that the Romans were impregnable. The legionary would have been vulnerable to shock cavalry, for example, but the heavy horsemen of their time lacked the capacity of medieval knights (lack of stirrups being a major problem). However, so far as Classical infantry was concerned, the legionary was supreme. Eventually, all Romans acquired pila and body armour (unlike in the Punic Wars, where some of the legionaries lacked substantial armour, and the veterans in reserve were still essentially equipped as hoplites – the object of the latter being either to guard a retreat with their long spears, or march through a disordered foe). With the defeat of Carthage and subsequent conquest of Greece, Rome was now ready to take on the world.

ROMAN PROFESSIONALISM

Unfortunately for Republican purists, the idea of the citizen in arms only really made sense when a relatively small area was being defended. As Roman territories spread beyond Italy, it became evident that legionaries would have to serve in the ranks for longer periods. Accordingly, the tradition of enlistment for just six years was allowed to lapse, with soldiers taking the opportunity to re-enlist for additional terms of service.

However, it was not just the soldiers who had to serve for long periods. Their commanders now became full-time generals, as opposed to the part-time approach favoured in the days of the citizen militia. One of these generals, Gaius Marius (who came to prominence in the war against Numidia from 112 BC to 105 BC), was instrumental in widening the property qualification for legionary service. Arms and armour were now provided by wealthy generals, or by the Republic itself. Accordingly, poor citizens were now recruited, and found a military career attractive. Moreover, they tended to serve particular generals, acquiring a loyalty towards their leaders in the process. All this tended to militate against Republicanism and in favour of a military dictatorship. As a result, Julius Caesar and his legions were able to crush the old Republic and replace it with the Empire. The army was now fully professional.

This trend naturally made the Romans even more of a force to be reckoned with. Not only was the legionary the most formidable Heavy Infantry soldier in existence, but the supporting arms were now considered in some detail. Whereas cavalry and light infantry had in the days of Marius and Caesar been recruited on an ad hoc basis from local barbarians, these same men were to find themselves embodied in regular units during the reign of the Emperor Augustus. These new auxiliary infantry and cavalry forces were able to cover the flanks of the legionaries effectively, and in the case of the new infantry (which fought in loose order) operate effectively in difficult terrain. Recruitment was guaranteed by offering the carrot of Roman citizenship at the end of 25 years' service in the ranks.

The new army was easily the most formidable military force in the Ancient world, and only proved vulnerable in rugged terrain (which was why the Germans were able to defeat the Romans in the Teutoburg Forest in AD 9), and even then only occasionally. The chief reason that the Empire was unable to conquer Germany and Parthia lay in the vast territorial areas of both entities: despite the Romans' many victories on the battlefield, the legions could not be supplied for long enough to conquer such recalcitrant foes. Nevertheless, the Roman Army was able to consolidate control over the imperial territories, and lay the foundations of the greatest civilisation of the Ancient world.

THE ROMAN MILITARY STATE

The provision of peace and order was the key to Roman success. Nobody within the Empire would be so foolish as to confront the army's military might, while the network of roads, originally built to facilitate legionary movement, served also as the basis of trade and administrative traffic. Moreover, the Empire adopted a pluralistic approach; Roman paganism allowed for not simply toleration, but even the encouragement of barbarian gods, provided that worship of the latter did not present a political challenge. In essence, all free men were encouraged to aspire to Roman citizenship, whose benefits included the right to vote for local magistrates, and service in the imperial administration. Cities vied with each other to provide the best public amenities, as Roman culture and tradition stressed service for the good of the people: so much so that all the aforementioned civic works were provided (and expected by all to be so endowed) at the private expense of leading citizens. In essence, the Roman Empire became entrenched owing to the desire of all its inhabitants that it would so remain.

Despite all this, the Empire endured a major crisis in the third century. Although Rome was able to grant citizenship to all its free men at the start of the century, this was no longer enough for some leading generals. With the Empire so large, their armies effectively became their own property, and Rome once again experienced the deadly threat of military men aspiring to the Imperial throne. Moreover, the Germanic tribes were now a serious danger, constantly raiding Roman territory. Although Dacia was abandoned to the (Germanic) Goths in 271, order was eventually restored after the accession of the Emperor Diocletian in 285.

The new imperial peace came at a price. With the Germanic threat now permanent, the army had to increase in size, and never be demobilised. Providing for imperial defence cost money, and economic stability had to be enforced by the state. This was done by means of punitive taxation, and also by insisting that men remain in their occupations without ever being allowed to change jobs;

moreover, a man's sons were expected to follow their father into his profession. Prices and wages were also fixed in an attempt to curb inflation. These drastic measures succeeded in ensuring the stability and revival of the Roman Empire; however, its character inevitably changed. It had now definitively become a military state, whose inhabitants had something of a siege mentality. Classical civilisation had undoubtedly survived thanks to Diocletian's edicts; it was, however, imperilled by the barbarian hordes, and would (as we shall see in Chapter 11) meet its demise with the onset of the Dark Ages.

PRIMARY SOURCES

Arrian (*c*. AD 160). *The Campaigns of Alexander* (tr. Aubrey de Sélincourt), Penguin, 1971

Caesar, Julius (*c*. 50 BC). *The Conquest of Gaul* (tr. S.A. Handford and rev. Jane F. Gardner), Penguin, 1982

Herodotus (*c*. 450 BC). *The Histories* (tr. Aubrey de Sélincourt and rev. A.R. Burn), Penguin, 1972

Plutarch (*c*. AD 90). *The Rise and Fall of Athens* (tr. Ian Scott-Kilvert), Penguin, 1960

Plutarch (*c*. AD 90). *The Age of Alexander* (tr. Ian Scott-Kilvert), Penguin, 1973

Plutarch (*c*. AD 90). *Fall of the Roman Republic* (tr. Rex Warner), Penguin, 1958

Polybius (*c*. 140 BC). *The Rise of the Roman Empire* (tr. Ian Scott-Kilvert), Penguin, 1979

Quintus Curtius Rufus (*c*. AD 40). *The History of Alexander* (tr. John Yardley), Penguin, 2001

Sallust (40 BC). *The Jugurthine War* (tr. S.A. Handford), Penguin, 1963

Suetonius (*c*. AD 120). *The Twelve Caesars* (tr. Robert Graves and rev. Michael Grant), Penguin, 1979

Tacitus (AD 98). *The Agricola and the Germania* (tr. Harold Mattingly and rev. S.A. Handford), Penguin, 1970

Tacitus (AD 120). *The Annals of Imperial Rome* (tr. Michael Grant), Penguin, 1989

Thucydides (*c*. 410 BC). *The Peloponnesian War* (tr. Rex Warner), Penguin, 1954

Xenophon (*c*. 365 BC). *The Persian Expedition* (tr. Rex Warner), Penguin, 1949

Xenophon (*c*. 355 BC). *A History of My Times* (tr. Rex Warner), Penguin, 1966

Vegetius (*c*. AD 390). 'The Military Institution of the Romans' in Phillips, T.R. (ed.) *Roots of Strategy*, Stackpole, 1985 (originally 1940)

SECONDARY SOURCES

Anglim, Simon et al. *Fighting Techniques of the Ancient World*, Greenhill, 2002

Barker, Phil. *The Armies and Enemies of Imperial Rome*, Wargames Research Group, 1981

Barrow, R.H. *The Romans*, Penguin, 1949

Burn, A.R. *The Pelican History of Greece*, Pelican, 1982

Carey, Brian Todd et al. *Warfare in the Ancient World*, Pen & Sword, 2005

Connolly, Peter. *Greece and Rome at War*, Greenhill, 1998

Ellis, John. *Cavalry*, Pen & Sword, 2004 (originally 1978)

Fuller, J.F.C. *Decisive Battles of the Western World: Volume 1*, Spa Books, 1993 (originally 1954)

Grant, Michael. *History of Rome*, Faber & Faber, 1993

Head, Duncan. *Armies of the Macedonian and Punic Wars*, Wargames Research Group, 1982

Montgomery, Field Marshal Viscount. *A Concise History of Warfare*, Wordsworth, 2000 (originally 1968)

Nelson, Richard. *Armies of the Greek and Persian Wars*, Wargames Research Group, 1978

JOURNAL ARTICLES

With such extensive coverage in primary and secondary sources, reference to journals is unnecessary for the general reader. In cases where articles are especially useful, they are cited in particular army lists.

Chapter 7

Classical Wargaming

Readers of *Wargaming: An Introduction* will experience a sense of familiarity when looking at my rules for Classical warfare, since they bear a very close relation to the Ancient wargames rules in my previous book. This is not in the least bit coincidental, as my old rules (and the vast majority of army lists) were primarily designed to cover the Classical period.

The prime development of warfare in this epoch lay in the field of infantry discipline. Foot soldiers were now able to withstand the disruptive effects of shooting far more than their Biblical predecessors. Accordingly, missile fire no longer has any effect upon morale; hand-to-hand combat is the area which will prove decisive, which is why a morale test is only taken when a base is lost in mêlée. Armies relying upon archery and javelins are best advised to avoid close combat as long as possible, using their missilry to deplete their foes before the mutual slaughter of hand-to-hand fighting.

Many troop types from the Biblical period appear in the Classical rules. Accordingly, for comments on Heavy Infantry, Auxiliary Infantry, Heavy Archers, Light Infantry, Heavy Cavalry, Light Cavalry, Heavy Chariots and Light Chariots, refer to Chapter 2. New categories of troops are listed below.

WARBAND

Readers of *Wargaming: An Introduction* should be aware that the old category of Warband referred both to barbarians in the Celtic tradition, and the Auxiliary Infantry described in Chapter 2 of this book. The new class of Warband now refers specifically to barbarians who rely upon loose formation and a ferocious charge. They accordingly move faster than Heavy Infantry, are much more effective in woods (where their formation is not disrupted, unlike Heavy Infantry), and are given a combat bonus in the first round of hand-to-hand combat. This latter rule is intended to simulate the impetuous charge that was such a feature of barbarian warriors. However, in the second and subsequent rounds of hand-to-hand combat, Warband troops are far less effective than Heavy Infantry. This reflects their lack of cohesion compared to disciplined regular troops.

The distinction between Auxiliary Infantry and Warband reflects a real difference between regular troops trained to fight in loose formation, and impetuous barbarians (the latter often being more lightly armoured than the former). It also gives Celtic armies a (realistically) greater capability.

SCYTHED CHARIOTS

These rather exotic weapons were effectively mobile battering rams. They had four horses, one driver, and vicious blades attached to the wheels. The driver would head towards the enemy at speed, and literally bale out of the vehicle before contact. With luck, the chariot would plough into the enemy and inflict great execution with its scythes. Unfortunately, such weapons were limited in number and could not operate in close order owing to their tendency to run into each other (this is why they only have one base in these rules; just 4 casualty points will wipe them out). Moreover, they were only effective upon impact (simulated by their being eliminated automatically after one round of combat). As a result, they tended to be targets for every single enemy missileman, and had little effect upon the course of battles. That notwithstanding, they are great fun to use.

ELEPHANT

Another irresistibly tempting weapon. Elephants are, like scythed chariots, few in number and have just one base with 4 casualty points accordingly. However, they do not die automatically after one round of combat, and can inflict terrible execution. Unfortunately, they often went berserk before dying, during which time they tended to run away from their enemy and charge into their own side, with serious consequences. Accordingly, this unfortunate tendency is taken account of in the rules. Elephants can be devastating; they are, however, very risky.

ARTILLERY

Ancient weapons either lobbed heavy stones towards the enemy, or fired huge arrows at them. In either event, they had a very long range, took a long time to reload (they only fire every other turn in the rules), could be inaccurate (the player rolls a die to determine the number of shots to be fired), but were very deadly if they hit (armour is useless against such weapons). Consisting of just one machine with a small crew, they would have no fighting capacity in hand-to-hand combat (which is why they are automatically eliminated when contacted by enemy units). Note that although Artillery often played a role in sieges, very few armies deployed it on the battlefield, which is why such weaponry seldom appears in my army lists.

Many military writers have taken the view that the art of Ancient warfare reached its zenith in the Classical period. Although this view has been challenged by those who like to attack orthodox arguments, one reason why traditional arguments become truisms is precisely because they are largely true. It is certainly the case that infantry reached its peak in the Classical period (the same in not true of cavalry), and for the gamer who enjoys using a wide variety of troop types, this wargaming epoch will often be the period of choice.

Chapter 8

Classical Wargames Rules

UNITS

Each unit generally consists of four bases, each of which has dimensions of 40mm × 20mm. Each base has a variable number of figures on it, depending upon the troop type, as listed below. (Note: the standard base size is ideal for 15–20mm figures. However, 25mm miniatures may require larger dimensions: 60mm × 40mm is suitable for these larger size figures.) As noted, units usually have four bases, which are aligned in two ranks of two bases. However, Elephant, Artillery, and Scythed Chariot units consist of a single base each.

Troop Type	Figures/models per base
Heavy Infantry, Heavy Archers	4
Auxiliary Infantry, Warband, Heavy Cavalry	3
Light Infantry, Light Cavalry	2
Heavy Chariots, Light Chariots, Scythed Chariots, Elephants	1
Artillery	1 artillery piece and 2–4 crew

HOW TO WIN

Victory is achieved as soon as one side is reduced to a strength of two remaining units.

a) *Exiting the map*. For every infantry unit (other than Light Infantry) exiting the mapboard on the enemy side, the enemy immediately withdraws *two* of his units. All three count as eliminated.

SEQUENCE OF PLAY

Each side follows the sequence listed below in each of its turns:

1) Charge sequence.
2) Movement.
3) Shooting.
4) Hand-to-hand combat.
5) Morale tests.

1) The Charge Sequence

Every time a general wishes a unit to enter into hand-to-hand combat with an enemy unit, the procedure is as follows:

1a) *Charge Declaration.* Declare the charge. Measure the distance between the units. If the charging unit can reach the enemy, move it into physical contact (bases touching).

1b) *Defensive fire.* If the defender is equipped with javelins, and if the attacker launched its charge from further than 8cm away the defender may fire at its assailant.

1c) *Initiate hand-to-hand combat.* After removing any losses caused by defensive fire, the two antagonists will fight in the hand-to-hand phase.

2) Movement

2a) *Movement allowances.* In general, units move the distance listed below during each turn. They do not have to use up all their movement allowance, but may not carry over any unused movement to the next turn.

Troop Type	Movement per turn
Light Cavalry, Light Chariots, Scythed Chariots	24cm
Heavy Cavalry, Heavy Chariots	20cm
Elephants, Warband, Auxiliary Infantry, Light Infantry	12cm
Heavy Infantry, Heavy Archers	8cm
Artillery	May not move

2b) *Turning.* If a Warband, Auxiliary Infantry, Elephant, Heavy Infantry, Heavy Archer, Heavy Chariot, Scythed Chariot or Heavy Cavalry unit wishes to deviate more than 30° from a straight line, it must use up half its movement allowance to do so.

i) Light Infantry, Light Chariots and Light Cavalry may turn without penalty.

2c) *Difficult terrain.* Ancient battles generally involved no more than three types of terrain; specifically hills, rivers and woods. They affect movement in varying ways.

    i) Hills have no effect on movement (they were usually gentle slopes).
    ii) All units take a complete turn to cross a river.
    iii) Cavalry, Chariots and Elephants may not enter woods.
    iv) Heavy Infantry and Heavy Archers have their movement reduced to 4cm every turn they move in a wood.
    v) Light Infantry, Auxiliary Infantry and Warbands are unaffected by woods, and may move up to their full movement allowance if desired.

2d) *Moving and firing.* Heavy troops may never move and fire. Light Infantry, Light Cavalry and Light Chariots may do so under certain circumstances.

    i) Light Infantry may move and fire if equipped with javelins. The firing may either precede or follow movement.
    ii) Light Cavalry and Light Chariots may move and fire if equipped with bows (firing must either precede or follow movement). However, Light Cavalry and Light Chariots equipped with javelins are allowed to split-move. That is to say, they may not only move and fire, but are allowed to fire at any point during their move (if the target is in range at the time of firing). They may for example move half their allowance, throw their javelins, turn around, and retire their remaining half-move away from the enemy they had just shot at.
    iii) No unit may ever fire if it is charging an enemy unit.

3) Shooting

3a) *Missile ranges.* When a unit wishes to shoot, it must first check to see if the enemy is in range.

Weapon	Range
Bow	24cm
Javelin	8cm
Artillery	48cm
Bow (on horseback), Sling	16cm

3b) *Rolling to hit.* Infantry and cavalry units with bows, slings or javelins roll one die for each base currently remaining. A successful hit may possibly inflict a casualty point on the defending unit.

    i)   Bowmen, slingers and javelinmen hit on a throw of 4–6.

    ii)   Units in woods only suffer half the number of hits registered.

3c) *Saving rolls.* However, the defender is permitted what is known as a saving roll for each potential casualty. This is dependent upon armour thickness. For every hit scored, the defender rolls a die. If the score achieves the required saving roll, the casualty is not inflicted.

Type of armour	Saving roll required
Elephant, extra-heavy armour	3–6
Heavy armour, Heavy Chariot	4–6
Medium armour, Light Chariot, Scythed Chariot	5–6
Light armour	6

3d) *Artillery fire.* This is resolved as follows:

    i)   Roll a die to determine the number of shots permitted.

    ii)   For every shot, roll a die. A hit is inflicted for every score of 4–6. Halve the number of hits if the target is in a wood.

    iii)   No saving roll is allowed. All hits cause a casualty point to be inflicted.

    iv)   Artillery may only fire every other move.

3e) *Base removal.* For every four casualty points inflicted on a unit remove a base (denote the current number of casualties using markers).

3f) *Elephant rules.* If 4 points are inflicted on an elephant unit, it goes berserk for 1 move before it dies. Roll a die:

1–2	Elephant moves left.
3–4	Elephant moves right.
5–6	Elephant moves directly to rear.

The elephant turns in the appropriate direction (without penalty) and moves its full allowance immediately. However, if any unit (friendly or enemy) is contacted, the elephant will cease moving and engage its victim in hand-to-hand combat.

4)   Hand-to-Hand Combat

4a)   *Procedure*. When units engage in hand-to-hand combat, the fight usually continues each turn until one side is eliminated (Cavalry, Light Chariots and Light Infantry may withdraw a full move after a round of combat, but only if their movement rate exceeds that of their assailants).

4b)   *Order of striking*. Blows are always struck simultaneously.

4c)   *Hand-to hand combat (open terrain)*. Each base in a unit rolls a variable number of dice, depending upon the type of opponent it is engaging.

Own unit	Enemy unit				
	Elephant	Heavy Infantry	Auxiliary Infantry Warband, Heavy Cavalry Heavy Chariots	Heavy Archers	Light Cavalry, Light Infantry, Light Chariots
Elephants	4	8	8	8	8
Scythed Chariots	4	8	8	8	8
Heavy Infantry	1	1	2	3	4
Warband	1	1	1	2	3
Auxiliary Infantry	1	1	1	2	3
Heavy Cavalry	1	1	1	2	3
Heavy Chariots	1	1	1	2	3
Heavy Archers	1	1	1	1	2
Light Cavalry	1	1	1	1	1
Light Infantry	1	1	1	1	1
Light Chariots	1	1	1	1	1

i)   Warband, Heavy and Light Chariots roll one extra die per base remaining in the first round of any combat.

ii)   Units uphill of their antagonists also roll one extra die per base remaining in the first round of any combat.

iii)   Units defending a river bank similarly roll one extra die per base remaining, if their assailants are crossing the river at the time. Again, this only applies during the first round.

iv)   Units attacking the flank or rear of an enemy always roll an additional die per base engaged.

v) Units hit in their flanks may turn to face their enemy in the second or subsequent rounds of hand-to-hand combat, but only if they are not simultaneously being engaged to their front.

vi) For every dice rolled, a 4–6 is needed to stand the chance of inflicting a casualty point loss on the enemy.

vii) Scythed chariots are automatically eliminated after one round of combat.

4d) *Saving roll.* As with shooting, the defending unit is entitled to a saving roll for each potential casualty. Use the same chart provided in the shooting section of these rules (see 3c above).

i) Troops engaged by Elephants or Scythed Chariots are never entitled to a saving roll.

ii) Artillery is defenceless in hand-to-hand combat, and is automatically exterminated if engaged.

4e) *Combat in woods.* This uses a (very) different hand-to-hand combat table.

Own unit	Enemy unit	
	Auxiliary Infantry, Warband	Other Troops
Auxiliary Infantry	1	2
Warband	1	2
Other troops	1	1

5) Morale Tests

5a) *Morale effects of hand-to-hand combat.* Whenever an infantry, cavalry or chariot unit loses a base in hand-to-hand combat, it must roll a die. If it fails to achieve the appropriate score, another base is removed (if two or three bases are removed in a single turn, roll two or three dice accordingly).

Class of unit	Morale roll
Elite	3–6
Average	4–6
Levy	5–6

Chapter 9

Classical Wargames Armies

With many wargamers taking an active interest in Classical history, this period will always be a very popular choice. I have included lists for the most prominent, or most interesting, armies in this chapter. As always, wargames forces comprise eight units. As with all periods, I would suggest that up to three terrain pieces should give a good game: hills, woods and rivers can all feature, with green being the colour of choice for the wargames table.

EARLY HOPLITE GREEK ARMY
(500 BC–450 BC)

Unit type	Number per army
City Hoplites (Heavy Infantry, heavy armour, Average)	4–7
Spartan Hoplites (Heavy Infantry, heavy armour, Elite)	0–2
Javelinmen (Light Infantry (javelin), light armour, Levy)	1–2
Cavalry (Light Cavalry (javelin), light armour, Average)	0–1

Hoplites inevitably form the core of Greek armies, and with good reason. Masses of heavily armoured infantry whose close combat skills are second to none, make for a difficult army to beat. However, the right-hand drift special rule can create difficulties (see below for details), and the hoplites are largely bereft of effective support. Levy javelinmen are – to say the least – not the most reliable or durable protectors of flanks, and the single permitted unit of cavalry is rather vulnerable against massed enemy horse.

SPECIAL RULES

1) *Phalanx*. Apply the following rules for all hoplite infantry:

    a) *Impact*. Hoplites add one to all their hand-to-hand combat dice rolls (so that they register hits on rolls of 3–6 rather than 4–6), until they lose a base. Once their first base is lost, hoplites no longer receive their bonus.

    b) *Loss of cohesion*. Hoplites defend as Auxiliary Infantry after they lose their first base. However, they continue to attack as Heavy Infantry.

2) *Right-hand drift* (optional rule). Whenever they advanced, each hoplite tended to instinctively inch to the right in order to obtain some protection from his neighbour's shield. Accordingly, whenever a hoplite unit moves forward between 5cm and 8cm all bases shift rightwards 1cm. They still face the same direction.

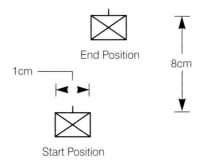

3) *Spartans*. These troops acquired an awesome reputation for their skills in combat as well as their morale. They always roll a single extra die (not one die per base) in every combat in which they participate.

4) *Cavalry* (optional). There has been much debate over the role of Greek cavalry. Although I believe they skirmished, some historians take the view that they were Heavy Cavalry. They may be reclassified as such if the gamer prefers.

SUGGESTED DEPLOYMENT

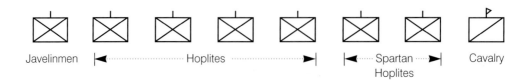

The Spartans are placed on the right in order to take advantage of the outflanking potential presented by the right-hand drift rule. This army should simply try to literally march through the opposition, with the javelinmen and cavalry harassing enemy outflanking attempts with skirmishing tactics.

The wargamer should however be aware that the javelinmen can come into their own (despite their Levy status) in wooded terrain. Always consider fielding an additional unit on such a battlefield, to replace either the cavalry or one of the hoplites.

CREATING THE ARMY IN MINIATURE

There is a wide availability of figures in 6mm, 15mm and 25mm scales. Coverage in plastic figures is also complete.

ALTERNATIVE ARMIES

There is absolutely no reason why hoplite figures from this army cannot be used in any force deploying heavy spearmen in the BC period. Purists would doubtless point out that later hoplites lacked greaves, but this need not prevent these figures appearing in any Greek army, and as mercenaries in Persian armies. Similar conditions apply to the cavalry.

The light infantrymen are sufficiently generic to appear in any army that features irregular javelinmen, although they are naturally enough best suited to states from the Mediterranean region.

PRIMARY SOURCES

Herodotus (c. 450 BC). *The Histories* (tr. Aubrey de Sélincourt and rev. A.R. Burn), Penguin, 1972

Plutarch (c. AD 90). 'Themistocles' (77–108) and 'Aristides' (109–39) in *The Rise and Fall of Athens* (tr. Ian Scott-Kilvert), Penguin, 1960

SECONDARY SOURCES

Burn, A.R. *The Pelican History of Greece*, Pelican, 1982

Connolly, Peter. *Greece and Rome at War*, Greenhill, 1998

Hanson, Victor Davis. *The War of the Ancient Greeks*, Cassell, 1999

Nelson, Richard. *Armies of the Greek and Persian Wars*, Wargames Research Group, 1978

RASHNESS AS A SAVING VIRTUE

The Athenians advanced at a run towards the enemy, not less than a mile away. The Persians, seeing the attack developing at the double, prepared to meet it, thinking it suicidal madness for the Athenians to risk an assault from either cavalry or archers. Well, that was what they imagined; nevertheless, the

Athenians came on, closed with the enemy all along the line, and fought in a way not to be forgotten.

Herodotus (*c.* 450 BC), *The Histories* (tr. Aubrey de Sélincourt and rev. A.R. Burn), Penguin, 1972, p. 429.

Herodotus' account of the Battle of Marathon (490 BC) shows how a rapid advance represented the best way of negating the effect of enemy archery.

HAUTE COUTURE

The Greeks saw their Persian enemies as being a remarkably effeminate bunch. This is because the Achaemenid armies were clad in trousers, whereas the Greeks maintained that real men always wore skirts.

EARLY ACHAEMENID PERSIAN ARMY
(500 BC–420 BC)

Unit type	Number per army
Persian Infantry (Heavy Archers, light armour, Average)	3–5
Levy Infantry (Light Infantry (bow), light armour, Levy)	1–3
Immortals (Heavy Archers, medium armour, Elite)	0–1
Persian Cavalry (Heavy Cavalry (bow), light armour, Average)	1–2
Horse Archers (Light Cavalry (bow), light armour, Average)	0–2

The Persians can deploy a huge quantity of archery, which means they should generally adopt a defensive posture. Delaying the moment of contact for as long as possible inevitably serves to maximise the casualties occurring to the enemy from shooting. However, the limited close combat skills of heavy archers can result in serious problems, especially against Greek hoplites – despite the Persian infantry having better defensive qualities than other bowmen (see special rules below). It is therefore vital to use the cavalry to outflank enemy units, thereby increasing potential damage in close combat.

SPECIAL RULES

1) *Persians in defence.* Persian infantry and Immortal units were equipped with large shields, which they propped up in front of them to form an impromptu barrier. Some of them (historians are constantly arguing over precisely how many) were also armed with long spears. All this resulted in an enhanced defensive capability. Accordingly, Persian infantry and Immortals should defend as Warband rather than Heavy Archers, when engaged in close

combat (however, they receive no such enhanced offensive capability, and only attack as Heavy Archers).

2) *Persian infantry armour* (optional rule). There is general agreement that the Immortals wore body armour, but historians are continually debating over whether this advantage extended to other infantry units. If the gamer thinks this is likely, treat all Persian infantry units (not Levy infantry) as having medium armour.

SUGGESTED DEPLOYMENT

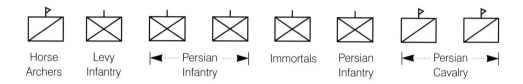

| Horse Archers | Levy Infantry | ◄······ Persian ······► Infantry | Immortals | Persian Infantry | ◄······ Persian ······► Cavalry |

The two Persian cavalry units are key to this deployment. They should be able to drive off opposing horsemen and Light Infantry (thanks to their combination of archery and close combat skills). All other troops should defend, although the horse archers can use their superior mobility to encircle an open flank, and the Levy infantry archers can prove very useful against other light foot troops.

Note the positioning of the Immortals. Their role in this deployment is not to assist any outflanking move, but to allow the centre to hold out for as long as possible. This should hopefully mean that the cavalry still has something left to attack once its flanking moves are completed.

CREATING THE ARMY IN MINIATURE
Many manufacturers of 6mm, 15mm or 25mm metal figures feature comprehensive ranges of Persians. There is also a complete selection of suitable plastic miniatures in 20mm scale.

ALTERNATIVE ARMIES
Provided that the wargamer follows my interpretation concerning the equipment of Kardakes infantry (see the list for the later Achaemenid Persians), there is absolutely no reason why Persian infantry units should not serve in the armies of the late Achaemenids. The same is also true of Heavy and Light Cavalry figures.

SOURCES
See the books listed in the Hoplite Greek army list. These also give good accounts of the Persian army. Readers may also find the following article of interest:

Head, Duncan, 'Xerses' Army in Greece, 480–479 BC' in *Slingshot* no. 181 (September 1995), 12–20

THE UTILITY OF CAVALRY

The Persian cavalry, being armed with the bow, were not easy to come to grips with; so when they moved forward, they harried all the Greek line with their arrows and javelins.

Herodotus (*c.* 450 BC), *The Histories* (tr. Aubrey de Sélincourt and rev. A.R. Burn), Penguin, 1972, p. 597.

Herodotus' comment on the Persian horse in action before the Battle of Plataea, reveals just how effective they were in combat.

THE MEN WHO LIVED FOREVER

Although the Immortals were an Elite unit, their title is not a comment upon their quality. It simply refers to the fact that if any member of the corps died, he was immediately replaced with a new recruit; the Immortals' strength accordingly remained at 10,000.

LATER HOPLITE GREEK ARMY
(450 BC–330 BC)

Unit type	*Number per army*
City Hoplites (Heavy Infantry, medium armour, Average)	4–7
Javelinmen (Light Infantry (javelin), light armour, Levy)	1–2
Peltasts (Auxiliary Infantry, light armour, Average)	0–2
Cavalry (Light Cavalry (javelin), light armour, Average)	0–1

Although hoplites had dispensed with much of their armour (the body protection was no longer metallic, and the greaves had been discarded) in order to enhance stamina and reduce their financial outlay, they remain at the heart of this army. However, the peltasts should be considered as an option; they not only make effective flank guards but are very potent in wooded terrain.

This army reflects the experience of war against the Persians. Although the Greeks took pride in the fact that their hoplites completely outclassed the Persian close-order infantry, it was apparent that lighter troops were rather weak. As a consequence, the peltasts were devised as a response: although they never challenged the supremacy of the hoplite, some Greek states used them to good effect, especially in woods and rocky areas.

SPECIAL RULES

1) *Phalanx*. See Early Hoplite Greek army list.
2) *Right-hand drift* (optional rule). See Early Hoplite Greek army list.
3) *Cavalry*. See Early Hoplite Greek army list.
4) *Hoplite armour* (optional rule). I have followed all previous wargames writers in downgrading hoplite protection in this period, to reflect their lighter equipment. However, it can be argued that the large shields, metal helmets and substantial (if non-metallic) body armour still made the hoplites formidable in defence. They may accordingly be reclassified as having heavy armour.
5) *Spartan army*. The following rules apply for gamers who wish to field a Spartan force:

   a) Add the following to the army list:

Unit type	Number per army
Spartan Hoplites (Heavy Infantry, medium armour, Elite)	1–3

These units enjoy the benefits of the Spartan special rule from the Early Hoplite Greek army list.

   b) The Spartan army may not field any units of cavalry or peltasts.

6) *Athenian Army*. If an Athenian force is deployed, add the following item to the army list:

Unit type	Number per army
Archers (Light Infantry (bow), light armour, Average)	0–1

7) *Theban Army*. The following units are added to any wargamer's army:

Unit type	Number per army
Theban Cavalry (Light Cavalry (javelin), light armour, Elite)	0–1
Sacred Band (Heavy Infantry, medium armour, Unbreakable)	0–1

   a) *Unbreakable unit*. The Sacred Band were the Elite of the Theban army, and despite not enjoying the training of the Spartans, had fanatical determination. Accordingly, the Sacred Band unit never has to check morale; it automatically passes all tests.

SUGGESTED DEPLOYMENT

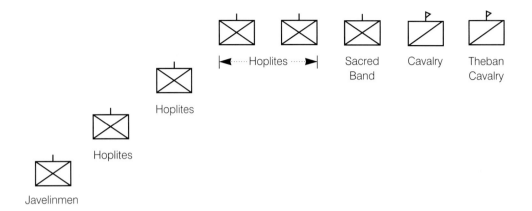

This Theban army attempts to replicate the successes of Epaminondas by reproducing his oblique order deployment. The weaker left flank is refused, whereas the right is strengthened with a strong force of hoplites supporting the Sacred Band; and cavalry concentrated to overwhelm any mounted foes, prior to outflanking the enemy. The wargamer could, of course, choose to copy Epaminondas directly by strengthening the left flank instead of the right.

CREATING THE ARMY IN MINIATURE

This army is covered extremely well by 6mm, 15mm and 25mm metal figure manufacturers. Plastic miniatures also provide suitable figures for this force.

ALTERNATIVE ARMIES

Most of these figures can be deployed in Early Greek armies, provided that the wargamer overlooks the lack of greaves on later hoplites. However, the latter make excellent mercenaries for service in Later Achaemenid Persian forces.

PRIMARY SOURCES

Plutarch (c. AD 90). *The Rise and Fall of Athens* (tr. Ian Scott-Kilvert), Penguin, 1960

Thucydides (c. 410 BC). *The Peloponnesian War* (tr. Rex Warner), Penguin, 1954

Xenophon (c. 375 BC). 'Spartan Society' in *Plutarch on Sparta* (tr. Richard J.A. Talbert), Penguin, 1988, 166–84

Xenophon (c. 365 BC). *The Persian Expedition* (tr. Rex Warner), Penguin, 1949

Xenophon (c. 355 BC). *A History of My Times* (tr. Rex Warner), Penguin, 1966

SECONDARY SOURCES

Connolly, Peter. *Greece and Rome at War*, Greenhill, 1998

SPARTAN PSYCHOLOGY

> Now as to their equipment for battle, he [Lycurgus] arranged that they should have a red cloak and a bronze shield, on the reckoning that the former presents the greatest contrast with any female dress, as well as the most warlike appearance; the latter certainly can be polished very quickly and is very slow to tarnish. He permitted those who had reached adulthood to wear their hair long too, in the belief that they would thereby look taller and have a nobler, more fearsome appearance.
>
> Xenophon (c. 375 BC), 'Spartan Society' in *Plutarch on Sparta* (tr. Richard J.A.Talbert), Penguin, 1988, p. 178.

Lycargus' legal code determined Spartan practice. Their reputation clearly owed much to techniques of intimidation, as well as their great military prowess.

THE MIGHTY 10,000

When the Persian prince Cyrus attempted to take the Achaemenid throne in 401 BC, he was winning the Battle of Cunaxa when he was killed. The 10,000 Greek hoplites he had hired promptly had to march across much of the Persian Empire to reach home – repelling attacks from the Achaemenid hordes as they did so. This exploit (subsequently recorded by Xenophon, who served as an officer in the Greek force, in *The Persian Expedition*) showed just how vulnerable the Persians were to Greek armies. It was a lesson that was not lost upon Alexander the Great.

LATER ACHAEMENID PERSIAN ARMY
(420 BC–330 BC)

Unit type	Number per army
Persian Cavalry (Heavy Cavalry, light armour, Average)	3–5
Paphlagonian Cavalry (Light Cavalry (javelin), light armour, Levy)	1–2
Scythed Chariots	0–1
Kardakes (Heavy Archers (bow), light armour, Levy)	2–4
Greek Mercenary Hoplites (Heavy Infantry, medium armour, Average)	0–2

Although the fighting power of Persian infantry had declined somewhat, this is quite a flexible army. If used offensively, both units of Greek mercenary hoplites should be in the vanguard of any advance, with the Persian cavalry forming a constant outflanking threat. If deployed defensively, the Kardakes can weaken any advance through the use of archery, while the Greeks form the rock upon which any advance can break. Meanwhile, massed Heavy Cavalry should be used to overwhelm enemy flanks.

SPECIAL RULES

1) *Phalanx*. See Early Hoplite Greek Army special rule no. 1.

2) *Kardakes* (optional rule). Many historians take the view that following the employment of Greek hoplites, the Persians neglected their traditional heavy archers. Instead, it is argued, the best part of the Persian Levy fought as auxiliaries in support of the Greeks. If the gamer prefers, Kardakes may be reclassified as follows:

    Kardakes   (Auxiliary Infantry, light armour, Levy)

I do not find these arguments persuasive. Although it is clear that Persian infantry declined under the later Achaemenids, I would argue that traditional heavy archery still played a part in Persian armies. For example, Arrian's account of the Battle of Issus refers specifically to Alexander's desire to reach the Persian lines before enemy archery had an effect. There is no obvious alternative source for this missilry apart from the Kardakes.

3) *Right-hand drift* (optional rule). See Hoplite Greek Army for details. I maintain that this rule is now redundant, given that the mercenaries employed by Persians were actually more akin to regular troops rather than citizen militia. Their drill and co-ordination were accordingly superior: as such, they were unlikely to deviate from a straight line. However, if the gamer believes that the Greeks retained their bad habits, then the right-hand drift rule may be used.

4) *Persian levies* (optional rule). A horde of levies was present at the battles of Issus and Gaugemela. This followed the Asiatic practice of fielding masses of troops, in an attempt to impress the enemy through numerical strength alone. In reality, such hordes were impossible to manoeuvre and of almost minimal fighting value. Despite this, it could (somewhat implausibly) be argued that the levies' presence did encourage other Persian troops to fight, by creating the impression of strength. Conversely, it is maintained that as soon as the levies ran away, other Persian troops suffered loss of morale. For those gamers who wish to paint masses of utterly useless troops, up to one unit of Persian levies may be fielded in their armies. The following rules apply:

    a) The levy comprises thirty bases (with three figures per base), deployed in two ranks.

b)   The levy may never move.

c)   The levy is equipped with javelins, and may use these to shoot with. It has 1–6 shots (roll a dice to determine the exact number).

d)   Similarly, the levy has from 1–6 dice rolls in hand-to-hand combat.

e)   The levy defends as Light Infantry.

f)   The levy is equipped with light armour.

g)   The levy has Levy morale. If the levy ever fails a morale test, the entire unit is eliminated.

h)   While the levy is present on the battlefield, other Persian units (apart from Greek mercenaries) add one to all morale test die rolls.

i)   Once the levy is eliminated, other Persian units (apart from Greek mercenaries) subtract one from all morale test die rolls.

SUGGESTED DEPLOYMENT

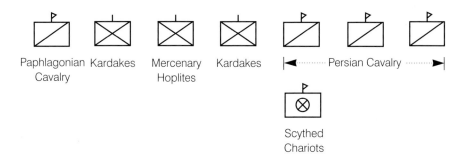

Paphlagonian Cavalry   Kardakes   Mercenary Hoplites   Kardakes |◄·········· Persian Cavalry ··········►|

Scythed Chariots

Although the prudent Persian general would doubtless maximise the number of Greek hoplites, scythed chariots often played a role in Achaemenid armies, and the fun guaranteed by their presence should be too much to resist for all but the most obsessively competitive players.

This army is best deployed with the Paphlagonians and the infantry adopting a defensive posture. The two cavalry units on the extreme right should set about outflanking the enemy from the start. The final cavalry unit has a dual role. Placed as it is in front of the scythed chariots, its first duty is to screen the latter from any enemy missilry. It should then advance to allow the chariotry to assail any attacking enemy unit, wrecking mayhem accordingly. The horsemen can then either join their comrades' outflanking move, or follow up the chariot assault.

CREATING THE ARMY IN MINIATURE

Metal figures are readily available in 6mm, 15mm and 25mm scales. 20mm plastic miniatures can also be used to create this army.

ALTERNATIVE ARMIES

All the Persian infantry and cavalry may be pressed into service as Early Achaemenids if desired. The mercenary hoplites may be fielded in any Greek army.

PRIMARY SOURCES

Xenophon (c. 370 BC). *The Persian Expedition* (tr. Rex Warner), Penguin, 1972
Other suitable primary sources can be found in the Alexandrian Macedonian army
    list.

SECONDARY SOURCES

Barker, Phil. *Alexander the Great's Campaigns*, Patrick Stephens, 1979
Head, Duncan. *Armies of the Macedonian and Punic Wars*, Wargames Research
    Group, 1982

DARIUS' BAD LUCK

His sound strategy, however, was shattered by fortune, which is more powerful than any calculation. Some of the Persians were too frightened to carry out their orders, others obeyed them to no effect – for when the parts give out, the entire structure collapses.

Quintus Curtius Rufus (c. AD 40), *The History of Alexander* (tr. John Yardley), Penguin, 2001, p. 40.

Curtius' summary of Darius' fate at Issus shows how important it was to enjoy good fortune. Napoleon observed that he always preferred to have lucky generals in command of his armies: he would never have recruited Darius.

A QUESTION OF NUMBERS

Classical historians tend to number Darius' armies in the hundreds of thousands. These assessments are invariably rejected by modern writers on the grounds that the numbers quoted seem too large. This rather neglects the obvious consideration that the Persian Empire was huge, and its levy would have been correspondingly big. It is, however, incontestable that numbers by themselves were insignificant; the Persians simply never realised that quality was far more important than quantity.

ALEXANDRIAN MACEDONIAN ARMY
(355 BC–320 BC)

Unit type	Number per army
Phalangites (Heavy Infantry, medium armour, Average)	3–5
Hypaspists (Heavy Infantry, medium armour, Elite)	0–1
Agrianians (Light Infantry (javelin), light armour, Average)	1–2
Cretans (Light Infantry (bow), light armour, Average)	0–2
Companions (Heavy Cavalry, light armour, Elite)	1–2
Thessalians (Light Cavalry (javelin), light armour, Elite)	0–1

It is often observed that Alexander the Great was a military genius. However, even the most gifted require help, and one look at their army list reveals why the Macedonians managed to conquer the mighty Persian Empire. Large numbers of Heavy Infantry pikemen who are exceptionally well drilled (and therefore no longer subject to the right-hand drift rule affecting other Greek armies), and some truly formidable Heavy Cavalry, combine to make a devastating attacking force. Even the light troops are very effective.

SPECIAL RULES

1) *Phalanx*. See Early Hoplite Greek army special rule no. 1. The phalangites and hypaspists are affected by the phalanx rule.

2) *Companions*. These cavalrymen were effectively the royal bodyguard, and as such tended to fight with fanatical determination. As a result, enemy horsemen invariably found themselves outclassed. To reflect this, Companions should always roll one additional die for every base engaged, when fighting enemy cavalry.

3) *Hypaspists* (optional rule). All historians agree that these troops were Elite infantrymen, and that they deployed on the right-hand side of the phalangites. Since this was the traditional place of honour for Greek hoplites, some historians (including me) believe that they should be classified as Heavy Infantry. However, other authorities believe that they adopted a more mobile posture, forming a link between the phalangites and the Companions. If the wargamer finds this view persuasive, then the hypaspists may be reclassified as Auxiliary Infantry.

4) *Thessalians* (optional rule). As with the hypaspists, there is much debate over how the Thessalians fought. It is agreed that their role was invariably to protect the passive (left) flank of the army from cavalry attack. I take the view that this task was best suited to Elite Light Cavalry. However, some historians

maintain that the Thessalians were actually close-combat specialists. Accordingly, the gamer may reclassify Thessalian horsemen as Heavy Cavalry if he or she desires.

5) *Armies in India*. By the time Alexander fought the Indian ruler Porus, many of his troops were getting thoroughly fed up with constant campaigning. The Thessalians especially were most discontented, and the vast majority had been sent home before the Indian adventure began. They were replaced with Light Cavalry (who may not be reclassified as Heavy Cavalry) known as hippakontistai. These are classified as follows:

Hippakontistai (Light Cavalry (javelin), light armour, Average)

SUGGESTED DEPLOYMENT

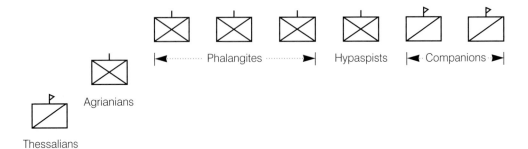

Thessalians

This represents Alexander's standard deployment, and as such represents the ideal model. The Heavy Infantry should be sent to drive through any opponents, or at least hold any enemy foot long enough for the Companions to play their part. The latter should concentrate upon destroying opposing enemy horse, before intervening in a flank attack upon any remaining opposition infantry.

Note that the Agrianians and Thessalians are refusing the left flank. This represents a conscious revival of Epaminondas' tactic, and is designed to ensure that the enemy has to travel a longer distance before enveloping the Macedonian left. In any event, the Agrianians and Thessalians are well equipped to fight a delaying action.

CREATING THE ARMY IN MINIATURE
Figures are readily available in all sizes of metal and plastic.

ALTERNATIVE ARMIES
All the figures can be pressed into service in Successor armies. The Agrianians may be deployed as Light Infantry in Hoplite Greek forces.

PRIMARY SOURCES

Arrian (*c.* AD 160). *The Campaigns of Alexander* (tr. Aubrey de Sélincourt), Penguin, 1971

Plutarch (*c.* AD 90). 'Alexander' in *The Age of Alexander* (tr. Ian Scott-Kilvert), Penguin, 1973, 252–334

Quintus Curtius Rufus (*c.* AD 40). *The History of Alexander* (tr. John Yardley), Penguin, 2001

SECONDARY SOURCES

Barker, Phil. *Alexander the Great's Campaigns*, Patrick Stephens, 1979

Fuller, J.F.C. *The Generalship of Alexander the Great*, Wordsworth, 1998 (originally 1958)

Head, Duncan. *Armies of the Macedonian and Punic Wars*, Wargames Research Group, 1982

SEIZING THE MOMENT

[Alexander] promptly made for the gap, and, with his Companions and all the heavy infantry in this sector of the line, drove in his wedge and raising the battle-cry pressed forward straight for the point where Darius stood. A close struggle ensued, but it was soon over.

Arrian (*c.* AD 160), *The Campaigns of Alexander* (tr. Aubrey de Sélincourt), Penguin, 1971, p. 169.

Arrian shows how, at the Battle of Gaugemela (331 BC), Alexander was able to identify the decisive point of the enemy line and apply overwhelming force against it. This proved the key to his success.

A MONUMENTAL FIGURE

Although the twentieth century saw its share of personality cults, Alexander made the likes of Stalin look positively modest. Although most people are aware of the Egyptian city bearing his name, at least eleven other Alexandrias were founded during his campaigns (according to Plutarch, seventy were built). This not only shows Alexander's conceit, but also the extent to which his empire was a house of cards built on nothing more than the force of his personality.

INDIAN ARMY
330 BC–320 BC

Unit type	Number per army
Infantry (Heavy Archers, light armour, Average)	2–5
Cavalry (Heavy Cavalry, light armour, Average)	1–3
Chariots (Heavy Chariots, Elite)	0–2
Elephants	2–4

This list has been included for wargamers who wish to simulate Alexander's campaign against King Porus (it may also cover the many wars within India itself between 400 BC and 180 BC). Its combination of Heavy Chariots and Elephants has often proved irresistible to tabletop generals; the latter inevitably form the focal point of this very exotic army. It certainly posed Alexander far more problems than the Persian hordes ever did.

SPECIAL RULES

1) *Indian longbow* (optional rule). Indian infantry were armed with a rudimentary longbow, rather than a composite bow. Although there is absolutely no evidence that this was any more effective than its rival, gamers who believe otherwise can impose an armour saving roll modifier of –1 for all troops hit by this weapon.

SUGGESTED DEPLOYMENT

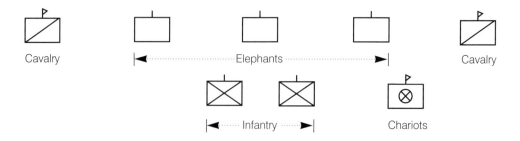

Tempting though it was to field the maximum number of elephants, this general has made some attempt to field a balanced army. The cavalry can provide flank support, and the chariot unit represents a potent reserve; as for the infantry, they can provide some supporting firepower if the elephant assault gets into difficulties. However, as with all Indian armies, the pachyderm blitzkrieg will be the key to success or failure.

CREATING THE ARMY IN MINIATURE

Although many metal manufacturers produce comprehensive ranges of Indians in 6mm, 15mm and 25mm, the same is not yet true of plastic figure suppliers.

ALTERNATIVE ARMIES

Indian troops generally cannot be used in other armies. Even the elephants are not really suitable, since most other forces soon protected their crewmen with wooden towers mounted on the back of the beasts – in contrast, Indian warriors sat astride their pachyderms.

SOURCES

The sources referred to in the Alexandrian Macedonian army list also contain information on Indian armies. Readers will also find the following secondary source extremely useful:

Jonas, Jeff. *Alexander the Great*, Warhammer Historical Wargames, 2003

A DOUBLE-EDGED SWORD

It was an odd bit of work – quite unlike any previous battle; the monster elephants plunged this way and that among the lines of infantry, dealing destruction in the solid mass of the Macedonian phalanx . . . while others, riderless and bewildered, ceased altogether to play their expected part, and, maddened by pain and fear, set indiscriminately upon friend and foe, thrusting, trampling, and spreading death before them.

Arrian (c. AD 160), *The Campaigns of Alexander* (tr. Aubrey de Sélincourt), Penguin, 1971, pp. 278–9.

Elephants may have been a deadly offensive weapon, but once rendered berserk either by wounds or the loss of their driver and his restraining influence, could prove just as dangerous to one's own side.

A TOWERING PERSONALITY

The Macedonians greatly admired Porus' bravery, but were also doubtless impressed by his stature. Arrian claims that he was over 7ft tall.

HELLENISTIC SUCCESSOR ARMY
320 BC–30 BC

Unit type	Number per army
Phalangites (Heavy Infantry, medium armour, Average)	2–4
Companions (Heavy Cavalry, light armour, Elite)	1–2
Elephants	1–3

This army list may seem very short. However, the reason for this will become clear upon consultation of the special rules below. For the Successor period saw the emergence of three main kingdoms (after a period of strife during which it became clear that no single ruler would succeed Alexander the Great). The Antigonid dynasty ruled Macedonia; the Ptolemaic family ran Egypt; and the Seleucids started off by controlling the rest of the Achaemenid Persian Empire, but soon found their effective control confined to what is now the Holy Land. All three kingdoms were eventually conquered by Rome.

Their fate notwithstanding, any army combining reliable Heavy Infantry and Heavy Cavalry with a force of elephants is bound to appeal to any wargamer. It is distinctly formidable when on the offensive.

SPECIAL RULES

1) *Phalanx*. See the Early Hoplite Greek army list special rule no. 1. All phalangites are affected by this rule.
2) *Antigonid armies*.

    a) Add the following items to the army list:

Unit type	Number per army
Peltasts (Auxiliary Infantry, light armour, Average)	1–2
Cretans (Light Infantry (bow), light armour, Average)	1–2

    b) Antigonid armies fighting in conflicts more recent than 260 BC may not field any elephants (without any native sources to replace the beasts originally brought to Macedonia after Alexander's campaigns, the elephant force died of old age).

3) *Ptolemaic armies*. Add the following items to the army list:

Unit type	Number per army
Egyptian Phalangites (Heavy Infantry, medium armour, Levy)	2–4
Skirmishers (Light Infantry (javelin), light armour, Average)	0–2

4) *Seleucid armies*.

   a)   Add the following items to the army list:

Unit type	Number per army
Scythed Chariots	0–2
Asiatic Levies (Light Infantry (bow), light armour, Levy)	2–4

   b)   Companions are equipped with medium armour.

SUGGESTED DEPLOYMENT (SELEUCID ARMY)

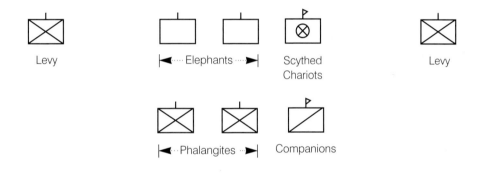

Levy |◄···· Elephants ····►| Scythed   Levy
                                            Chariots

                |◄···Phalangites ···►| Companions

For the wargamer, the Seleucid army has everything – infantry phalanxes, Elite armoured Heavy Cavalry, elephants and even the mayhem-inducing scythed chariot. Unfortunately, it also has some rather useless Levy infantry. These are deployed on the flanks, with a sizeable gap between them and the centre. This is to allow a wide field of fire for their bows. The elephants and chariot should charge the enemy as soon as possible, with the phalangites and Companions seeking to follow up the initial assault.

CREATING THE ARMY IN MINIATURE

Some metal manufacturers produce a range of suitable figures in 6mm, 15mm and 25mm miniatures. For those who like to game with plastic figures, Macedonian infantry and cavalry can be combined with Carthaginian elephants to produce an acceptable mix. The Seleucid levies can be fielded by using Persian infantry figures.

ALTERNATIVE ARMIES

Infantry and cavalry figures can often be used in Alexandrian Macedonian armies.

PRIMARY SOURCE

Polybius (c. 140 BC). *The Rise of the Roman Empire* (tr. Ian Scott-Kilvert), Penguin, 1979

SECONDARY SOURCES

Connolly, Peter. *Greece and Rome at War*, Greenhill, 1998

Head, Duncan. *Armies of the Macedonian and Punic Wars*, Wargames Research Group, 1982

Walbank, F.W. *The Hellenistic World*, Fontana, 1992

THE HUMAN BATTERING RAM

We can easily picture the nature and the tremendous power of a charge by the whole phalanx, when it advances sixteen deep with levelled pikes. Of these sixteen ranks those who are stationed further back than the fifth cannot use their pikes to take an active part in the battle. . . . Once the charge is launched, these rear ranks by the sheer pressure of their bodily weight greatly increase its momentum and make it impossible for the foremost ranks to face about.

Polybius (c. 140 BC), *The Rise of the Roman Empire* (tr. Ian Scott-Kilvert), Penguin, 1979, p. 510.

The sheer power of a phalanx's frontal charge was clearly awesome. However, Polybius went on to point out that once the formation was disrupted, it became distinctly vulnerable.

CULTURAL IMPERIALISM

The Hellenistic kingdoms insured that Greek culture and ideas spread throughout Asia (greatly to the artistic and intellectual benefit of the latter). However, the only ruler to take the trouble to learn any native language was the last of the Ptolemies, Cleopatra VII. Although she has acquired historical notoriety as a femme fatale (captivating as she did both Julius Caesar and Mark Antony), Cleopatra was a noted linguist who spoke at least nine languages, including Egyptian.

GALLIC ARMY
(300 BC–50 BC)

Unit type	Number per army
Warriors (Warband, light armour, Average)	3–6
Skirmishers (Light Infantry (javelin), light armour, Levy)	1–2
Cavalry (Heavy Cavalry, light armour, Elite)	1–3
Chief's Bodyguard (Warband, light armour, Elite)	0–1
Archers (Light Infantry (bow), light armour, Levy)	0–1

Gallic armies are now rather more effective than in *Wargaming: An Introduction*, thanks to the enhanced offensive power of Warbands. Gamers would, however, be well advised to take advantage of the special rules for terrain, and putting as many units in woods as possible. Note that early armies, with a combination of cavalry and chariots (see special rules below), can cause a potent threat to the flanks of any enemy force.

SPECIAL RULES

1) *Terrain*. Gallic armies may place two additional woods anywhere on the battlefield.
2) *Early armies*. Forces deployed in battles before 200 BC may add the following item to the army list:

Unit type	Number per army
Chariots (Light Chariots (javelin), Elite)	1–2

SUGGESTED DEPLOYMENT

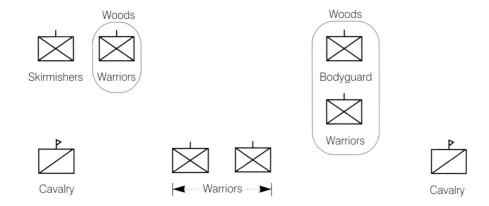

This general has maximised the potential of the terrain rule. Note especially how the Gallic commander has sought to deceive his enemy counterpart by making the left flank appear stronger than the right. His intention is to encourage an attack on the latter flank, thereby guaranteeing extreme consternation when the enemy discovers a second hidden unit in the woods. Should the enemy choose to assault the centre, the fact that this is refused allows for flanking attacks from the Gallic units in the woods.

CREATING THE ARMY IN MINIATURE

Metal and plastic gamers are catered for extremely well by most manufacturers (although chariots are rather hard to track down in plastic). For those who like to play on a truly grand scale, plastic infantry and cavalry are available in 54mm size figures.

PRIMARY SOURCES

Caesar, Julius (c. 50 BC). *The Conquest of Gaul* (tr. S.A. Handford and rev. Jane F. Gardner), Penguin, 1982

Plutarch (c. AD 90). *Fall of the Roman Republic* (tr. Rex Warner), Penguin, 1958

Polybius (c. 140 BC). *The Rise of the Roman Empire* (tr. Ian Scott-Kilvert), Penguin, 1979

SECONDARY SOURCES

Barker, Phil. *The Armies and Enemies of Imperial Rome*, Wargames Research Group, 1981

Head, Duncan. *Armies of the Macedonian and Punic Wars*, Wargames Research Group, 1982

Wilcox, Peter. *Rome's Enemies 2: Gallic and British Celts*, Osprey, 1985

FAKING A RETREAT

Whenever a [Roman] cohort made a charge out of the circle, the enemy retreated at full speed. A temporary gap was bound to be left in the circle, so that the unit which stood next was exposed to missiles on its right flank; and when the cohort began to return to its original place, it was surrounded by the Gauls who had fallen back and by the nearest of those who had remained in position.

Caesar, Julius (c. 50 BC), *The Conquest of Gaul* (tr. S.A. Handford and rev. Jane F. Gardner), Penguin, 1982, pp. 120–1.

It is often assumed that the Gauls were unthinking louts who simply charged their nearest opponents at the earliest possible opportunity. Caesar was well aware that they were a good deal more subtle than that.

CARTHAGINIAN ARMY
(270 BC–200 BC)

Unit type	Number per army
African Infantry (Heavy Infantry, light armour, Average)	1–3
Gallic or Spanish Infantry (Warband, light armour, Average)	1–3
Skirmishers (Light Infantry (javelin), light armour, Levy)	1–2
Elephants	0–2
Numidian Cavalry (Light Cavalry (javelin), light armour, Average)	1–3
Gallic or Spanish Cavalry (Heavy Cavalry, light armour, Elite)	1–2

Given the range of possible selections that can be fielded in any Carthaginian army, it is difficult to define overall strengths and weaknesses. However, the gamer would be well advised to use his or her (formidable) cavalry to guarantee superiority on the flanks. Players should also consider that elephants are rather erratic, and should therefore be provided with support. The Gallic and Spanish foot is useful, but brittle; if not succeeding initially, it is inclined to suffer in sustained combat with Heavy Infantry.

SPECIAL RULES

1) *Phalanx*. See Early Hoplite Greek army list special rule no. 1. The African Infantry and Hannibal's Veterans are affected by this rule.

2) *Hannibal in Italy*. If gamers wish to simulate engagements involving Hannibal's army (is there anyone who doesn't?), the Carthaginian army list should be modified as follows:

   a) *African veterans*. Hannibal's African foot became distinctly formidable during his campaign, and were moreover re-equipped with captured Roman armour. The African Infantry entry should therefore be replaced with the following:

Unit type	Number per army
Hannibal's African Veterans (Heavy Infantry, medium armour, Elite)	1–3

   b) No elephants may be fielded in Hannibal's army (see below for explanation).

3) *The Zama campaign*. The end of the Second Punic War saw a beleaguered Hannibal face Scipio Africanus' Romans outside Carthage itself. To fight

battles from this campaign, the standard army list should be changed as follows:

a) *Numidian cavalry.* Most of these horsemen had changed sides after one of their leading nobles, Prince Masinissa, had (correctly) perceived that Rome was in the ascendant. Accordingly, only 0–1 Numidian cavalry units may be fielded at Zama.

b) *Citizen cavalry.* Although the Carthaginian nobles invariably preferred to pay mercenaries to do their fighting for them, the extreme crisis of Zama forced them to come out and fight. The following addition may therefore be made to the Carthaginian army list for the Zama campaign.

Unit type	*Number per army*
Carthaginian Citizen Cavalry (Heavy Cavalry, medium armour, Elite)	0–1

c) *Hannibal's veterans.* Although few in number, Hannibal's remaining old soldiers were both fanatically loyal to their leader, and very well equipped. Add the following entry to the Carthaginian army list for the Zama campaign:

Unit type	*Number per army*
Hannibal's Veterans (Heavy Infantry, medium armour, Elite)	0–1

SUGGESTED DEPLOYMENT

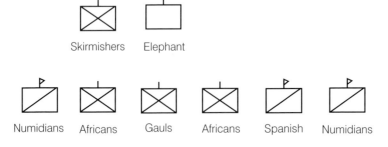

Tempting though it was to illustrate Hannibal's army, I could not resist the lure of the elephants. Only one is fielded here. Note how it is placed in front of the Gauls. The object of this is to allow the pachyderm to advance ahead of the infantry lines, rendering the latter out of range should the beast stampede. The skirmishers need not be protected; being expendable, they are assigned the role of providing support for the elephants. Should they survive, they can disengage from any enemy infantry, and head for the left flank to assist the Numidians.

The cavalry on the right flank should meanwhile seek to defeat its enemy counterparts. It can threaten an assault upon the flank and rear of the enemy centre. With the damage inflicted by elephants and horsemen, the Africans and Gauls will hopefully find their eventual assault made much easier.

As is inevitable in any army with strengths lying in cavalry and pachyderms, but whose infantry possesses only moderate abilities, this plan is of necessity rather intricate. It is accordingly prone to the occasional mishap, but nevertheless represents a fascinating challenge.

CREATING THE ARMY IN MINIATURE
Figures are readily available in all scales, in both metal and plastic. Some plastic figures are even obtainable in 54mm scale.

ALTERNATIVE ARMIES
The Gallic infantry may be used in any Gallic, Ancient British or German barbarian army. The elephants may take their place in the ranks of any Successor army. As for the Numidians, they may serve in Republican or Caesarian Roman armies, and also (astonishingly enough) in Numidian armies.

PRIMARY SOURCES
Polybius (140 BC). *The Rise of the Roman Empire* (tr. Ian Scott-Kilvert), Penguin, 1979

SECONDARY SOURCES
Bath, Tony. *Hannibal's Campaigns*, Patrick Stephens, 1981
Connolly, Peter. *Greece and Rome at War*, Greenhill, 1998
Curtis, Allen E. *Hannibal and the Punic Wars*, Warhammer Historical Wargames, 2005
Head, Duncan. *Armies of the Macedonian and Punic Wars*, Wargames Research Group, 1982
Wise, Terence. *Armies of the Carthaginian Wars 265–146 BC*, Osprey, 1982

CARTHAGE'S ONLY HOPE
It is impossible to withhold our admiration for Hannibal's leadership, his courage and his ability in the field, when we consider the duration of his campaigns . . . the difficulties he encountered at various times, and, in short, the whole scope of his design and its execution.

Polybius (140 BC), *The Rise of the Roman Empire* (tr. Ian Scott-Kilvert), Penguin, 1979, p. 427.

As Polybius realised, Hannibal was a military genius. Without him, the Carthaginians would have lost the Second Punic War long before they did.

A WASTED EFFORT

Many are aware that when Hannibal crossed the Alps at the start of his campaign, he took thirty-seven elephants with him. The fact that all had died by the time the Carthaginians reached Italy is not so well known.

REPUBLICAN ROMAN ARMY
(270 BC–105 BC)

Unit type	Number per army
Hastati and Principes (Heavy Infantry, medium armour, Average)	4–7
Triarii (Heavy Infantry, heavy armour, Elite)	0–1
Velites (Light Infantry (javelin), light armour, Average)	1–2
Roman cavalry (Heavy Cavalry, medium armour, Average)	0–1

This army is distinctly similar to that of the Hoplite Greeks. It relies almost entirely upon highly effective Heavy Infantry, but has very limited cavalry and light infantry support. Accordingly, the army needs to march through the enemy centre (a task that can be facilitated by use of the optional manipular formation special rule) before the flanks cave in. To be a true Roman citizen, the wargamer must seize the initiative and act aggressively.

SPECIAL RULES

1) *Manipular formation* (optional rule). Classical historians point out that the Republican legions deployed in a chequerboard formation, which looked something like this:

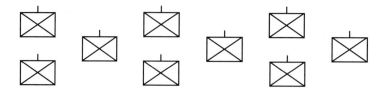

This deployment allowed troops in the second line to relieve their front-line comrades by advancing through the gaps and confronting the enemy while the erstwhile front-line troops retreated, in order to rally. For those who wish to simulate the manipular legion, use the following rule:

a) Roman Heavy Infantry units may be supported by another Heavy Infantry unit facing the same direction directly to the rear. The supporting unit must be within 4cm of the front-line unit, must not itself be engaged in combat, and must be of at least an equal number of bases as the unit it is supporting. If all these conditions are met, the front line unit enjoys the following benefits:

    i) It adds a modifier of +1 to all close combat dice scores.
    ii) It adds a modifier of +1 to all morale die rolls.

Although Classical historians speak highly of the manipular formation's utility, I am not entirely convinced of its effectiveness. In particular, the idea that the enemy would remain conveniently passive while the complicated manipular manoeuvres were ongoing, seems somewhat unconvincing. It is certainly instructive that the much more efficient Imperial Roman armies do not seem to have used the manipular formation. However, it is possible that the Republican units may have benefited from some form of rear support, which is why this rule is included as an option.

2) *Numidian cavalry*. As has already been noted, the Romans employed these African horsemen during the Zama campaign. Their effectiveness was so great, that they were in great demand in subsequent wars. Accordingly, add the following entry to the army list for all campaigns fought from 202 BC to 105 BC.

Unit type	*Number per army*
Numidian cavalry (Light Cavalry (javelin), medium armour, Average)	1–2

SUGGESTED DEPLOYMENT

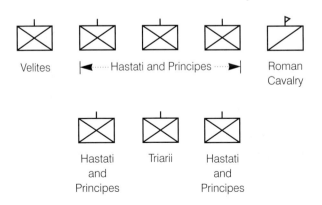

Velites |◄······ Hastati and Principes ······►| Roman Cavalry

Hastati and Principes   Triarii   Hastati and Principes

This layout is intended to take full advantage of the manipular special rule; the front and second lines must accordingly be no more than 4cm apart. This army has just one objective – the Heavy Infantry must destroy the enemy centre, and send enough units off the enemy side of the battlefield to trigger panic. Note the location of the triarii unit. By being placed in the centre of the second line it will be protected from flank attack, and be in a position to intervene in any front-line crisis.

This army is naturally very vulnerable to flank attack. This is not simply because of the limited support from cavalry and Light Infantry, but is also due to the narrow frontage of the main infantry lines. This inevitable problem of manipular tactics would only be solved with the employment of Numidian cavalry, from the Zama campaign onwards.

CREATING THE ARMY IN MINIATURE
The Republican Romans are another very popular army, and figures are readily available in all scales, both in metal and plastic. As with the Carthaginians, plastic figures are also obtainable in 54mm.

ALTERNATIVE ARMIES
In all honesty, Republican Romans are not particularly suitable for use in other armies of the period – their equipment was simply unique. However, hastati may be pressed into service as imitation legionaries in Numidian armies. In addition, hastati or principes with mail body armour may be used as Caesarian legionaries.

PRIMARY SOURCES
See the Carthaginian army list.

SECONDARY SOURCES
Grant, Michael. *History of Rome*, Faber & Faber, 1993
For other secondary sources, see the Carthaginian army list.

TACTICAL INITIATIVE
The Roman formation is highly flexible. Every Roman soldier, once he is armed and goes into action, can adapt himself equally well to any place or time and meet an attack from any quarter. . . . Accordingly, since the effective use of the parts of the Roman army is so much superior, their plans are much more likely to achieve success than those of others.

Polybius (140 BC), *The Rise of the Roman Empire* (tr. Ian Scott-Kilvert), Penguin, 1979, p. 513.

Roman generalship was not always brilliant, but the qualities of the Roman legionary were such that the Republic always won its wars – even (as Polybius was describing in this passage) when pitted against the mighty Macedonian phalanx.

DIVIDE AND CONQUER

For eminently sound constitutional reasons, the Republic elected two consuls every year, in order to avoid the risk of dictatorship. Unfortunately, both consuls were expected to exercise joint command in the field. When the combination of the cautious Paulus and the rash Varro was instrumental in creating the rout against Hannibal at the Battle of Cannae, the Republic came to realise that single commands tended to make military sense – even if they offended political rectitude.

PARTHIAN ARMY
(250 BC–AD 225)

Unit type	Number per army
Nobles (Heavy Cavalry, extra-heavy armour, Elite)	2–4
Horse Archers (Light Cavalry (bow), light armour, Average)	4–6
Militia (Light Infantry (javelin), light armour, Levy)	0–2

For cavalry lovers, the Parthians have to be the army of choice. These heirs to Achaemenid territory (and monarchical style of government) shared the Persian predilection for mounted warfare to a truly spectacular degree. The wargames general should be aware that getting the balance right between the fire and shock combat is essential, if success is to ensue.

SPECIAL RULES

1) *Parthian nobles.* With both man and horse enjoying the benefits of heavy armour, the nobles' movement was inevitably compromised. Accordingly, their movement rate is reduced to 12cm per turn.
2) *Foot archers.* The Parthians seem to have made some use of archery in their militia. If two units are fielded, one of them may be equipped with bows instead of javelins.

SUGGESTED DEPLOYMENT

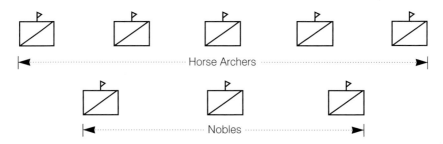

This Parthian army is designed to soften up the enemy lines with a shower of arrows, following this up with a charge from the nobles. Note that the centre consists of two units (one of horse archers and one of nobles): these can support either flank assault as appropriate, or may alternatively distract the attention of the enemy front line while the other Parthian units destroy the opposing flank forces.

CREATING THE ARMY IN MINIATURE
Although there are no suitable plastic figures for this army, coverage in all metal scales is ample.

ALTERNATIVE ARMIES
Parthian horse archers frequently wore Scythian dress, and may serve in that army accordingly (and vice versa). Similarly, Sassanid Persian cataphracts and Parthian nobles dressed similarly; figures may double up accordingly.

PRIMARY SOURCES
Plutarch (c. AD 90). *Fall of the Roman Republic* (tr. S.A. Handford and rev. Jane F. Gardner), Penguin, 1982
Tacitus (AD 120). *The Annals of Imperial Rome* (tr. Michael Grant), Penguin, 1989

SECONDARY SOURCES
Barker, Phil. *The Armies and Enemies of Imperial Rome*, Wargames Research Group, 1981
Miranda, Joseph. 'Trajan's Parthian War' in *Strategy and Tactics* no. 145 (September 1991), 5–12

COMBINED ARMS
The [Parthian army] then got to work. Their light cavalry rode round the flanks, shooting their arrows in on the Romans, while their armoured cavalry attacking from in front with their long spears kept driving then closer and closer together.
　　Plutarch (c. AD 90), *Fall of the Roman Republic* (tr. S.A. Handford and rev. Jane F. Gardner), Penguin, 1982, p. 147.

This account of Rome's calamitous defeat at the Battle of Carrhae (53 BC) shows how a combination of archery and shock action could have a devastating effect upon even the most formidable of Parthia's enemies.

NUMIDIAN ARMY (120 BC–AD 25)

Unit type	Number per army
Cavalry (Light Cavalry (javelin), light armour, Average)	2–6
King's Bodyguard (Light Cavalry (Javelin), light armour, Elite)	0–1
Infantry (Light Infantry (javelin), light armour, Average)	2–4
Imitation Romans (Heavy Infantry, light armour, Levy)	0–2
Elephants	0–1

The Numidians laid great stress upon the effectiveness of their Light Cavalry, which could easily run rings around any enemy. Given the rather unreliable support provided by the elephants and the Imitation Romans, skirmishing tactics were always going to be the most effective approach for any Numidian king. The same is likely to be true of the wargames general; he or she would do well to consider that Numidia's successes in her revolt against Rome (the most effective of which was led by Jugurtha 120 BC–105 BC) only occurred when skirmishing held sway. As soon as the Numidians relied upon close-quarter combat, they were defeated.

SPECIAL RULES

1) *Imitation Romans* (optional rule). I have downgraded the armour of these troops to reflect their inferior drill (undisciplined men tend to lose their formation and present their unshielded bodies to the enemy). If the wargamer is feeling charitable, Imitation Romans may be reclassified as having medium armour.

SUGGESTED DEPLOYMENT

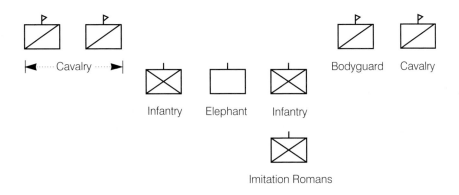

Cavalry   Bodyguard   Cavalry

Infantry   Elephant   Infantry

Imitation Romans

This wargamer could not resist the allure of the elephants and Imitation Romans. The cavalry is deployed to the fore, in order to assail the enemy flanks and create general mayhem. The infantry can provide supporting fire for the elephants, and the Imitation Romans are kept in reserve (note that they are out of the way at the berserk movement of a dying pachyderm), to assault a weakened enemy line.

CREATING THE ARMY IN MINIATURE

Figures exist in the mediums of both metal and plastic. However, Carthaginian war elephants will have to be fielded to represent their Numidian equivalents. The Imitation Romans are best provided for by purchasing figures representing Republican hastati (these lack body armour).

ALTERNATIVE ARMIES

The cavalry and infantry may serve in Carthaginian armies; the horsemen may also fill the ranks of Marian Roman forces. As stated above, elephants do serve as Carthaginians, and Imitation Romans can be used in Republican Roman armies.

PRIMARY SOURCES

Plutarch (c. AD 90). *Fall of the Roman Republic* (tr. S.A. Handford and rev. Jane F. Gardner), Penguin, 1982
Sallust (40 BC). *The Jugurthine War* (tr. S.A. Handford), Penguin, 1963
Tacitus (AD 120). *The Annals of Imperial Rome* (tr. Michael Grant), Penguin, 1989

SECONDARY SOURCES

Head, Duncan. *Armies of the Macedonian and Punic Wars*, Wargames Research Group, 1982

KINGS OF MANOEUVRE

Jugurtha's horsemen had been given careful instructions beforehand. Whenever a squadron of the Roman cavalry began a charge, instead of retiring in a body in one direction, they retreated independently, scattering as widely as possible. In this way they could take advantage of their numerical superiority. If they failed to check their enemy's charge, they would wait till the Romans lost their formation, and then cut them off by attacks in their rear or on their flanks.

Sallust (40 BC), *The Jugurthine War* (tr. S.A. Handford), Penguin, 1963, p. 87.

The Numidian use of dispersal (which drew an enemy charge) and subsequent rapid concentration proved the downfall of many rash opponents.

AN UNRELIABLE PEOPLE

When Rome wanted an alliance with the Numidians during the Second Punic War, they sent a military mission to train King Syphax's infantry in the legionary style (in 213 BC). As soon as his men had been trained, Syphax promptly fought on the Carthaginian side. This sort of behaviour was common practice in Numidia.

MARIAN ROMAN ARMY
(105 BC–25 BC)

Unit type	Number per army
Legionaries (Heavy Infantry, heavy armour, Average)	2–5
Veteran Legionaries (Heavy Infantry, heavy armour, Elite)	1–2
Gauls (Heavy Cavalry, light armour, Average)	1–2
Numidians (Light Cavalry (javelin), light armour, Average)	0–1
Skirmishers (Light Infantry (javelin), light armour, Average)	1–2

Following the reforms of Marius, the Roman army was much strengthened, thanks to the widespread use of heavy armour, and the increased proportion of Elite veterans. Cavalry and Light Infantry support was provided by assorted tribesmen, who were often willing to fight on the winning side. With much more effective flank protection than the Republican Roman army Marius succeeded in creating a rather awesome (if not yet perfect) military machine.

SPECIAL RULES

1) *Gauls* (optional rule). I have downgraded Gallic morale to reflect the fact that the Romans saw them simply as effective mercenaries – in some contrast to their accustomed position as the social elite of their tribes. If the gamer believes that Gallic élan was unimpaired by this minor humiliation, Gauls may be reclassified as having Elite morale.

SUGGESTED DEPLOYMENT

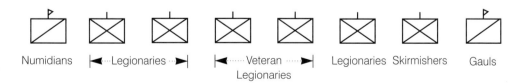

Numidians　　|◄····Legionaries ···►|　　　|◄······Veteran ······►|　Legionaries Skirmishers　　Gauls
　　　　　　　　　　　　　　　　　　　　　　Legionaries

This army relies upon the power of the legionaries. It is designed to smash through the centre of the enemy lines. This task is rendered easier than would be the case with a Republican Roman army, thanks to the enhanced flank protection provided by the Numidians and Gauls (the latter unit being given missile support by the skirmishers).

CREATING THE ARMY IN MINIATURE
Suitable metal figures can be obtained for this army. Unfortunately for the plastic figure gamer, Marian legionaries are not yet available.

ALTERNATIVE ARMIES
Cavalry and skirmishers may be used in appropriate barbarian forces; the Numidians may serve in Carthaginian armies.

PRIMARY SOURCES
Caesar, Julius (c. 50 BC). *The Conquest of Gaul* (tr. S.A. Handford and rev. Jane F. Gardner), Penguin, 1982

Plutarch (c. AD 90). *Fall of the Roman Republic* (tr. Rex Warner), Penguin, 1958

Suetonius (c. AD 120). *The Twelve Caesars* (tr. Robert Graves and rev. Michael Grant), Penguin, 1979

SECONDARY SOURCES
Barker, Phil. *The Armies and Enemies of Imperial Rome*, Wargames Research Group, 1981

Fuller, J.F.C. *Julius Caesar: Man, Soldier and Tyrant*, Wordsworth, 1998 (originally 1965)

Goldsworthy, Adrian. 'Roman Strategic Thought and Practice, 100 BC–AD 200' Part 1 in *Slingshot* no. 185 (May 1996), 4–7

Goldsworthy, Adrian. 'Roman Strategic Thought and Practice, 100 BC–AD 200' Part 2 in *Slingshot* no. 186 (July 1996), 2–5

LEADING FROM THE FRONT
Caesar was a most skilful swordsman and horseman, and showed surprising powers of endurance. He always led his army, more often on foot than in the saddle, went bareheaded in sun and rain alike, and could travel for long distances at incredible speed in a gig, taking very little luggage. If he reached an unfordable river he would either swim or propel himself across it on an inflatable skin; and often arrived at his destination before the messengers whom he had sent ahead to announce his approach.

Suetonius (c. AD 120), *The Twelve Caesars* (tr. Robert Graves and rev. Michael Grant), Penguin, 1979, p. 29.

Caesar's toughness made a great impression on his men, and inspired the personal loyalty that allowed him to usurp power.

HOLLYWOOD HISTORY

Roman legionaries of Caesar's time actually wore chain mail. This minor detail seems to have escaped the notice of many film producers, whose Caesarian Romans sport the overlapping metal strips (known as *lorica segmentata*) that did not equip the legions until the first century AD.

GERMAN ARMY
(70 BC–AD 250)

Unit type	Number per army
Nobles (Heavy Cavalry, light armour, Elite)	1–2
Warriors (Heavy Infantry, light armour, Average)	3–6
Skirmishers (Light Infantry (javelin), light armour, Average)	1–3
Archers (Light Infantry (bow), light armour, Average)	0–2

Without wishing to indulge in national stereotypes, it is interesting to note that Germany differed from other barbarian nations in having a well-organised and rigidly disciplined infantry (they also had a distinctly anti-authoritarian outlook, which comprehensively debunks the pernicious myth about Germans having a predilection for dictatorship). This makes the army rather formidable; unlike forces based around Warbands, it can withstand initial reverses with great fortitude. Although the cavalry can be effective (see special rule below), any German army will always rely upon the endurance of its warriors.

SPECIAL RULE

1) *Noble fanaticism* (optional rule). These horsemen were noted for their exceptional bravery, and their belief that cavalry with saddles were effeminate: accordingly, the latter were always charged on sight. Nobles may be reclassified as Fanatics if desired, with the following effects:

    a) Morale tests are passed on a die roll of 2–6.
    b) Nobles must always head towards the nearest enemy unit at full speed, and seek to engage it in hand-to-hand combat.

SUGGESTED DEPLOYMENT

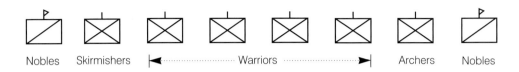

Nobles   Skirmishers |◄⋯⋯⋯⋯⋯⋯ Warriors ⋯⋯⋯⋯⋯⋯►| Archers   Nobles

The warriors should engage the enemy as soon as possible, with the Light Infantry providing whatever supporting fire it can. The nobles can meanwhile wreck havoc among unsupported enemy horse.

CREATING THE ARMY IN MINIATURE

Figures are readily available in all sizes of metal miniatures. Plastic infantrymen can be purchased, but the nobles can only be provided for by using Gallic cavalry figures.

ALTERNATIVE ARMIES

German figures can serve in Gallic or British armies if desired, provided that the wargamer has no violent objection to their being based as Heavy Infantry rather than Warband.

PRIMARY SOURCES

Caesar, Julius (c. 50 BC). *The Conquest of Gaul* (tr. S.A. Handford and rev. Jane F. Gardner), Penguin, 1982

Tacitus (AD 98). 'The Germania' in *The Agricola and the Germania* (tr. Harold Mattingly and rev. S.A. Handford), Penguin, 1970

Tacitus (AD 120). *The Annals of Imperial Rome* (tr. Michael Grant), Penguin, 1989

SECONDARY SOURCES

Barker, Phil. *The Armies and Enemies of Imperial Rome*, Wargames Research Group, 1981

Miranda, Joseph. 'Germania: The Roman Campaign Beyond the Rhine, 1st Century AD' in *Strategy and Tactics* no. 175 (July 1995), 5–16

Wilcox, Peter. Rome's Enemies 1: *Germanics and Dacians*, Osprey, 1982

DISCIPLINED WARRIORS

The battle-line is made up of wedge-shaped formations. To give ground, provided that you return to the attack, is considered good tactics rather than cowardice. They bring back the bodies of the fallen even when a battle hangs in the balance. To throw away one's shield is the supreme disgrace, and the man who has thus dishonoured himself is debarred from attendance at sacrifice or assembly. Many such survivors from the battlefield have ended their shame by hanging themselves.

Tacitus (AD 98). *The Germania* in *The Agricola and the Germania* (tr. Harold Mattingly and rev. S.A. Handford), Penguin, 1970, 106–7.

The discipline, cohesion and *esprit de corps* revealed by this extract shows just how formidable German tribesmen could be, in sustained combat with the enemy.

BRITISH ARMY
(55 BC–70 AD)

Unit type	Number per army
Nobles (Light Chariots (javelin), Elite)	2–4
Cavalry (Light Cavalry (javelin), light armour, Average)	1–2
Warriors (Warband, light armour, Average)	2–5
Slingers (Light Infantry (sling), light armour, Average)	0–3

The chariots are undoubtedly the most eye-catching part of this army, and can be the most effective. However, any wargamer tempted to recreate the 'Ancient British Panzer Division' so reviled in the pages of *Wargaming: An Introduction*, should be aware that foot warriors must always be at the core of any efficient army.

SPECIAL RULES

1) *Terrain*. British armies may place two additional woods anywhere on the battlefield.

SUGGESTED DEPLOYMENT

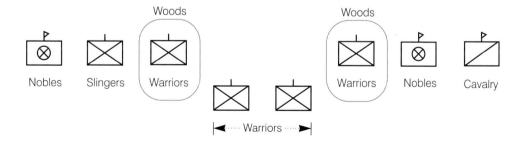

This wargamer has exploited woods in the same way as the Gallic general featured earlier. Any attacker has the unenviable choice of confronting the Warbands in the woods; or ignoring them, and risking a flank attack as they assault the British centre. Although the chariots are few in number, they can still cause a good deal of damage thanks to support from the slingers and the cavalry.

CREATING THE ARMY IN MINIATURE

Figures are widely available in metal. Coverage in plastic is problematic: foot warriors are provided for, but little else.

ALTERNATIVE ARMIES

Foot warriors may serve in Gallic or German armies. Chariots can also equip the early Gallic forces. However, British cavalry is more lightly equipped than the other barbarian armies, and therefore cannot make up a Gallic or German roster.

PRIMARY SOURCES

Caesar, Julius (c. 50 BC). *The Conquest of Gaul* (tr. S.A. Handford and rev. Jane F. Gardner), Penguin, 1982

Tacitus (AD 98). *The Agricola* in *The Agricola and the Germania* (tr. Harold Mattingley and rev. S.A. Handford), Penguin, 1970

Tacitus (AD 120). *The Annals of Imperial Rome* (tr. Michael Grant), Penguin, 1989

SECONDARY SOURCES

Barker, Phil. *The Armies and Enemies of Imperial Rome*, Wargames Research Group, 1981

Peddie, John. *Conquest: The Roman Invasion of Britain*, Sutton, 1987

Wilcox, Peter. *Rome's Enemies 2: Gallic and British Celts*, Osprey, 1985

HITTING AND RUNNING

In chariot fighting the Britons begin by driving all over the field hurling javelins, and generally the terror inspired by the horses and the noise of the wheels are sufficient to throw their opponents' ranks into disorder. Then, after making their way between the squadrons of their own cavalry, they jump down from the battle and place the chariots in such a position that their masters, if hard pressed by numbers, have an easy means of retreat to their own lines. Thus they combine the mobility of cavalry with the staying power of infantry.

Caesar, Julius (c. 50 BC), *The Conquest of Gaul* (tr. S.A. Handford and rev. Jane F. Gardner), Penguin, 1982, pp. 102–3.

Caesar was somewhat exasperated by the British chariots, but was clearly impressed with their effectiveness in battle. A surprise attack, followed by rapid withdrawal before the enemy recovered from their initial disorder, often paid dividends.

NOBILITY IN DEFEAT

When the Romans finally captured Caratacus (their greatest British foe), in AD 51, he was taken to Rome with his family. The tradition on these occasions was for the defeated enemies of Rome to be paraded through the city in chariots – grovelling for mercy as they went (to no great effect, as the Emperor invariably ordered their execution). Caratacus was altogether more dignified; while his family behaved with the spinelessness the Romans had come to expect, Caratacus himself marched through the city with his head held high. Moreover, his appeal for clemency did not display the usual sycophancy, but simply took the form of regret that he was not strong enough to defeat the Romans. This nobility and courage so impressed the Emperor Claudius that he granted Caratacus and his family an Imperial pardon: they spent the rest of their lives in Rome.

IMPERIAL ROMAN ARMY
(25 BC–AD 300)

Unit type	Number per army
Legionaries (Heavy Infantry, heavy armour, Elite)	3–6
Auxiliary Infantry (Auxiliary Infantry, medium armour, Average)	1–4
Auxiliary Cavalry (Heavy Cavalry, medium armour, Elite)	1–3
Auxiliary Archers (Light Infantry (bow), light armour, Average)	0–1
Artillery	0–1

The Marian army may have been formidable, but it still had weaknesses. These were comprehensively addressed by the time the Empire was created: all legionaries now had Elite status, and supporting troops were recruited and trained on a regular basis, which made them much more reliable. The Romans even took artillery onto the battlefield, in the shape of bolt throwers (effectively gigantic bows). This is possibly the most formidable army featured in this book – which is why some of the most interesting battles can be those depicting the periodic Imperial civil wars, rather than conflicts against barbarians.

SPECIAL RULES

1) *Auxiliary veterans.* Many Auxiliary Infantry units became distinctly formidable thanks to extensive experience of battle. Up to two Auxiliary Infantry units (not Auxiliary archers) may be reclassified as having Elite morale.

2) *Auxiliary Heavy Infantry* (optional rule). Some historians now believe (as stated in *Wargaming: An Introduction*) that Auxiliary Infantry were trained as Heavy Infantry, but were simply given all the dirty jobs (such as entering woods to clear out barbarian warriors) by their commanders. Although I find such arguments exceptionally unpersuasive, since there was a very real need for infantry who specialised in fighting in loose-order formation, readers may reclassify Auxiliary Infantry as Heavy Infantry if they so desire.

SUGGESTED DEPLOYMENT

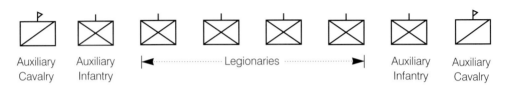

| Auxiliary
Cavalry | Auxiliary
Infantry | ◄ ·············· Legionaries ·············· ► | Auxiliary
Infantry | Auxiliary
Cavalry |

With their flanks protected by reliable supporting troops, the legionaries can march straight through the enemy lines. It really can be as simple as that. However, the Auxiliary Infantry has a very important role to play in difficult terrain, and gamers who enjoy a touch of variety can derive much merriment from replacing one of the units with an artillery piece.

CREATING THE ARMY IN MINIATURE
With almost every metal and plastic figure manufacturer producing Imperial Romans, this army is by far the easiest to obtain.

ALTERNATIVE ARMIES
Remember that the early years of the Empire saw legionaries still equipped on the Marian pattern with chain mail (the famous *lorica segmentata* metal strips only appeared from AD 40 onwards), so any spare Marian legionaries can serve in this army. Other troops cannot serve anywhere else: Romans were Romans. It is as simple as that.

PRIMARY SOURCES
Suetonius (AD 120). *The Twelve Caesars* (tr. Robert Graves and rev. S.A. Handford), Penguin, 1970

Tacitus (AD 98). 'The Agricola' in *The Agricola and the Germania* (tr. Harold Mattingly and rev. S.A. Handford), Penguin, 1970

Tacitus (AD 120). *The Annals of Imperial Rome* (tr. Michael Grant), Penguin, 1989

SECONDARY SOURCES

Barker, Phil. *The Armies and Enemies of Imperial Rome*, Wargames Research Group, 1981

Connolly, Peter. *Greece and Rome at War*, Greenhill, 1998

Grant, Michael. *History of Rome*, Faber & Faber, 1993

THE ROUT OF BOUDICCA

[Suetonius] chose a position in a defile with a wood behind him. There could be no enemy, he knew, except at his front, where there was open country without cover for ambushes. Suetonius drew up his regular troops in close order, with the light-armed auxiliaries at their flanks, and the cavalry massed on the wings. On the British side, cavalry and infantry bands seethed over a wide area in unprecedented numbers. . . . At first the regular troops stood their ground. Keeping to the defile as a natural defence, they launched their javelins accurately at the approaching enemy. Then in wedge formation, they burst forward. So did the auxiliary infantry. The cavalry, too, with lances extended, demolished all serious resistance. . . . It was a glorious victory, comparable with bygone triumphs.

    Tacitus (AD 120). *The Annals of Imperial Rome* (tr. Michael Grant), Penguin, 1989, pp. 330–1.

Suetonius (who was a general, not the historian who wrote *The Twelve Caesars*) smashed the Boudiccan revolt of AD 60 by deploying in a position that could not be outflanked by the British horde. The discipline of his troops was then sufficient to overcome barbarian valour.

SHIVERING ITALIANS?

Children's books always used to point out that Italian Roman legionaries suffered terribly while garrisoning Hadrian's Wall in winter. In reality, the fortification in question was manned by auxiliaries (not legionaries), many of which units were recruited from areas of Europe accustomed to distinctly chilly weather.

Chapter 10

Classical Battle Report

The Classical period is a fascinating one for any wargamer, blessed as it is with many intriguing battles involving a huge range of armies. Few campaigns are however more fascinating than the clash between Alexander the Great's Macedonians, and the mighty empire of the Achaemenid Persians. Accordingly, this battle report is an attempt to recreate the Battle of Issus, fought in 333 BC.

THE BATTLE IN HISTORY

Alexander the Great started his attempt at world conquest by moving against Asia Minor (present-day Turkey) in 334 BC. Persian Emperor Darius III was not initially unduly concerned with the Macedonian invasion; he felt that he could rely upon his regional governors, or satraps, to stop the Greek upstarts in their tracks.

Unfortunately for Darius, things did not go according to plan. The satraps were defeated at the Battle of Granicus, and much of Asia Minor proceeded to fall to the invaders. This left the Great King (such being the official title bestowed upon Darius) with a strategic dilemma: whether to campaign on land, or adopt a maritime approach.

The naval strategy certainly appeared to have much to recommend it. If the Persians could capture one or more of the many islands off the coast of Asia Minor, they could launch amphibious operations (using the formidable Greek mercenary hoplites) against the Macedonian line of communications, and ultimately threaten Greece itself. This would force Alexander to retreat, and effectively prevent any further offensive moves against the Persian heartland. Not surprisingly, Darius decided upon a naval campaign; the alternative land strategy would have meant mobilising a huge levy, to be led personally by the Great King himself. Any lost battle could have disastrous strategic and political implications; whereas a maritime campaign offered decent prospects of success, without unduly cataclysmic results in the event of failure.

The Persian offensive made a good start by capturing the islands of Chios and (after stiff resistance) Lesbos. Unfortunately, the Persian commander (the Greek mercenary leader Memnon of Rhodes) fell ill and died during the Lesbos campaign. His replacement proved less than competent, leading to the abandonment of further offensive moves, and the consequent adoption of a land strategy in June 333 BC. Darius accordingly set about mobilising a large army of Persians and Greek mercenaries, and headed westwards from Babylon.

Alexander meanwhile headed from Asia Minor into Phoenicia (present-day Syria) through a group of mountain passes known as the Syrian Gates, doubtless believing that the Persian horde could never mobilise in time to stop him. However, Darius was certainly an accomplished organiser; and the Macedonians soon made the spectacularly unwelcome discovery (in September 333 BC) that the Persian army had arrived in their rear, and was proceeding to seal off the Syrian Gates.

Fortunately for Alexander, not all the passes were cut off, and the Macedonians were able to escape northwards and unite with their remaining comrades in Asia Minor. Darius was nevertheless able to choose a good position for the inevitable battle, fought near Issus in early November 333 BC.

Darius had a steep hill covering his left flank, up which he sent 20,000 Light Infantry. The remainder of his army was drawn up behind the River Pinarus. The left flank was manned by a small contingent (specific numbers are not known, but presumably under 1,000) of Light Cavalry. The centre was held by 30,000 Greek mercenary hoplites with two bodies of Kardakes (each of 30,000) on either side of the Greeks. Darius placed the vast bulk of his cavalry, of the order of 30,000 horsemen, on his right flank. To the rear were positioned 160,000 levies of no fighting value, save only that of numerical size. Their role was simply to intimidate the enemy by the impression of strength. Darius' plan was to hold the centre and the left, and use his horde of cavalry on the right to roll up the Macedonian flank. It was undoubtedly a good approach to take; unfortunately for Darius, Alexander had no intention of co-operating.

The future world conqueror was well aware of the Persian cavalry threat, and sent 2,000 Thessalian cavalry and 1,500 Light Infantry to defend his left, reinforcing the 750 Light Cavalry already there. 18,000 Heavy Infantry were detailed to assault the Kardakes and mercenary hoplites. Alexander realised that the latter would prove a tough nut to crack, but that the Persian infantry would once again show its vulnerability to Greek Heavy Infantry, and cave in accordingly. Of equal importance was the Macedonian right; Alexander was undeterred by the Persian light infantry on the hills, and positioned 2,000 Companion cavalry to assault the Persian left. The Macedonian king believed that a rapid cavalry assault (led as always by himself in person) could overwhelm the Persian left, and then proceed to outflank the centre. Moreover, if Darius himself could (positioned as he was behind his mercenary hoplites) be captured or killed, there would be an excellent chance of political cataclysm in Persian circles.

The battle itself saw a bitter infantry struggle. The Macedonian phalangites and hypaspists did suffer from the Kardakes' archery, but were eventually able to cross the Pinarus and gain the upper hand against the Persian foot. However, the remaining phalangites were not so fortunate, given that they had to cross the river (which was actually more of a stream) and then fight the Greek mercenaries, who were an altogether tougher proposition than the Kardakes. Indeed, Darius' mercenaries fought so well, that the result of the battle was in the balance. Much depended upon what was happening on the flanks.

Overwhelming numbers notwithstanding, the Persian cavalry, despite inflicting serious losses upon the Macedonian Light Infantry and Thessalian cavalry, was unable to engage the phalangite flanks effectively. The time taken to cross the river, combined with the brilliant harassing tactics of the Thessalians, had proved crucial.

The Macedonian companions met with rather more success. Their rapid advance negated Persian missilry utterly, and they soon drove the meagre cavalry force from their path. Alexander then turned to his left and hit the Kardakes in the flank, smashing these and moving on to the hoplites and Darius himself. The Persian Great King promptly fled; what was left of his army (including the horde of useless levies) routed with him. It had been a close-run thing, but the Macedonians were victorious.

Although Alexander was able to capture the Persian royal family, Darius himself managed to escape. In the short term, the Macedonians captured the rest of Phoenicia (not only Syria but what is now Israel, Lebanon and Jordan as well) and Egypt. By 331 BC, Alexander advanced into the Persian heartland and fought Darius again at Gaugemela, routing him again and winning control of the Persian Empire itself. Darius met the miserable fate of being murdered by one of his own commanders, Bessus, who did not benefit from his disloyalty, being captured and put to death by Alexander shortly after perpetrating his misdeed. One can surmise that the new Macedonian emperor did not wish to reward regicide, lest one of his own subordinates follow Bessus' precedent by assassinating Alexander himself.

RECREATING THE BATTLEFIELD

With only two terrain pieces affecting the action at Issus, constructing a wargames battle was very straightforward. I used a 4ft × 2ft board covered in grass matting, with ready-made hills from Games Workshop and a (narrow) river from S & A Scenics. A simple alternative would be to drape a green cloth over a convenient table, placing books under it to represent the hill. The Pinarus can be depicted using either a pair of old jeans cut into narrow strips, or alternatively sections of thin card painted blue. The Gulf of Issus, on the extreme right of the Persian line, did not need to be depicted, since (naturally enough) no troops could enter any body of deep water. It was simply assumed that the Gulf was bordering the battlefield on the Persian right (and Macedonian left).

ARMY COMPOSITION

The army lists for Macedonians and Persians were able to give a good impression of their historical equivalent. Taking the Macedonians first, the strong influence of the Companions on the battle was reflected by allocating two units to the order of battle. The spine of the army inevitably comprised Heavy Infantry, so four units of these (three phalangites and one hypaspist) were fielded. That left two units to illustrate the significance of light troops, best exemplified by allowing one unit of Agrianan foot javelinmen, and one of Thessalian cavalry, to take their place in the line of battle.

So far as the Persians were concerned, the importance of cavalry units had to be illustrated by fielding four units of horsemen; three Heavy Cavalry units, and one of Paphlagonian light horsemen, fitted the bill. However, Darius placed great importance upon infantry at Issus, so the remainder of the army consisted of infantrymen. As with the Macedonian Companions, the effect of the various foot soldiers had to be considered when deciding upon army composition. Given the significance of the mercenary hoplites in the real battle, it was decided to field two of these Greek infantrymen on the wargames table, together with two Kardakes units. Although this does not depict the historical facts of 60,000 Kardakes compared with 30,000 hoplites, it certainly best reflected the relative effectiveness of the mercenaries compared with the indigenous Persians. The importance of this cannot be emphasised enough; my wargames armies do not necessarily depict raw numbers, but instead reflect the effectiveness of the various units in the historical engagement simulated in the battle reports.

With the effectiveness a primary consideration, two units had to be omitted from the Persian order of battle. The horde of levies, playing as it did no part in the historical battle, was removed accordingly (this is customary wargames practice, there being little point in painting masses of figures to represent troops that tend to run away at the first contact with the enemy). The Light Infantry deployed on the hill also had to be removed. Their role seems to have been to harass the Macedonian right, but the rapid advance of the latter made the Persian light infantrymen ineffective. Given that the hills seem to have provided a formidable obstacle to movement for all troops save Light Infantry, it was also decided to treat the former terrain as mountainous, and hence impassable to all units. This may have prevented the Persian Light Infantry from threatening the Macedonian right flank, but also screened the Persian left from any outflanking moves by Alexander's army. This again reflects what happened in the historical battle.

PLANS AND DEPLOYMENT

Given that Alexander the Great always showed great flexibility and the ability to respond quickly to any opposition moves, it was felt that the Persians should deploy first, with the Macedonians allowed the luxury of responding to Darius' set up.

Our wargaming Great King decided to reflect his historical predecessor by massing three units of heavy cavalry on his right flank. These were to be used aggressively, crossing the Pinarus and hopefully outflanking the Macedonian line. As for his infantry, Darius placed the hoplite units in the centre, flanked on either side by the Kardakes. He felt that the hoplites, aided by the Pinarus, would form a formidable obstacle to the expected Macedonian infantry assault. Unfortunately for Darius, the same could not really be said of the Kardakes, whose archery was undoubtedly useful, but whose close-combat weakness left them vulnerable. Accordingly, the Persian commander decided that on no account would his infantry cross the Pinarus. For by remaining behind the stream, the Kardakes could maximise the effect of their missiles (given that the Macedonian foot would take a full move just to cross the Pinarus), and also use the river obstacle to their advantage during the first round of combat. Our wargaming Darius hoped that the Kardakes would hold their position long enough for the combined effects of the hoplites and the heavy cavalry to win the battle. The one remaining point of vulnerability was the left flank, and our Great King knew it. He decided to block the hole with his Paphlagonian light cavalry, hoping that the harassing effect of javelin fire and the obstacle to movement presented by the Pinarus, would blunt the power of any Macedonian outflanking moves. The Persian commander did consider weakening his right flank assault by deploying a Heavy Cavalry unit in support of his light horsemen, on the left, but rejected this idea. Our wargaming Darius worked on the principle that it was foolish to imperil his one offensive move by relying too heavily upon defending his line; that would serve only to hand the initiative to Alexander.

Speaking of which, our would-be world conqueror took one look at the Persian deployment and saw that his opponent intended to adopt the approach of his historical predecessor. This was actually rather unwelcome, for our wargaming Alexander knew full well that the historical Darius, notwithstanding the ribaldry directed against him by Classical historians, was in reality an effective tactician. Accordingly, the Macedonian army would adopt Alexander's battle plan, on the grounds that there was no finer model. As a result, the four Heavy Infantry units were deployed facing the hoplites and the Kardakes. Their role was to assault the Persian line, even though this meant crossing the Pinarus. The alternative of standing and waiting for a Persian assault, only to be picked off by the Kardakes' archery in the meantime, proved a distinctly unsatisfactory option. The flanks presented the chief problem. Alexander soon decided that the Agrianians and

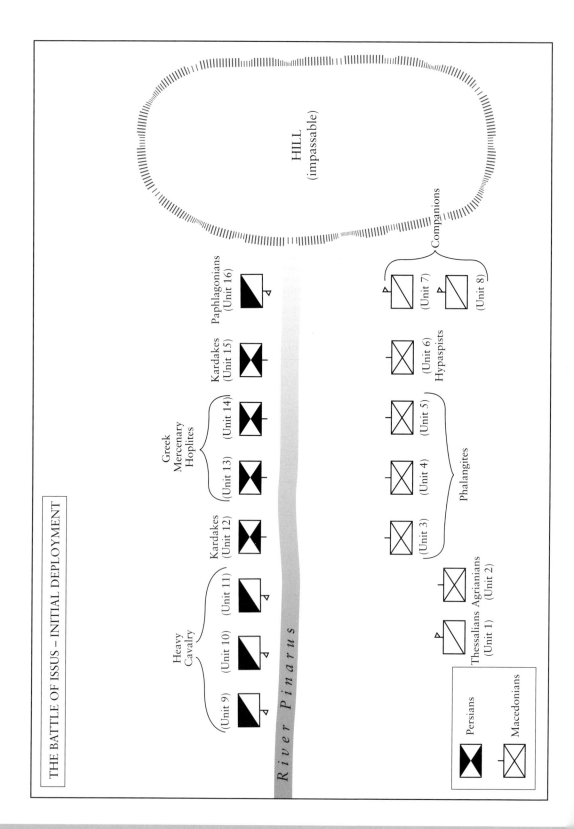

THE BATTLE OF ISSUS – INITIAL DEPLOYMENT

HILL
(impassable)

River Pinarus

Heavy Cavalry
(Unit 9)
(Unit 10)
(Unit 11)

Kardakes
(Unit 12)

Greek Mercenary Hoplites
(Unit 13)
(Unit 14)

Kardakes
(Unit 15)

Paphlagonians
(Unit 16)

Thessalians
(Unit 1)

Agrianians
(Unit 2)

Phalangites
(Unit 3)
(Unit 4)
(Unit 5)

Hypaspists
(Unit 6)

Companions
(Unit 7)
(Unit 8)

Persians

Macedonians

Thessalians would have to screen his left flank from the massed Persian cavalry. He could have added one of his Companion units as reinsurance; however, such a cautious approach would have been disdained by the historical Alexander, and our wargamer would have been mortified to be castigated as a poltroon by his fellow gamers. Accordingly, both Companion units were placed on the Macedonian right, with orders to drive away the Paphlagonians, and engage the flanks of the Persian infantry with all possible speed.

In essence, both commanders intended to attack the opposition left flank, but the Macedonians hoped to seize the initiative by assaulting the Persian centre with Heavy Infantry. Time would tell whether Greek aggression or Persian guile would prove victorious.

TURN-BY-TURN ANALYSIS

Turn 1 saw the Macedonian Heavy Infantry and Companions advance. The Companions did not move their full allowance straight ahead, since to do so would have subjected them to javelin fire from the Paphlagonians and archery from the Kardakes (unit 15) as well. As for the light units, the Agrianians advanced in echelon behind the leftmost phalangite unit (3), while the Thessalians seized the opportunity to take advantage of the split-move role, by moving to the river bank, engaging one of the Persian Heavy Cavalry units (11) with javelin fire, then retiring to safety. The value of such nuisance tactics would prove increasingly apparent as the battle continued.

The Persians responded by sending their Heavy Cavalry (units 9–11) across the Pinarus. This took an entire move. The Kardakes units meanwhile used their archery; unit 12 engaged its opposing phalangite unit (3) with little effect (thanks to some good armour saving dice rolls from Alexander), but unit 15 assailed the leading Companion unit (7) and inflicted rather more damage. The Macedonian decision to limit his Companions' advance, thereby preventing combined fire from the Kardakes and the Paphlagonian light horse, was proving to be wise.

On turn 2, the Macedonians continued their infantry advance, but the Companions lead unit (7) reached the Pinarus by advancing its full move. This would mean that it would only have to face the fire of the Paphlagonian Light Cavalry (unit 16) since the Kardakes unit (15) could not fire at the acute angle now presented by the Companions. The second Companion unit (8) followed on behind. Meanwhile, the Agrianians (unit 2) and Thessalians (unit 1) were able both to cover the flank of the nearest phalangite unit (3) and fire at the closest Persian Heavy Cavalry unit (11), which lost its first base as a result of accumulated casualty points.

When it came to their turn, the Persian Heavy Cavalry (unit 11) promptly exacted retribution on the Agrianians, engaging them in hand-to-hand combat. However, they first had to endure javelin fire from the infantrymen, and suffered so severely that another base was removed. The other Persian Heavy Cavalry units (9 and 10) had now positioned themselves in a flanking position, but were not yet anywhere near the Macedonian phalangites. The half-move penalty for turning at an angle of greater than 30° was slowing the Persian assault considerably. The missilry of both Kardakes units (12 and 15) had a limited effect upon the opposing Macedonian infantry (units 3 and 6), whereas the Paphlagonian light horse, which fired at the Companion unit on the river bank (unit 7), had even less effect. Nor did the hand-to-hand combat phase go well for the Persians. Although the Agrianians suffered at the hands of their cavalry opponents, they were able to inflict yet another base loss on the Persian horse (unit 11). Although the latter passed its morale test, it was now reduced to a single base.

Turn 3 saw the Macedonian Heavy Infantry reach the Pinarus, while the Companions (unit 7) crossed the river (the Paphlagonian horse having prudently retired after firing its javelins on the previous turn). The second Companion unit (8) reached the river bank. The Thessalians transferred their harassing intent to the second Persian cavalry unit (10), while the Agrianians inevitably began to suffer in hand-to-hand combat, losing a base to their Persian cavalry assailants (unit 11). It should be remembered that the Agrianians could not retire from combat (normally a sensible course of action for light troops) because their movement rate did not exceed that of their mounted opponents.

On their turn, the Persians were able to advance the second Heavy Cavalry unit (10) to hit the Agrianian flank. Being engaged in both front and flank, the Macedonian Light Infantry could not be expected to survive for long, but had certainly done their job: the phalangites and hypaspists (units 3-6) would cross the Pinarus without being engaged in any flank. For the remaining Persian cavalry unit (9) was finally in a position to charge, but would be unable to reach their infantry targets before the latter crossed the river. However, the firing phase saw some good news for the Persians. Although their leftmost Kardakes unit (15) had little effect on the hypaspists, their right-hand comrades (unit 12) inflicted enough casualties to cause a base to be removed from their phalangite target (unit 3). The hand-to-hand combat phase saw predictable carnage, with two bases removed from the Agrianians (unit 2); however, owing to remarkable fortitude (both morale tests being passed) the Macedonian Light Infantry remained in the fight.

Turn 4 saw Alexander's Heavy Infantry (units 3–6) cross the Pinarus and engage the Persian foot (units 12–15). Crucially, the leading Companion unit (7), having crossed the river on turn 3, was now able to engage the nearest Kardakes unit (15) in flank, in conjunction with a frontal assault from the hypaspists (unit 6). The second Companion unit (8) crossed the Pinarus too, but was not yet in range of any opponents. Nevertheless, the Elite Macedonian Heavy Cavalry was certainly making its presence felt.

The hand-to-hand combat phase finally saw the elimination of the Agrianians, which left its two assailants (Persian cavalry units 10 and 11) free to intervene elsewhere, but now on the south side of the Pinarus – and all the important action was occurring on the north bank. However, things were not going entirely the Macedonians' way. The leftmost phalangite unit (3) had a particularly difficult time against the Kardakes (unit 12) losing one base after hand-to-hand combat, and having to remove another as a result of a failed morale test. The Greek mercenary hoplites (units 13 and 14) also had the better of the initial exchanges against their phalangite opponents (units 4 and 5). Our wargaming Darius was beginning to feel reassured, convinced as he was of the efficacy of river obstacles as an aid to defence.

Unfortunately for the Persian commander, the Hypaspists (unit 6) and the Companions (unit 7) combined with horrific effect. Despite vigorous defence from the Kardakes (unit 15), which saw the Hypaspists lose two bases (one in combat, and one after a failed morale test) the Macedonians inflicted a total of eight casualty point losses upon the Persian foot. That meant the removal of two bases, which saw a calamitous collapse in the Kardakes' ranks; two morale test failures saw the elimination of the Persian infantrymen. Thus did Darius' worst nightmare come to pass: the Kardakes' fragile morale and limited hand-to-hand combat skills left them horribly exposed once archery ceased to play a part, and led to the elimination of unit 15.

When it came to the Persian turn, our wargaming Great King had his cavalry to consider. Two units of Heavy Cavalry (9 and 10) were ordered to the south bank of the Pinarus, behind two units of phalangites (3 and 4); the horsemen would be able to assault the Macedonian rear on the following turn. That left one Persian heavy cavalry unit (11). It will be recalled that this had been reduced to just one base thanks to the combined efforts of the Thessalians and Agrianians. Moreover, the Thessalian Light Cavalry (unit 1) was now in charge range. The Persian commander, goaded beyond endurance, found himself unable to resist temptation and charged. This proved a disastrous miscalculation, since the Macedonian light horse were able to fire javelins at their assailants, which they did with considerable effect. Darius really should have been more wary: he was well aware of just how useful javelin fire could be from the efforts of his own Paphlagonian Light Cavalry (unit 16), which was indulging in harassing tactics against the lead Companion unit (7), and beginning to inflict significant casualties.

The hand-to-hand combat phase saw further attritional combat between Greek mercenaries (units 13 and 14) and Macedonian phalangites (units 4 and 5), with neither side yet able to gain the upper hand. As for the remaining Kardakes unit (12) they predictably began to suffer. Despite inflicting losses on the remaining phalangite base (from unit 3) they themselves had to remove a base, which promptly became two following a morale failure.

End of Turn 4	Eliminated Units
Macedonians	One unit (2)
Persians	Two units (11 and 15)

With the onset of turn 5, Alexander had some important decisions to make on his right flank. The elimination of the Kardakes (unit 15) allowed the lead Companion unit (7), which had launched the flanking attack upon the Persian heavy archers, to assault the nearest hoplite unit's (14) flank in turn. The hypaspists (unit 6) now advanced straight ahead, aiming to reach the Persian baseline and thereby eliminate two enemy units. This would not happen until turn 8; our wargaming Alexander nevertheless believed that the long march would still bring useful dividends, given that the hypaspists' path to other enemy units was comprehensively blocked. The remaining Companion unit (8) had meanwhile turned 45° to its left and was advancing towards the main battle. Meanwhile, the Thessalians (unit 1) indulged in some largely ineffective firing against the nearest Persian Heavy Cavalry (unit 10), before themselves contacting the river bank. This would (in an extreme situation) allow the light horsemen to intervene in hand-to-hand combat if necessary.

Speaking of which, Darius let out a hearty cheer when the remaining Kardakes unit (12) eliminated their phalangite opponents (unit 3). Alexander gritted his teeth at this point, but derived some comfort from the continued indecisive combat between his central phalangite unit (4) and its hoplite opponent (unit 13). Our would-be emperor was especially looking forward to the results of the Companions' (unit 7) flank attack on the remaining hoplite unit (14), in combination with a frontal assault from the remaining phalangites (unit 5). Nor was our wargaming Alexander disappointed; a base was eliminated from the hoplites, which became two bases following the failure of the resulting morale test.

During the Persian turn, the remaining Heavy Cavalry units (9 and 10) crossed the Pinarus, with unit 10 engaging one of the phalangite units (4) in the rear. This was in combination with one of the hoplites (unit 13), currently embroiled in a continuing mêlée against the phalangites' front. The remaining Kardakes unit (12), having eliminated its erstwhile opponents, turned 90° to its left in readiness for engaging the somewhat beleaguered phalangites, assailed as they already were in front and rear. Thanks to the Kardakes' move, they now had a flank attack to anticipate in addition. The results were predictably bloody, with one phalangite base lost in combat, and another added following a morale failure. The remaining combat saw final hoplite unit (14) hold off the Macedonian front and flank attack (from units 5 and 7) without further losses. The situation at this stage can be seen on the map provided.

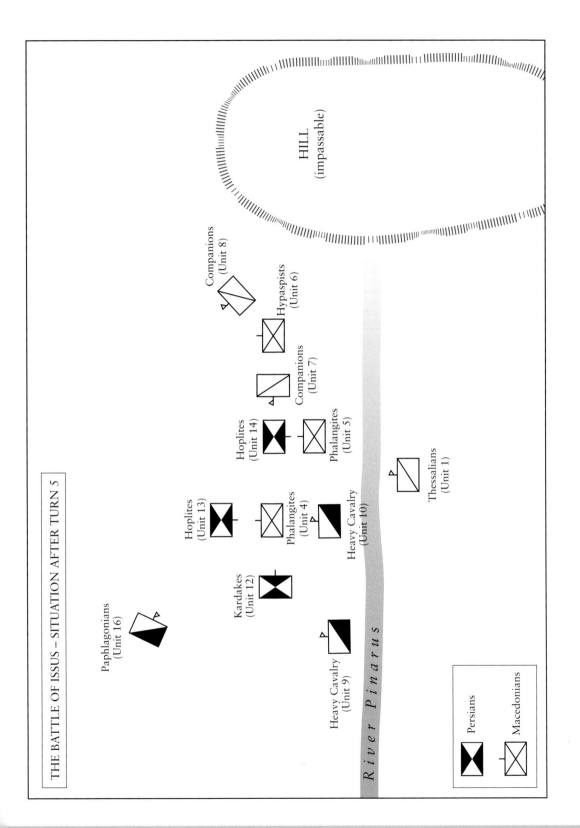

THE BATTLE OF ISSUS – SITUATION AFTER TURN 5

HILL
(impassable)

Companions
(Unit 8)

Hypaspists
(Unit 6)

Companions
(Unit 7)

Hoplites
(Unit 14)

Phalangites
(Unit 5)

Thessalians
(Unit 1)

Hoplites
(Unit 13)

Phalangites
(Unit 4)

Heavy Cavalry
(Unit 10)

Kardakes
(Unit 12)

Paphlagonians
(Unit 16)

Heavy Cavalry
(Unit 9)

River Pinarus

Persians

Macedonians

End of Turn 5	**Eliminated Units**
Macedonians	Two units (2 and 5)
Persians	Two units (11 and 15)

Alexander was rather worried at the start of turn 6. The hypaspists were still heading for the Persian baseline, but would not exit the board until turn 8; the unengaged Companion unit (8) was meanwhile continuing to turn to its left and head towards the Persian flank and rear, but would not be able to intervene until the following turn. Things were so desperate that our would-be emperor sent the Thessalian Light Cavalry (unit 1) across the Pinarus, and against the rear of the Persian heavy horse (unit 10).

The ensuing hand-to-hand combat phase saw both flank and rear combats bear fruit; the phalangites (unit 4) assaulted by the hoplites (unit 13) and Heavy Cavalry (unit 10) were eliminated, but so too were the hoplites (unit 14) under attack from the remaining phalangites (unit 5) and the Companions (unit 7). Moreover, the Thessalians were able to take full advantage of the rear assault, managing to eliminate a base from their Heavy Cavalry opponents (unit 10).

The Persians had to realign their troops to meet the new threat. Given that the cavalry (unit 10) and hoplite (unit 13) combination had eliminated their phalangite (unit 4) opponents in the previous Macedonian turn, this was now possible. The hoplites accordingly turned to face the as yet uncommitted Companions (unit 8). The unit in question was meanwhile being harassed by the Paphlagonian Light Cavalry (unit 16), losing a base to javelin fire in the process. Darius was also in a position to inflict serious damage upon the Thessalian cavalry unit (1), by simply turning his now unengaged heavy horsemen (unit 10) to face the Macedonians, and charging the Thessalians' flank using the similarly unengaged Kardakes (unit 12). The resultant combat saw the Thessalians lose two bases, plus an extra one following the failure of one of the mandatory morale tests (the other one being passed). This left the Macedonian light horse with only one base remaining, but crucially still in being as a functioning unit. The situation at this critical stage of the battle is illustrated on the map provided.

End of Turn 6	**Eliminated Units**
Macedonians	Three units (2, 4 and 5)
Persians	Three units (11, 14 and 15)

Our wargaming Alexander had a great opportunity at the start of turn 7, and he seized it with alacrity. A consultation of the rules revealed that the remaining phalangites (unit 5) could turn up to 30° and still advance a full move, and that doing so would contact one of the Persian cavalry units (10) in the flank. The effects of this were likely to be extremely bloody for the Achaemenids. Moreover,

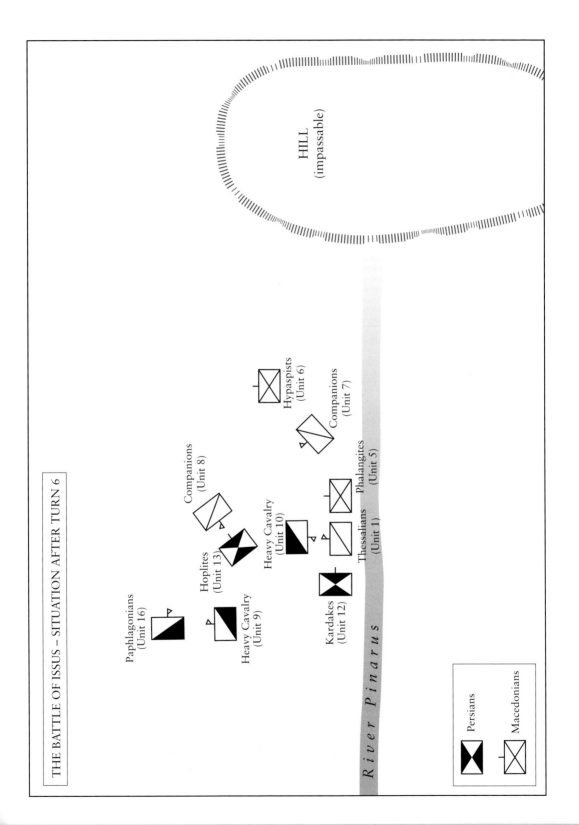

THE BATTLE OF ISSUS – SITUATION AFTER TURN 6

Paphlagonians
(Unit 16)

Companions
(Unit 8)

Hoplites
(Unit 13)

Heavy Cavalry
(Unit 9)

Heavy Cavalry
(Unit 10)

Kardakes
(Unit 12)

Hypaspists
(Unit 6)

Companions
(Unit 7)

Phalangites
(Unit 5)

Thessalians
(Unit 1)

HILL
(impassable)

River Pinarus

Persians

Macedonians

this allowed both Companion units (7 and 8) to engage Darius' mercenary hoplites (unit 13), one frontally and one in flank. Meanwhile the Thessalians (unit 1), their job having been done, elected to withdraw from hand-to-hand combat in order to survive; this retreat was permitted because their movement rate exceeded that of their assailants (cavalry unit 10 and Kardakes unit 12). The hypaspists continued towards the baseline, and would be able to exit the map during the next turn.

The hand-to-hand combat phase saw the phalangites (unit 5) engage the Persian Heavy Cavalry (unit 10) with devastating results. Two bases were removed following the fight, and the failure of one of the mandatory morale tests saw a third base depart. Given that the Persian horsemen had started the mêlée with just three bases, they were now eliminated – despite causing the removal of two bases (one after combat, the second after a failed morale test) from the phalangites, themselves reduced to just one remaining base. However, the assault by the Companions (units 7 and 8) was not as effective. Their hoplite target (unit 13) showed just how durable Heavy Infantry could be, achieving better than average armour saving rolls against the Macedonian attacks, and eliminating a base from one of the Companion units (8). Unfortunately for the Persians, the Elite Macedonian cavalry passed their morale test, preserving them from further losses.

The Persian turn saw Darius in serious difficulties. Having seen that he could not prevent the hypaspists from exiting the map, our wargaming Great King knew that he had to destroy some units quickly. Accordingly, the Kardakes (unit 12) engaged the phalangites (unit 5) (who were an available target having just wiped out the Persian heavy horse (unit 10)) with archery. Their missilry was supported by that of the Paphlagonian Light Cavalry (unit 16), which indulged in the customary tactic of galloping towards its target, firing its javelins, and retiring. The combined fire saw the removal of three casualty points from the Macedonians – not quite enough to remove the one remaining base. The Persians were soon to have cause to regret this failure.

Darius was nevertheless not finished yet. His remaining Heavy Cavalry unit (9) was now able to assist the outnumbered hoplites (unit 13) by attacking a Companion unit (8) in its flank, following a rightwards turn and charge to contact. The ensuing hand-to-hand combat phase saw another base removed from the Companions (unit 8), but once again another successful morale test – never was the efficacy of Elite status more effectively proven. The Great King was now staring defeat in the face.

End of Turn 7	*Eliminated Units*
Macedonians	Three units (2, 4 and 5)
Persians	Four units (10, 11, 14 and 15)

Turn 8 was very brief. Although the phalangite unit (5) decided to escape the Persian missilry by the novel expedient of charging the beleaguered mercenary hoplites (unit 13) in the rear, the hypaspists (unit 6) were now in a position to exit the board. This necessitated the removal of two Persian units: Darius selected the Kardakes (unit 12) and the Paphlagonians (unit 16). However, with only two units now remaining on the battlefield, the Persians had to concede defeat. Our wargaming Alexander had managed to emulate his conquering predecessor.

End of Turn 8	**Eliminated Units**
Macedonians	Four units (2, 4, 5 and 6)
Persians	Six units (10, 11, 12, 14, 15 and 16)

CONCLUSIONS AND SUMMARY

Our battle was a bitter struggle, just as the real-life Battle of Issus had been. Just as in the real thing, Alexander's Companions played a decisive role. They aided the Macedonian Heavy Infantry by controlling the right-hand side of the battlefield, and launching murderously effective assaults upon the Persian flanks. However, the real stars of the show were the Thessalian light horsemen. Their harassing tactics served to weaken the Persian heavy horse, and our wargaming Alexander showed great initiative by committing them in hand-to-hand combat at a decisive point. Their assaults upon the rear of the Persian cavalry target inflicted telling losses, and their timely retreat insured that they stayed in the battle as a functioning (albeit much weakened) unit. Any wargamer should always be aware that a gamble can be justified, and that fortune frequently favours the brave.

As for the Persians, our wargaming Darius again stuck to historical tactics. He was acute enough an analyst to realise that the Classical historians, notwithstanding their rather contemptuous dismissal of Darius' perceived cowardice in the battle, actually reveal the Great King to be a shrewd tactician. Accordingly, historical tactics were followed: the one exception being that the assault on the Macedonian left was carried out with greater force. Our Darius nearly won the battle; he was unfortunate enough to come up against an opponent equally well versed in history, and able to command the Macedonians with vigour and aggression.

In essence, our re-enactment showed just how crucial it is to seize the initiative. By taking advantage of his superior troops and having the confidence to assault the Persian lines, our Alexander always ensured that the wargaming Darius was always responding to Macedonian moves. However strong a defensive position is, it must always be remembered that the attacker has the initiative on the wargames table – and if he or she is able to seize it, there will always be a good chance of victory.

PRIMARY SOURCE

Arrian (*c*. 160 AD). *The Campaigns of Alexander* (tr. Aubrey de Sélincourt), Penguin, 1971

SECONDARY SOURCES

Barker, Phil. *Alexander the Great's Campaigns*, Patrick Stephens, 1979

Fuller, J.F.C. *The Generalship of Alexander the Great*, Wordsworth, 1998 (originally 1958)

Chapter 11

Dark Age Warfare 300–1100

KEY EVENTS

Date	Event
312–37	Reign of Emperor Constantine I. Christianity becomes official Roman religion, and Constantinople constructed.
378	Battle of Adrianople. Goths destroy Roman army and kill Emperor Valens. Rome loses control of Northern Balkans.
395	Formal division of Roman Empire into Western and Eastern sections.
410	Goths under Alaric sack Rome. Roman army abandons Britain.
440–55	Huns invade Eastern and Western Roman Empires. Saxons begin conquest of England.
451	Battle of Chalons. Romano-Gothic army under Aetius defeats Huns.
453	Death of Attila the Hun. Disintegration of Hunnic Confederacy.
470–520	Destruction of Western Empire. Italy falls to Ostrogoths, France to Franks and Spain to Visigoths.
c. 495	Battle of Mount Badon. Romano-British under King Arthur rout Saxons. British revival.
527–65	Reign of Justinian I in East Roman (Byzantine) Empire. Inconclusive wars with Sassanid Persians, and re-conquest of Italy.
540–600	Romano-British undermined by plague and internal divisions. Saxons seize control of England.
565–600	Lombards invade and ravage Northern Italy.
603–28	War between Byzantines and Sassanid Persians ends in Byzantine victory.
610–32	Creation of Islamic faith by the Prophet Muhammad. Arabia falls under control of Muslims.
633–42	Muslims seize Middle East and Egypt from Byzantines.

636	Battle of Yarmuk. In the greatest military victory of the Arab Conquest, the Byzantine army in Syria is smashed.
638–650	Muslims overrun Sassanid Persia.
643–710	Muslims eject Byzantines from North Africa.
661	Establishment of Islamic Caliphate.
711–15	Muslims destroy Visigothic Kingdom and conquer Spain.
732	Battle of Tours. Franks under Charles Martel defeat and destroy Arab invading force. Muslim armies retreat from France, and never return.
750–800	Carolingian kings consolidate power in France. Franks defeat and incorporate Saxons into their empire. Avars also crushed by Carolingians.
790–820	Vikings start raiding Britain, Ireland and France.
800	Charlemagne crowned Holy Roman Emperor by Pope Leo III.
814	Death of Charlemagne.
870–99	Reign of King Alfred the Great of Wessex. Vikings defeated, and Saxon primacy established in England.
877–900	Disintegration of Carolingian Empire.
930–50	Viking raiders seize control of what became Normandy.
936–60	Germanic Saxon Empire created under Otto I.
955	Battle of Lechfield. Otto I crushes Magyar army. Magyar power destroyed.
962	Otto I crowned Holy Roman Emperor by Pope John XII. Holy Roman Empire remains under control of German kings until its abolition in 1806.
976–1025	Byzantine Empire revives under Basil II, who became known as the 'Bulgar Basher' after destruction of latter barbarians.
997	End of Carolingian rule in France. Capetian dynasty seizes power. Normans still control Western France.
1066	Battle of Hastings. Duke William the Bastard of Normandy becomes King William the Conqueror of England, following Norman victory over Saxons.
1071	Battle of Manzikert. Byzantine army routed by Seljuk Turks. Byzantines lose much of Anatolia, and most of their power.

THE STRAINS UPON ROME

Chapter 6 has already covered the difficulties experienced by the Emperor Diocletian when restoring order at the end of the third century. The fourth century saw an intensification of the problems besetting Rome that were to result in its partial collapse during the fifth century. These pressures were both ideological (or theological, to be precise) and strategic.

It was Christianity that presented the greatest intellectual challenge to the Roman ethos. As has already been noted, paganism was remarkably pluralistic:

gods co-existed, and new ones were worshipped all the time. Several emperors saw the potential of this, and their posthumous deification allowed the growth of an imperial cult that served to cement Roman authority. However, Christianity was universalist in scope, and intrinsically dictatorial. With only one God (albeit in the trinitarian form of Father, Son, and Holy Spirit) to worship, Christians were unwilling to accept that other faiths had any validity. This refusal to acknowledge the existence of other gods understandably aroused much ire among pagans, and led to sporadic persecution of Christian believers.

Nevertheless, Christians were able to withstand such attacks. One reason is that the crackdown upon their faith was not carried out with sufficient consistency or persistence to eradicate it. There were more positive reasons for Christianity's fortitude, in the face of hostile action from the imperial authorities, however. One important factor was the religion's exclusivity – all believers anticipated the imminent return of Christ and the consequent judgement of mankind. Moreover, when this occurred it was only Christians who would be saved: non-believers had to face the rather unenviable prospect of burning in hell for all eternity. This doctrine strengthened Christian solidarity, but only served to antagonise pagans further. The same was not true of the egalitarianism inherent in Christianity, which was by far its most attractive, and ultimately most influential feature.

Anyone who reads the Gospels today is struck by Jesus' tendency to preach to the poor, consort with the pariahs of society, and challenge those established religious authorities who placed an emphasis upon social status and ritual, rather than following God's message. The Christian belief that all men were equal in the sight of God gave hope to the poor; it also brought compassion into existence. In essence, Christians helped the poor for the sake of the latter; Roman public works, in contrast, were intended for the personal glory of the benefactor and (by extension) the Roman state. Although the achievements of pagan Rome were mighty, they could be argued to have lacked heart. Christian egalitarianism acted in direct contrast to pagan glories, and provided a remarkable potential social glue. The Emperor Constantine realised this when he effectively made Christianity the official Roman religion.

Unfortunately, the negative aspects of universalism and exclusivity wrought havoc upon the intellectual and cultural life of Rome, sapping its vitality. The death of pagan pluralism meant an end to intellectual speculation: all thought now led to the contemplation of God, rather than the consideration of mankind – theology effectively replaced philosophy. Moreover, the culture of public service was replaced by obsession with the condition of individual believers' souls. In essence, the growth of Christianity meant that the Roman Empire found its heart and lost its mind.

Rome's strategic problems stemmed, as Chapter 6 has already mentioned, from its sheer size. The shift to the defensive resulted in static frontier garrisons being supported by mobile armies consisting of cavalry and the old auxiliary infantry. It must be stressed that although the static forces were often of indifferent quality (as befitting their sedentary role), the mobile forces remained as strong as ever. Unfortunately for them, they had a large frontier to cover, and a state that lacked the ideological coherence to support the army (despite Diocletian's rather draconian planned economy). Eventually, the de facto division into western and eastern empires implemented by Diocletian, became a formal de jure construct in 395.

As was the case in the later Republic, a large Empire led to dispersed armies, some of which had generals with imperial ambitions. The resultant coup attempts led not only to ruinous civil wars – the Emperor Constantine came to power after one such conflict, for example – but to opportunistic barbarian invasions too. For when a putative emperor headed towards Rome, taking his army with him, the garrisons left behind had great difficulties coping with invaders. Britain proved especially vulnerable: being so far from Rome, it was a favourite base for ambitious generals to foment their plots far from the imperial gaze. The constant civil wars led to a situation whereby the Emperor Honorius withdrew all troops from Britain in 410, not merely to defend the embattled Gallic frontier, but also to prevent Britain being used as the launching point for yet another coup.

As for the barbarians themselves, they were now more mobile. Whereas some forces such as the Franks and Saxons relied upon infantry, the Goths and especially the Huns used far greater numbers of cavalry – which increased both the breadth and destructiveness of their raids. By the end of the fifth century the Western Empire had collapsed. However, the Eastern Empire survived and prospered, maintaining the Christian Roman inheritance (along with some of the old Classical texts and learning). It was only after the calamitous rout at Manzikert in 1071 that saw the East Roman Empire begin its decline. It is important to note that the title of 'Byzantine' Empire was a neologism coined by later historians. Its citizens saw themselves as 'Romans', and were likewise regarded as such by the medieval world.

THE CAVALRY CHALLENGE

Social distinctions were very significant in barbarian society. Nobles believed in displaying their wealth, and one way of doing this was to ride a horse into battle. Moreover, the barbarian elite had time on its hands to devote itself to military training. The result was a core of heavy cavalry with armoured riders, in both the Gothic armies of central Europe, and the Sassanid Persian Empire.

The heavy cavalryman had common features. His armour allowed him to engage in close-quarter combat, and the long thrusting spear provided a potent threat against any troops who lost their cohesion. The Sassanids went a stage farther than the Goths: whereas the Germanic invaders had armoured riders, the

Persians covered their horses in armour too. Although this made the horses rather slow, it could produce a very durable and powerful form of cavalry, which became known as cataphracts. As has been mentioned earlier, the Romans also needed to adopt cavalry on a large scale in order to protect their frontiers. The Byzantines continued this tradition. In many ways the best weapon to confront a warrior on horseback was another cavalry force; it could not be outmanoeuvred in the way an infantry army would have been.

The Huns adopted a different route. They were very much heirs to the Scythians, both in their destructive savagery and their mode of fighting. They relied almost entirely upon horse archery, but there was one crucial difference from the Scythians. Although both armies adopted open-order formation, the Hunnic cavalry was equipped with a light spear in addition to bows. As a result, the latter were far more willing to enter close combat than the Scythians had been. The combination of fire combat and ferocity made for a deadly combination. Troops in close order could undoubtedly repel the Huns if they retained their tight formation; however, archery tended to disrupt this, resulting in gaps which the Huns could ride into and wreak havoc.

Although many armies used a combination of Heavy and Light Cavalry in order to maximise the impact of each, two technical innovations served to make horsemen even more potent. The first of these was the stirrup, which appeared during the eighth century. By improving the rider's control of his mount, and generally creating a more stable combat platform, Heavy Cavalry charges became more effective. Instead of the previous overarm thrusts, the stirrups allowed horsemen to brace their spears (which developed into fully fledged long lances by the end of the Dark Ages) underarm, allowing horses to provide the motive force for the weapons. It is however important not to overstate the role of the stirrup: it would not allow horses to charge an enemy unit in disciplined close-order formation. However, an unsteady body of men would often lose their close alignment when confronted by a cavalry unit advancing with murderous intent; and this was when the new mounted lancers could wreak havoc. Stirrups simply allowed horsemen to control their steeds for longer, when in the heat of battle: since victory in mêlée combat always went to the side which retained its cohesion under pressure, this extra time proved vital. It is not true, as some writers suggest, that cavalry charges were impossible before the invention of the stirrup; it simply made shock action more likely to succeed.

The second innovation to revolutionise cavalry warfare was the nailed horseshoe, which became widespread during the tenth century. Before the use of the shoe, horses could only perform efficiently if their hooves remained hard. This was not a problem in dry climates; however, the somewhat wetter regions of Western Europe created softer ground, and hooves became softer in turn. When the ground dried out following a period of rain, the horses' now tender feet proved unequal to the load of their rider. Accordingly, the scope of combat operations was curtailed somewhat. Although it is true that rudimentary horse-shoes appeared as early as the fourth century, it was only with the introduction of the nailed version that cavalry operations could be wide ranging irrespective of climatic changes.

The Dark Ages therefore saw cavalry come of age. Although traditional Light Cavalry skirmishing was still very effective, shock action by heavy horsemen became widespread – the combination of the technological innovations to the horse, and the prestige attached to the fact that their riders came from the social elite, gave the Heavy Cavalry both status and effectiveness.

THE DECLINE OF INFANTRY

All this emphasis upon cavalry had an unfortunate effect upon the foot soldiery. Traditional Heavy Infantry on the Roman legionary pattern suffered, as the societal elite fought on horseback. With their role confined to a passive one, legionaries and their equivalents became much less important: they simply supported cavalry, and no longer won the battles. Morale and training inevitably suffered, and the latter deficiency proved crucial. Without the same levels of discipline and drill, Heavy Infantry could not retain its formation in the advance, and close-order foot lost much of its offensive potential.

Nevertheless, the legionaries and their successors were still effective in defence. Many armies developed a tactic known as the shieldwall. As its name suggests, this took the form of having the infantry units bunch up very tightly, taking advantage of the protection resulting from an impenetrable shield barrier. Although this tactic made movement very slow at best (a slow walk was the only feasible approach), the defensive protection was great. This gave Dark Age Infantry impressive potential endurance, which went some way towards negating the decline in offensive ability.

Heavy Infantry may have been on the decline, but the Warband was still very much a part of some armies – the Vikings being the most notable example. This traditional brand of barbarian warfare could be very effective, since the Dark Age Heavy Infantry was no more useful in close combat than the Warband, and lacked the impetuous charge of the latter. A massed barbarian charge could still, as the Vikings showed, have a remarkable impact on the battlefield.

On a strategic level, some infantry units took to riding horses on the march. In so doing, infantry elites (such as the Anglo-Saxon huscarls) were able greatly to increase their scope of operations, acting in support of local militias either to repel invaders, or to mass quickly on an offensive. Mounted infantry were also able to keep up with cavalry on the march. It must be stressed that these soldiers may have marched on horseback, but they always fought their battles on foot. Their adoption simply allowed for more rapid strategic movement.

It can therefore be seen that infantry still had a significant role to play on the battlefield. However, it is important to be aware that the decline of Heavy Infantry (shieldwall tactic notwithstanding) not only increased the potency of the Warband, but helped make cavalry not only the weapon of glamour and status, but also that of first choice and greatest effectiveness.

BARBARIANS AND MUSLIMS

After the fall of the Western Roman Empire, chaos initially ensued as the barbarians took over. Fortunately for the ultimate fate of Western civilisation, many of these peoples (such as the Goths and the Franks) were awestruck by the glories they found, and did their best to preserve the Roman ways. Unfortunately, they lacked the knowledge to run the old imperial bureaucracy, which as a consequence suffered; where it functioned at all, it took on a decidedly ramshackle appearance. As a result, the somewhat flummoxed barbarians turned to the only intact intellectual force, namely the Roman Catholic Church. Post-Roman states were created in France, Italy and Spain. It has to be said that these bore little resemblance to Rome in its heyday, but were at least able to give Western Europe an ideological identity, based upon Christianity.

Other barbarians were less enlightened. They were simply bent on plunder, and it was only after they settled down in the areas they occupied (if they ever did; the Huns for example remained resolutely immune to the blandishments of civilised life) that they began to make any constructive contribution to society. Raiders such as the Huns, Magyars and Avars were largely based upon cavalry; but the Vikings and early Saxons used ships to reach their destination (often Britain). In so doing, the latter effectively became the Dark Age equivalent of the Biblical Sea Peoples.

There was one new force in the intellectual firmament of the Dark Ages, and it came from a totally unexpected source. The Arabian desert peoples had not hitherto made any contribution to civilisation, and their military efforts had been distinctly unimpressive, with the partial exception of the Midianite Arabs in Biblical times. All this was to change with the advent of Islam.

It is one of history's supreme ironies that the Prophet Muhammad did not see himself as a revolutionary thinker. Islam can essentially be seen as a new interpretation of Judaism: it retained the one God of the Jewish faith, but no longer expected the arrival of a messiah on Earth. Islam also took the Christian tenet of universalism, applying itself to the cause of converting all mankind, rather than a single race. A very potent force was nevertheless created, which was to conquer the Middle East, North Africa and Spain.

Islam's chief strength lay in its theological coherence. All the divine revelations that Muhammad believed had inspired him were collected in one book (the *Koran*), which made their dissemination – even in a world with limited literacy and no printing presses – fairly easy. Moreover, the belief in one God was easy to grasp, and avoided the often poisonous theological disputes over the nature of the Holy Trinity, that so bedevilled the Byzantine world (even to the point of weakening its political unity). Moreover, there was none of the pacifism so inconveniently espoused by Jesus: Islam was all for a spot of military conquest, provided that the faith was spread as a result. All this gave the Arab peoples a great deal of self-respect; Islam had provided them with a cause, and a specific philosophical outlook. Both these qualities are, of course, the essential prerequisites for the development of a viable civilisation.

Another trait aiding the spread of the Islamic faith was the nature of the obligations upon believers. Specifically, there was never any requirement for a Muslim to attend a mosque: the faithful simply had to pray five times daily, and stick to obligations such as fasting from dawn to dusk during the month of Ramadan. In a very real sense, Islam was always centred upon the believer. The only authority was that of the *Koran*. Influential sects and divisions did arise; but without the existence of a figure like the Pope, in accordance with the stipulation that Islam had no ruling religious authority, the faith remained centred upon its believers rather than institutions. Doctrinal unity was thereby achieved without schisms.

Islam was, however, only one faith: others had to be confronted – not merely the Christianity of the Byzantine Empire, but also Judaism, and the Zoroastrianism practised in Sassanid Persia. Muhammad accordingly preached a message of toleration: in his eyes, Muslims should co-exist with believers of other faiths. This was an absolute necessity, given that any Islamic military conquests would involve controlling areas where other religions held sway. It must be stressed that toleration was for the Muslims a rather limited notion – it was emphatically not a case of enlightened pluralism, but instead took the form of putting up with unpalatable realities. For example, other faiths were allowed to exist in the Islamic world, but their believers had to pay a special poll tax, and were in addition not allowed to seek converts (anyone who converted from Islam to Christianity could in theory be put to death). Similarly, slaves had rights under Islam, but their status as slaves could not be questioned; women also had specific rights, but were still regarded as being inferior to men. In essence Islamic toleration represented an advance upon medieval Christian practice, but could not be described as enlightened: bigotry was rife, and an intellectual straitjacket present.

However, the combination of theological unity, glorification of military achievement, and (limited) toleration created great military vigour. The Arab armies developed their traditional cavalry skills to the point of creating a mounted strike force with a combination of lance and bow. The ability to combine fire and shock often proved decisive; the period of the great conquests also saw the mounted force supported most effectively by infantry Warbands. Moreover, the Arab armies benefited greatly from the fact that the Byzantine and Sassanid empires were weakened by constant wars with each other. As a consequence, the Muslims conquered all of Persia, the Middle East, North Africa and also Spain (the Visigothic kingdom falling in the process).

FEUDALISM

The twin threat from barbarians and Muslims presented a mortal challenge to Europe. It became evident that overall political unity was essential, and many looked back longingly to the glories of Rome. Imperial unity and cultural self-confidence provided a great contrast to Dark Age Europe, suffering as it did from a political shambles and a cultural vacuum – in some contrast to the Byzantine Empire, whose continued splendours reminded Western Europe of its inferiority.

However, although Rome was a memory, Christianity was very much alive. Despite its lack of intellectual vitality, the Catholic Church provided the only functioning source of administrative and cultural unity. Moreover, the Christian religion did, as has already been stated, insist upon the unity of mankind – and especially the obligation to feel compassion towards, and provide charity for, the poor.

Militarily, all this had significant implications. Patches of territory were defended by warlords, who had a sense of obligation not only to their retinues, but also to the people who fell under their control. As a result, a system of offering service in return for protection, developed into feudalism.

On a political level, powerful nobles linked themselves together on an essentially tribal basis, and agreed that the strongest of their number should become king. Given the absence of the Roman monetary economy, creating an empire based upon landholding and protection thereof, was the only viable option. Christianity provided the essential social and ideological bonding agent for the new system: the poor had to respect their masters, and the nobles had to protect the poor. All had a duty to worship the Christian God. This system of interlocking social obligations based upon the control of real estate, became known as feudalism.

It has to be said that many feudal regimes lacked political sophistication. The empire of Charlemagne did for example base its unity upon the fact that its ruler constantly had to tour his dominions. In this way, royal power could be asserted. Moreover, the Carolingian empire was to break up, owing to the practice of sub-division of kingdoms among a ruler's heirs. However, the system had enough political vitality for Pope Leo III to crown Charlemagne Holy Roman Emperor in 800. The new Emperor now had the responsibility of defending Christendom – the concept of Rome as a political entity had died, but it is fascinating to note how men in the Dark Ages were always looking back to the glories of Empire.

Nevertheless, early feudalism had the vitality to develop a force strong enough to repel Islam, defeat many barbarian invaders, and assimilate the rest into

Christian civilisation (albeit after much devastation first). A new and viable military force had developed, based upon mobile armies (with either Heavy Cavalry, or mounted infantry Warbands at their core). This new brand of militarised Christianity had been created against all the odds, and was to reach its zenith in the Medieval period.

PRIMARY SOURCES

Ammianus Marcellinus (*c.* 390). *The Later Roman Empire* (tr. Walter Hamilton), Penguin, 1986

Asser (880–900). *Alfred the Great: Asser's Life of King Alfred and Other Contemporary Sources* (tr. Simon Keynes and Michael Lapidge), Penguin, 1983

Bede (731). *Ecclesiastical History of the English People* (tr. Leo Sherley-Price), Penguin, 1990

Einhard (829–36) and Notker the Stammerer (884–7). *Two Lives of Charlemagne* (tr. Lewis Thorpe), Penguin, 1969

Gildas (*c.* 540). *The Ruin of Britain* (tr. Michael Winterbottom), Phillimore, 1978

The Koran (644–56) (tr. N.J. Dawood), Penguin, 1999

Nennius (*c.* 800). *History of the British* (tr. John Morris), Phillimore, 1980

Procopius (550). *The Secret History* (tr. G.A. Williamson), Penguin, 1966

Psellus, Michael (1060–80). *Fourteen Byzantine Rulers* (tr. E.R.A. Sewter), Penguin, 1966

Sturluson, Snorri (*c.* 1235). *King Harald's Saga* (tr. Magnus Magnusson and Hermann Pálsson), Penguin, 1966

SECONDARY SOURCES

Barker, Phil. *The Armies and Enemies of Imperial Rome*, Wargames Research Group, 1981

Bennett, Matthew et al. *Fighting Techniques of the Medieval World*, Spellmount, 2005

Contamine, Phillipe. *War in the Middle Ages* (tr. Michael Jones), Blackwell, 1984

Davis, R.H.C. *A History of Medieval Europe*, Longman, 1970

Ellis, John. *Cavalry*, Pen & Sword, 1993 (originally 1978)

Ellis, Peter Berresford. *Celt and Saxon*, Constable, 1993

Evans, Stephen S. *Lords of Battle*, Boydell, 1997

Fletcher, Richard. *The Cross and the Crescent*, Penguin, 2003

Fuller, J.F.C. *Decisive Battles of the Western World, Volume 1*, SPA Books, 1993 (originally 1954)

Heath, Ian. *Armies of the Dark Ages*, Wargames Research Group, 1980

Hildinger, Erik. *Warriors of the Steppe*, Spellmount, 1997

Karasulas, Antony. *Mounted Archers of the Steppe 600 BC–AD 1300*, Osprey, 2004

Keen, Maurice (ed.). *Medieval Warfare*, Oxford, 1999

Montgomery, Field Marshal Viscount. *A Concise History of Warfare*, Wordsworth, 2000 (originally 1968)

Nicolle, David. *The Armies of Islam 7th–11th Centuries*, Osprey, 1982

Nicolle, David. *The Age of Charlemagne*, Osprey, 1984

Nicolle, David. *Arthur and the Anglo-Saxon Wars*, Osprey, 1984

Wise, Terence. *Saxon, Viking and Norman*, Osprey, 1979

JOURNAL ARTICLES

Bath, Tony. 'The Age of the Barbarian' Part 1 in *Slingshot* no. 238 (November 2004), 16–20

Bath, Tony. 'The Age of the Barbarian' Part 2 in *Slingshot* no. 240 (March 2005), 27–33

Patrick, Stephen B. 'Empires of the Middle Ages' in *Strategy and Tactics* no. 80 (May 1980), 23–32

Chapter 12

Dark Age Wargaming

The Dark Ages were noted chiefly for the decline of infantry and the growth of cavalry. Accordingly, the old category of Heavy Infantry is no longer appropriate, and is replaced by Dark Age Infantry in these rules (much in the same way that Biblical Infantry was included as a separate and inferior classification in the Biblical wargames rules). As a result, close-order infantry is potentially vulnerable to assaults from Warband, and from Heavy Cavalry and Cataphracts.

Nevertheless, some beneficial traces of the Classical heritage remained, and are reflected in the rules. In particular, shooting still only has a disruptive effect, and will never trigger a morale test. Heavy and Light Cavalry were also as effective as before.

Some of the old Classical favourite troop types no longer played a role in warfare, which is why Auxiliary Infantry, Heavy Infantry, all types of chariots, and Artillery have disappeared from these rules. New troop types are covered below; for those categories already covered in previous rules, refer to Chapters 2 and 7.

DARK AGE INFANTRY

Although rather less well drilled than the old Heavy Infantry, and thereby less effective when attacking, some (by no means all) armies were able to make the most of their close-order foot by deploying them in shieldwall formation. Although bunching up in an even closer order than usual inevitably reduced movement, it did greatly enhance a unit's protection (which is why the saving roll improves so markedly). However, whenever a unit left a shieldwall formation to revert to normal close order, extreme disruption and indeed demoralisation could occur. This is why leaving a shieldwall results in a morale test. Wargamers would therefore be advised to keep their units in shieldwall upon adopting the formation.

CATAPHRACTS

These extremely heavily armoured cavalry essentially represented a mobile shieldwall. With both rider and horse protected with heavy armour, Cataphracts had great endurance. However, they were so burdened as to be incapable of moving at a speed greater than a (usually slow) trot, and can therefore be outmanoeuvred by traditional Heavy Cavalry.

Although there are only two new troop types in these rules, there is a new missile weapon. The Dark Ages saw the first appearance of the crossbow in Europe. This had special characteristics that must be reflected in the rules. Although the crossbow is ostensibly less accurate than standard bows (only hitting its target on a roll of 5–6 rather than 4–6), this actually reflects the slower reloading time of the crossbow, rather than inferior performance. However, the crossbow bolt hit its target with much greater velocity than the ordinary arrow, which is reflected in its greater armour-piercing capacity.

Although battles between armies consisting of shieldwalls tend to be somewhat tedious affairs, many Dark Age forces contain cavalry elements that add greatly to the excitement. Also, suffused as it is by legends such as Arthurian myths and Viking Sagas, Dark Age armies can have a great allure for any wargamer who has a taste for heroic deeds.

The Biblical elite. Egyptian chariots on the march. *(Kevin Dallimore)*

The Mycenean Greeks and Trojans face each other outside the walls of Troy. *(®Miniature Wargames)*

Trojan light infantry in action. *(Kevin Dallimore)*

Assyrian infantry prepare to attack. A sight to terrify any foe. *(Brush Strokes)*

An Achaemenid Persian force arrayed for battle. *(Brush Strokes)*

The business end of a Hoplite Greek phalanx. *(GJM Figurines)*

The hordes of Persian cavalry and chariots on the right bank of the stream may look impressive, but are unlikely to prevail against the Macedonian pikemen. *(®Miniature Wargames)*

The Battle of the Hydaspes (326 BC). The Indian elephants are preparing to assault the Macedonian lines. (®*Miniature Wargames*)

Indian army elephants made a big impression on the Macedonians, and were enlisted by the Hellenistic Successor kingdoms. This is a Seleucid example. *(Kevin Dallimore)*

Above: The Republican Roman and Carthaginian armies prepare for hand-to-hand combat. *(®Miniature Wargames)*

Left: Hail Caesar! The Roman Emperor Claudius reviews his troops. *(Kevin Dallimore)*

Top right: Imperial Roman legionaries in close-up. *(Kevin Dallimore)*

Centre: These Imperial Roman cavalrymen will play a vital role in protecting the flanks of the legionary infantry. *(Brush Strokes)*

Right: Imperial Roman legionaries set about destroying another barbarian horde. *(®Miniature Wargames)*

A Late Imperial Roman auxiliary infantry unit. These troops were the backbone of the army. *(Brush Strokes)*

The Romans were the first army to deploy field artillery. This example is serving in a Late Imperial force. *(Brush Strokes)*

Alaric's Gothic cavalry marching onwards towards Rome. *(GJM Figurines)*

The Sassanid Persian cataphracts combined heavy armour and opulent display, which is why many wargamers cannot resist collecting them! *(Brush Strokes)*

Above left: The Scourge of God. Attila encourages his Hunnic hordes to commit further depredations. *(Kevin Dallimore)* **Right:** A group of Romano-British infantry (painted and photographed by Kevin Dallimore) rallies around their standard. *(®Miniature Wargames)*

This Anglo-Saxon shieldwall provides a formidable obstacle for any attacker. *(GJM Figurines)*

The Swords of Allah. Arab infantry prepares to charge the infidel. *(Kevin Dallimore)*

Carolingian cavalrymen assault Saxon infantry. *(®Miniature Wargames)*

These Vikings may look somewhat disordered, but they are no less deadly for all their impetuosity. *(Brush Strokes)*

These Varangian Guards formed the backbone of later Byzantine armies. *(Kevin Dallimore)*

In this re-enactment of the Battle of Bannockburn (1314) the Scottish spearmen are about to destroy the English knights. *(®Miniature Wargames)*

The English combined battle line of archers and men-at-arms frequently proved successful in the Hundred Years War – as the French mounted knights in the background are about to find out. *(®Miniature Wargames)*

Ottoman Turkish Sipahis launch an attack. *(Kevin Dallimore)*

Not all Medieval cavalry was of noble birth. Hobilars like these often served in English armies of the period. *(Brush Strokes)*

When the English armies fought each other during the Wars of the Roses, the battle invariably started with an archery duel. (®*Miniature Wargames*)

Following the exchange of arrows, Wars of the Roses armies engaged each other in a savage mêlée. (®*Miniature Wargames*)

Assaults on towns were very rare during the Ancient and Medieval periods. The Battle of St Albans (1461) was an exception. *(®Miniature Wargames)*

This bombard represents the cutting edge of Late Medieval technology, although it could easily misfire – with fatal results for its unfortunate crew! *(GJM Figurines)*

Chapter 13

Dark Age Wargames Rules

UNITS

Each unit generally consists of four bases, each of which has dimensions of 40mm × 20mm. Each base has a variable number of figures on it, depending upon the troop type, as listed below. (Note: the standard base size is ideal for 15–20mm figures. However, 25mm miniatures may require larger dimensions: 60mm × 40mm is suitable for these larger size figures.) As noted, units usually have four bases, which are aligned in two ranks of two bases. However, Elephant units have only one base.

Troop Type	Figures/models per base
Dark Age Infantry, Heavy Archers	4
Warband, Cataphracts, Heavy Cavalry	3
Light Infantry, Light Cavalry	2
Elephants	1

HOW TO WIN

Victory is achieved as soon as one side is reduced to a strength of two remaining units.

a)   *Exiting the map.* For every infantry unit (other than Light Infantry) exiting the mapboard on the enemy side, the enemy immediately withdraws *two* of his units. All three count as eliminated.

SEQUENCE OF PLAY

Each side follows the sequence listed below in each of its turns:

1) Charge sequence.
2) Movement.
3) Shooting.
4) Hand-to-hand combat.
5) Morale tests.

1) The Charge Sequence

Every time a general wishes a unit to enter into hand-to-hand combat with an enemy unit, the procedure is as follows:

1a) *Charge declaration*. Declare the charge. Measure the distance between the units. If the charging unit can reach the enemy, move it into physical contact (bases touching).

1b) *Defensive fire*. If the defender is equipped with javelins, and if the attacker launched its charge from further than 8cm away the defender may fire at its assailant.

1c) *Initiate hand-to-hand combat*. After removing any losses caused by defensive fire, the two antagonists will fight in the hand-to-hand phase.

2) Movement

2a) *Movement allowances*. In general, units move the distance listed below during each turn. They do not have to use up all their movement allowance, but may not carry over any unused movement to the next turn.

Troop Type	Movement per turn
Light Cavalry	24cm
Heavy Cavalry	20cm
Elephants, Cataphracts, Warband, Light Infantry	12cm
Dark Age Infantry, Heavy Archers	8cm

2b) *Turning*. If a Warband, Elephant, Cataphract, Dark Age Infantry, Heavy Archer or Heavy Cavalry unit wishes to deviate more than 30° from a straight line, it must use up half its movement allowance to do so.

i) Light Infantry and Light Cavalry may turn without penalty.

2c) *Difficult terrain.* Ancient battles generally involved no more than three types of terrain; specifically hills, rivers and woods. They affect movement in varying ways.

> i)   Hills have no effect on movement (they were usually gentle slopes).
> ii) All units take a complete turn to cross a river.
> iii) Cavalry, Elephants and Cataphracts may not enter woods.
> iv) Dark Age Infantry and Heavy Archers have their movement reduced to 4cm every turn they move in a wood.
> v)   Light infantry and Warbands are unaffected by woods, and may move up to their full movement allowance if desired.

2d) *Moving and firing.* Heavy troops may never move and fire. Light Infantry and Light Cavalry may do so under certain circumstances.

> i)   Light Infantry may move and fire if equipped with javelins. The firing may either precede or follow movement.
> ii) Light Cavalry may move and fire if equipped with bows (firing must either precede or follow movement). However, Light Cavalry equipped with javelins are allowed to split-move. That is to say, they may not only move and fire, but are allowed to fire at any point during their move (if the target is in range at the time of firing). They may, for example, move half their allowance, throw their javelins, turn around, and retire their remaining half-move away from the enemy they had just shot at.
> iii) No unit may ever fire if it is charging an enemy unit.

3) Shooting

3a) *Missile ranges.* When a unit wishes to shoot, it must first check to see if the enemy is in range.

Weapon	Range
Bow and crossbow (on foot)	24cm
Javelin	8cm
Bow and crossbow (on horseback), sling	16cm

3b) *Rolling to hit.* Infantry and cavalry units with bows, crossbows, slings or javelin roll one die for each base currently remaining. A successful hit may possibly inflict a casualty point on the defending unit.

i)   Bowmen, slingers and javelinmen hit on a throw of 4–6.

ii)   Crossbowmen hit on a throw of 5–6.

iii)   Units in woods only suffer half the number of hits registered.

3c) *Saving rolls*. However, the defender is permitted what is known as a saving roll for each potential casualty. This is dependent upon armour thickness. For every hit scored, the defender rolls a die. If the score achieves the required saving roll, the casualty is not inflicted.

    i)   When assessing casualties from crossbow fire, the defender suffers a –2 dice-roll modifier on its saving roll.

Type of armour	Saving roll required
Elephant, extra-heavy armour	3–6
Heavy armour	4–6
Medium armour	5–6
Light armour	6

3d) *Base removal*. For every four casualty points inflicted on a unit, remove a base (denote the current number of casualties using markers).

3e) *Elephant rules*. If 4 points are inflicted on an elephant unit, it goes berserk for 1 move before it dies. Roll a die:

1–2 Elephant moves left.
3–4 Elephant moves right.
5–6 Elephant moves directly to rear.

The elephant turns in the appropriate direction (without penalty) and moves its full allowance immediately. However, if any unit (friendly or enemy) is contacted, the elephant will cease moving and engage its victim in hand-to-hand combat.

4) Hand-to-Hand Combat

4a) *Procedure*. When units engage in hand-to-hand combat, the fight usually continues each turn until one side is eliminated (cavalry or Light Infantry may withdraw a full move after a round of combat, but only if their movement rate exceeds that of their assailants).

4b) *Order of striking*. Blows are always struck simultaneously.

4c) *Hand-to-hand combat (open terrain)*. Each base in a unit rolls a variable number of dice, depending upon the type of opponent it is engaging.

Own unit	Enemy unit			
	Elephant	Dark Age Infantry, Warband, Cataphracts, Heavy Cavalry	Heavy Archers	Light Cavalry, Light Infantry
Elephant	4	8	8	8
Dark Age Infantry	1	1	2	3
Warband	1	1	2	3
Cataphracts	1	1	2	3
Heavy Cavalry	1	1	2	3
Heavy Archers	1	1	1	2
Light Cavalry	1	1	1	1
Light Infantry	1	1	1	1

i) Warband roll one extra die per base remaining in the first round of any combat.

ii) Units uphill of their antagonists also roll one extra die per base remaining in the first round of any combat.

iii) Units defending a river bank similarly roll one extra die per base remaining, if their assailants are crossing the river at the time. Again, this only applies during the first round.

iv) Units attacking the flank or rear of an enemy always roll an additional die per base engaged.

v) Units hit in their flanks may turn to face their enemy in the second or subsequent rounds of hand-to-hand combat, but only if they are not simultaneously being engaged to their front.

vi) For every dice rolled, a 4–6 is needed to stand the chance of inflicting a casualty point loss on the enemy.

4d) *Saving roll.* As with shooting, the defending unit is entitled to a saving roll for each potential casualty. Use the same chart provided in the shooting section of these rules (see 3c above).

i) Troops engaged by Elephants are never entitled to a saving roll.

4e) *Combat in woods.* This uses a (very) different hand-to-hand combat table.

Own unit	Enemy unit	
	Warband	Non-Warband
Warband	1	2
Non-Warband	1	1

5) Morale tests

5a) *Morale effects of hand-to-hand combat.* Whenever an infantry, cavalry or chariot unit loses a base in hand-to-hand combat, it must roll a die. If it fails to achieve the appropriate score, another base is removed (if two or three bases are removed in a single turn, roll two or three dice accordingly).

Class of unit	*Morale roll*
Elite	3–6
Average	4–6
Levy	5–6

6) Shieldwall

6a) *Shieldwall formation.* Some Dark Age Infantry units (specified in the relevant army lists) may adopt this formation at the start of any move. It has the following characteristics:

    i)   Movement is reduced to 4cm.

    ii)   A unit in shieldwall formation may not enter a wood.

    iii)   A unit in shieldwall formation may not cross a river.

    iv)   The unit's saving roll is improved to 3–6 (irrespective of its original saving roll).

    v)   Although a unit may enter or leave shieldwall formation at the start of any move, it must take a morale test every time it leaves the shieldwall (never when it enters the formation). If the morale test is failed, the unit loses a base.

Chapter 14

Dark Age Wargames Armies

Obscurity notwithstanding, the Dark Ages feature a wide range of some rather exotic armies. As a result, the period is growing increasingly popular with wargamers. Lists for the most prominent armies are included in this chapter; as always, forces comprise eight units. So far as terrain is concerned, I would suggest that up to three pieces should be fielded; hills, woods and rivers may feature in mainland Europe; hills alone put in an appearance in deserts.

LATE IMPERIAL ROMAN ARMY
(300–475)

Unit type	Number per army
Cavalry (Heavy Cavalry, medium armour, Average)	2–4
Cataphracts (Cataphracts, extra-heavy armour, Average)	0–1
Horse Archers (Light Cavalry (bow), light armour, Levy)	0–1
Auxiliaries (Warband, medium armour, Elite)	2–4
Legionaries (Dark Age Infantry, medium armour, Average)	1–2
Militia (Dark Age Infantry, medium armour, Levy)	1–2
Archers (Heavy Archers, light armour, Levy)	0–2

Although the strains of constant warfare meant that the Roman army was past its best, it could still be very formidable. The combination of cavalry and auxiliaries makes for a useful offensive force, and the legionaries can (decline in status and training notwithstanding) provide effective defensive support. Note that the auxiliaries are actually better than their Classical forebears; whereas the legionaries had declined, the previously lowly auxiliaries had become a hardened elite accustomed to frequent warfare – hence their reclassification as Warband, with its augmented hand-to-hand capability.

SPECIAL RULES

1) *Shieldwall.* Legionaries may adopt shieldwall formation (militia do not receive the benefit, owing to their lack of training).
2) *Integral archers.* Auxiliaries often had a contingent of archers attached to the unit. Accordingly, one base of any auxiliary unit may fire (with bows) each turn. The auxiliaries may move and fire; firing occurs after movement.
3) *Artillery* (optional rule). Late Roman armies occasionally had bolt throwers in the roster. Up to two artillery units may be fielded; use the rules provided in the Classical wargames rules (Chapter 8).
4) *Later armies* (425–75). These frequently suffered from low morale, and also had a much greater influx of barbarian recruits. Apply the following rules:

   a) Downgrade all troops one morale class (Elites become Average; Average become Levy; Levy does not change).
   b) After the army has been selected, roll a die for each unit. It only appears on a 4–6. Any resultant shortfall may be made up of equal numbers of Gothic gentry and Gothic archers (see Gothic army list for details), so that the final army will comprise eight units.

SUGGESTED DEPLOYMENT

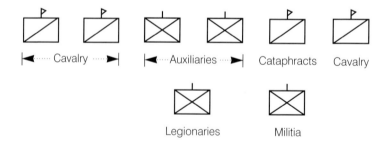

With such a range of troop types, Late Roman armies can be constructed to fit the temperament of the wargamer. This tabletop commander clearly favours an aggressive approach; the front-line units are to advance towards the enemy and engage as soon as possible. Note how the auxiliaries are supported by the legionary unit, which can plug any gaps and adopt a shieldwall formation if things go wrong. Similarly, the Cataphracts are aided by the militia: guarding the rear can give troops of inferior morale a significant role in the army.

CREATING THE ARMY IN MINIATURE

The Late Romans are catered for extremely well by most metal figure manufacturers. Infantry and Cataphracts are now available in plastic.

ALTERNATIVE ARMIES

Cavalry may serve as auxiliary cavalry in Imperial Roman armies, and vice versa. This allows for a Late Roman army to be fielded entirely from plastic figures (with Imperial Roman cavalry serving in the Late Roman army).

PRIMARY SOURCE

Ammianus Marcellinus (c. 390). *The Later Roman Empire* (tr. Walter Hamilton), Penguin, 1986

SECONDARY SOURCES

Barker, Phil. *The Armies and Enemies of Imperial Rome*, Wargames Research Group, 1981

Connolly, Peter. *Greece and Rome at War*, Greenhill, 1998

Lambshead, John and Newsom, Leslie. *Fall of the West*, Warhammer Historical Wargames, 2000

MacDowall, Simon. *Twilight of the Empire: The Roman Infantryman 3rd to 6th Century AD*. Osprey, 1994

Miranda, Joseph. 'The Fall of Rome' in *Strategy and Tactics*, no. 181 (July 1996), 4–16

VICTORY THROUGH ENDURANCE

Suddenly there leapt forward, burning for the fight, a troop of notables which included even the kings. With their men behind them they burst upon our line and forced their way as far as the Legion of Primari, which was stationed in the centre of our position. . . . Here our troops were drawn up in close formation and in several ranks. They stood as firm as towers and renewed the battle with increased spirit. Taking care to avoid being wounded and covering themselves like gladiators, they plunged their swords into the barbarians' sides, which their wild rage left exposed. The enemy, who were ready to squander their lives for victory, tried repeatedly to find weak spots in the fabric of our line. As they perished one after another and the confidence of the Romans who were striking them down increased, fresh hosts took the place of the slain, till the incessant cries of the dying stupefied them with fear. Then at last they gave way under the stress of disaster and put all their energy into attempts at flight.

Ammianus Marcellinus (c. 390), *The Later Roman Empire* (tr. Walter Hamilton), Penguin, 1986, p. 113.

This account of the Battle of Strasbourg (357) shows how a shieldwall formation could defeat an impetuous barbarian Warband assault.

INTRIGUE AND DISASTER

Two of the most effective generals of the late Empire were Stilicho and Aetius. The emperors Honorius and Valentinian III ordered the assassination of each (in 408 and 454 respectively), fearing their political ambitions. Such myopic action served only to hasten the Western Empire's demise.

SASSANID PERSIAN ARMY
(350–640)

Unit type	Number per army
Nobles (Cataphracts, extra-heavy armour, Elite)	2–4
Allied Cavalry (Light Cavalry (bow), light armour, Average)	1–3
Levies (Dark Age Infantry, medium armour, Levy)	2–4
Archers (Light Infantry (bow), light armour, Average)	0–4
Elephants	0–2

Ancient wargamers have always been drawn to the Sassanids, and with good reason. No other army provides the exotic combination of Cataphracts and elephants, offering as it does the potential literally to steamroller its way through any opposition. If one can get past the allure of glamorous troop types and ornate apparel (at least in the case of the nobles), the history of Sassanid Persia has its own fascination too – the Empire saw itself as the heir to the Achaemenids, and modelled many of its institutions on the template provided by the latter.

SPECIAL RULES

1) *Nobles*. These augmented the power of their lances with short bows, which they fired at close range prior to entering hand-to-hand combat. To take account of this, nobles always hit on dice rolls of 3–6 in the first round of any hand-to-hand combat.

2) *Levies*. The Sassanid levy infantry was notorious for its lack of training. Accordingly, levies only fight as Heavy Archers (despite their classification as Dark Age Infantry).

SUGGESTED DEPLOYMENT

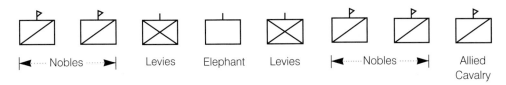

| ◄····· Nobles ·····► | Levies | Elephant | Levies | ◄······ Nobles ······► | Allied Cavalry |

This gamer could not resist the allure of the Cataphracts, and has fielded the maximum number of nobles permitted. Although the allied cavalry can provide some useful supporting fire, this army must march through the opposition lines if it is to succeed. Note how the levies are positioned on either side of the elephant; this is to insure that if the latter goes berserk, it will crush a Levy unit rather than a noble one.

CREATING THE ARMY IN MINIATURE

Many metal figure manufacturers provide a range of Sassanids in their repertoire. Plastic figure gamers will have to improvise. Provided that they are not too fussy about exact historical accuracy, Parthian cavalry can double as Sassanid nobles, Achaemenid infantry as levies and archers, and Carthaginian elephants as their Sassanid equivalents (taking the precaution of using Achaemenid infantry as crew).

ALTERNATIVE ARMIES

As has just been stated, Sassanid figures can serve in Parthian and Achaemenid armies if desired.

PRIMARY SOURCES

Ammianus Marcellinus (c. 390). *The Later Roman Empire* (tr. Walter Hamilton), Penguin, 1986

Procopius (550). *The Secret History* (tr. G.A. Williamson), Penguin, 1966

SECONDARY SOURCES

Barker, Phil. *The Armies and Enemies of Imperial Rome*, Wargames Research Group, 1981

Halewood, Phil. 'Heirs of the Achaemenids' in *Slingshot* nos. 184–9 (March 1996–January 1997); nos. 191–193 (May–September 1997); no. 196 (March 1996)

Nicolle, David. *Sassanid Armies*, Montvert, 1996

CLASS WARFARE

Their military training and discipline, and their constant practice of manoeuvres and arms drill, which I have often described, make them formidable even to large armies. They rely especially on their cavalry, in which all their nobility and men of mark serve. Their infantry are armed like gladiators, and obey orders like soldiers' servants. These people follow behind their masters in a mass condemned as it were to perpetual servitude and never remunerated either by pay or presents.

Ammianus Marcellinus (c. 390), *The Later Roman Empire* (tr. Walter Hamilton), Penguin, 1986, p. 265.

Formidable as the Sassanid army was, its total neglect of infantry could leave it distinctly vulnerable on occasion.

STANDING FAST

Sassanid levies were all too inclined to run away when the going got tough. Some generals got around this unfortunate propensity, by taking the precaution of chaining their levies to the ground before the battle commenced.

GOTHIC ARMY
(350–600)

Unit type	Number per army
Nobles (Heavy Cavalry, medium armour, Elite)	1–2
Gentry (Heavy Cavalry, light armour, Elite)	2–4
Warriors (Warband, light armour, Average)	2–4
Archers (Light Infantry (bow), light armour, Average)	1–2

Rome's conquerors usually relied upon an aggressive approach in order to succeed. The combination of formidable shock cavalry and impetuous barbarian foot, can cause an opponent many difficulties. For those of a more passive bent, a Wagon Fort can be used to good effect (as it was at the Battle of Adrianople in 378).

SPECIAL RULE

1) *Wagon Fort*. Up to four infantry units may deploy behind this barrier (represented by a circle of suitable models). This has the following effects:

a) The units enjoy a saving roll of 3–6.
b) Warriors no longer receive the Warband bonus in the first round of hand-to-hand combat (they are assumed to be standing behind the wagon, not charging the enemy).
c) If units choose to leave the Wagon Fort, they may not return.

SUGGESTED DEPLOYMENT

| Gentry | Nobles | Archers | ◀······Warriors······▶ | Archers | Nobles | Gentry |

This general has shunned the Wagon Fort as being unmanly. However, our would-be Alaric has still adopted a touch of subtlety to his aggression. Note how the archers are carefully positioned to provide supporting fire to the left or right, as necessary. Also, the nobles have their outward flanks protected by the gentry, in order to maximise the effectiveness of the Goths' most potent cavalry.

CREATING THE ARMY IN MINIATURE
Several metal figure companies produce ranges of Goths in all the main scales. Suitable plastic miniatures are also available.

ALTERNATIVE ARMIES
Gothic infantry may (if equipped with oblong shields) serve in Gallic or British armies. Gothic Gentry may fill the ranks of Gallic or German forces from the Classical period.

PRIMARY SOURCES
Ammianus Marcellinus (c. 390). *The Later Roman Empire* (tr. Walter Hamilton), Penguin, 1986

SECONDARY SOURCES
Barker, Phil. *The Armies and Enemies of Imperial Rome*, Wargames Research Group, 1981
Fredholm von Essen, Michael. 'The Gothic Art of War', in *Slingshot* no. 219 (January 2002), 33–42
Fredholm von Essen, Michael. 'The Gothic Art of War', in *Slingshot* no. 220 (March 2002), 47–50
Lambshead, John and Newsom, Leslie. *Fall of the West*, Warhammer Historical Wargames, 2000
Wilcox, Peter. *Rome's Enemies 1: Germanics and Dacians*, Osprey, 1982

A SAVAGE FIGHT

The barbarians, after taking their customary oath to stand by one another, attempted to reach some hilly ground from which they could rush down as if on wheels and carry all before them by the impetus of their attack. . . . The barbarians with their usual nimbleness and alacrity hurled at our men huge clubs hardened in the fire, plunged their daggers in the breasts of those who put up a stout resistance, and broke through our left wing. This gave way, but a strong body of reserves made a fierce counter-attack. . . . Stubborn though the conflict was, neither side gave way to exhaustion and neither gained the upper hand.

Ammianus Marcellinus (*c.* 390), *The Later Roman Empire* (tr. Walter Hamilton), Penguin, 1986.

This account of the Battle of Salices (377) shows how the Goths tried to use terrain to their advantage. It reinforces the point that although they may have been uncultivated, they were emphatically not stupid.

PICTISH ARMY
(380–1100)

Unit type	Number per army
Warriors (Dark Age Infantry, light armour, Average)	3–5
Archers (Light Infantry (bow), light armour, Average)	2–4
Crossbowmen (Light Infantry (crossbow), light armour, Average)	0–1
Cavalry (Light Cavalry (javelin), light armour, Average)	1–2

Pictish armies appear to have possessed the stoical temperament for which their medieval Scottish descendants were famed. Accordingly, they deployed large numbers of spearmen relying upon the shieldwall tactic. However, they also took pains to support these with a substantial contingent of archers. The latter included crossbowmen: it may seem astonishing that the most sophisticated missile weapon of the Dark Ages should appear in the ranks of one of the most penurious nations, yet there is incontrovertible archaeological evidence of its presence. It is likely that the Picts captured some Roman examples, and manufactured their own copies.

SPECIAL RULES

1) *Shieldwall.* Warriors may adopt shieldwall formation.
2) *Terrain.* The Pictish player may add two additional woods anywhere on the battlefield.

3) *Nobles*. Units may be upgraded or modified as follows:

    a)   *Early armies* (380–800). One of the warrior units may be upgraded to Elite status.

    b)   *Later armies* (800–1100). One of the cavalry units may be modified as follows:

Nobles (Heavy Cavalry, medium armour, Elite)

SUGGESTED DEPLOYMENT (EARLY PICTISH ARMY)

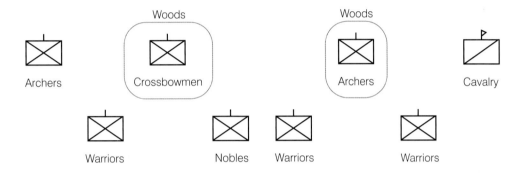

The missile units are deployed to the fore, in order to weaken any enemy assault (given the likely Pictish superiority in long-range weaponry, it would be suicidal for most foes to adopt a defensive posture). The nobles and warriors should remain in shieldwall, ready to confront the enemy. Note how the woods are used to channel any hostile assault, and simultaneously protect the flanks of the noble and warrior units making up the centre of the Pict battleline.

CREATING THE ARMY IN MINIATURE

Pictish figures are fairly widely available in all metal scales. Plastic infantry can also be purchased, but suitable cavalry provision is a problem. The best option is to buy some Classical Celtic horsemen, although it should be stressed that these are only really suitable for later nobles (commoner cavalry lacked the armour worn by Celtic cavalry).

ALTERNATIVE ARMIES

Given their distinctive shields, Pictish infantry cannot really be used in other armies. Cavalry can be used as light horsemen in British forces from the Classical period.

PRIMARY SOURCES

Bede (731). *Ecclesiastical History of the English People* (tr. Leo Sherley-Price), Penguin, 1990

Gildas (*c.* 540). *The Ruin of Britain* (tr. Michael Winterbottom), Phillimore, 1978

SECONDARY SOURCES

Aitchison, Nick. *The Picts and the Scots at War*, Sutton, 2003

Barker, Phil. *The Armies and Enemies of Imperial Rome*, Wargames Research Group, 1981

Ellis, Peter Berresford. *Celt and Saxon*, Constable, 1993

Morris, John. *The Age of Arthur*, Phoenix, 1973

SAVAGE RAIDERS

As the Romans went back home, there eagerly emerged from the coracles that had carried them across the sea-valleys the foul hordes of Scots and Picts, like dark throngs of worms who wriggle out of narrow fissures in the rock when the sun is high and the weather grows warm. They were to some extent different in their customs, but they were in perfect accord in their greed for bloodshed: and they were readier to cover their villainous faces with hair than their private parts and neighbouring regions with clothes. . . . So they seized the whole of the extreme north of the island from its inhabitants, right up to the wall.

Gildas (*c.* 540), *The Ruin of Britain* (tr. Michael Winterbottom), Phillimore, 1978.

Gildas describes the poverty and the savagery of the Picts. They were certainly well able to seize the opportunity provided by the Roman departure from Britain, to grab substantial areas of territory. For the Scots, see the Appendix to this list.

THE PAINTED PEOPLE

The word 'Picti' means 'painted'. The Picts tended to paint or tattoo themselves with blue-green dye from the woad plant. This penchant can be explained by the fact that the leaves of the woad plant are shaped like arrowheads; therefore, the dye was believed to protect its wearer from enemy archery.

APPENDIX: SCOT RAIDER ARMY (380–600)

The Scots originally come from Ireland, but eventually gave their name to Scotland after they succeeded in settling in Pictish territory (to eventually form a unified kingdom with the Picts in 846). Although I take the view that the Scots soon adopted Pictish military organisation, other wargames writers believe that they followed a more disorderly (but nonetheless effective) approach. For those who wish to experiment, however, I have included an army list for a Scot raider force below:

Unit type	Number per army
Nobles (Warband, light armour, Elite)	1–3
Rabble (Warband, light armour, Levy)	3–5
Skirmishers (Light Infantry (javelin), light armour, Levy)	1–2

ANGLO-SAXON ARMY
(380–1100)

Unit type	Number per army
Nobles (Dark Age Infantry, medium armour, Elite)	1–3
Peasants (Dark Age Infantry, light armour, Average)	4–6
Archers (Light Infantry (bow), light armour, Levy)	0–1

An army consisting almost entirely of infantry in shieldwall formation is not the most exciting, but can be very effective (for those who are of a more dashing temperament, the Early Saxon army covered in the special rules below, is likely to have more appeal). Saxon commanders relied upon their great resilience of their men, to grind any foe into submission. The wargamer would be advised to follow their example.

SPECIAL RULES

1) *Shieldwall*. Nobles and Peasants may adopt shieldwall formation.
2) *Integral archers* (optional rule). Saxons seem to have added some bowmen to their infantry units, in order to assail the enemy with close-range archery. To reflect this, noble and peasant units may roll one additional die in the first round of any hand-to-hand combat.
3) *Cavalry* (optional rule). For those gamers who believe the Saxons used cavalry, one unit of nobles may be reclassified as follows:

   Cavalry (Heavy Cavalry, light armour, Elite)

4) *Early armies* (380–600). Armies from this period relied upon rapid assaults. To reflect this, nobles and peasants are reclassified as Warband, and they may not adopt shieldwall formation. Similarly, neither integral archers nor cavalry may be deployed.

SUGGESTED DEPLOYMENT

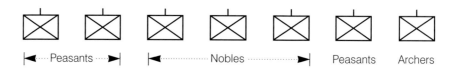

◄····Peasants····► ◄················Nobles················► Peasants Archers

Peasants

This force should form shieldwall when within charging range of the enemy, and try to march through the opposition, rather in the manner of the Classical Greek phalanx. Note, however, that the right flank is protected by the archers, and the left by refusing a peasant unit. This means that any enemy flanking manoeuvres will take time, thereby maximising the chances of a Saxon victory in the meantime.

CREATING THE ARMY IN MINIATURE

The Saxons have always been a very popular wargames army, and figures are readily available in all scales – both in metal and plastic.

ALTERNATIVE ARMIES

Bizarre as it may seem, Saxons and Vikings often wore similar attire, so that the former may become the latter if desired.

PRIMARY SOURCES

Asser (880–900). *Alfred the Great: Asser's Life of King Alfred and Other Contemporary Sources* (tr. Simon Keynes and Michael Lapidge), Penguin, 1983

Bede (731). *Ecclesiastical History of the English People* (tr. Leo-Sherley-Price), Penguin, 1990

SECONDARY SOURCES

Bath, Tony. 'The Saxon Conquest of England' in *Slingshot* no. 246 (May 2006), 20–31

Ellis, Peter Berresford. *Celt and Saxon*, Constable, 1993

Heath, Ian. *Armies of the Dark Ages*, Wargames Research Group, 1980

Wise, Terence. *Saxon, Viking and Norman*, Osprey, 1979

ENDURANCE AND ENDEAVOUR

When the next morning dawned he [Alfred] moved his forces and came to a place called Edington, and fighting fiercely with a compact shield-wall against the entire Viking army, he persevered resolutely for a long time; at length he gained the victory through God's will. He destroyed the Vikings with great slaughter, and pursued those who fled as far as the [Viking] stronghold, hacking them down.

Asser (893), 'Life of King Alfred' in *Alfred the Great: Asser's Life of King Alfred and Other Contemporary Sources* (tr. Simon Keynes and Michael Lapidge), Penguin, 1983, p. 84.

The Battle of Edington (878) saw one of Alfred the Great's most significant victories over the Vikings. This brief account shows how the Saxons were able to grind their foes into submission.

DID THEY OR DIDN'T THEY?

The debate over whether or not Saxons used cavalry has been one of military history's more animated discussions. Some medieval chroniclers maintain that English armies did not deploy cavalry at all; others that they were most ineffective when they tried it. However, Snorri Sturluson's *King Harald's Saga* (c. 1235) not only gives an account of Saxon cavalry in action, but also records them using authentic contemporary tactics (from 1066) of overarm spear thrusts. I have therefore allowed for some cavalry to be used as an optional rule, but have downgraded its effectiveness (by reducing its armour classification) in relation to its European contemporaries.

HUNNIC ARMY
(400–460)

Unit type	Number per army
Hun Nobles (Heavy Cavalry (bow), medium armour, Elite)	0–1
Huns (Light Cavalry (bow), light armour, Average)	3–7
Allied Cavalry (Heavy Cavalry, light armour, Average)	0–2
Allied Infantry (Dark Age Infantry, light armour, Levy)	0–2

When fighting without assistance, the Huns acted rather like a more effective Scythian army. However, Attila forcibly recruited some barbarian subjects, which make up the allied elements here. They have been downgraded to reflect their lack of enthusiasm for the Hunnic cause: both cavalry and infantry have lower morale than usual, and the foot have been reclassified from Warband to Dark Age Infantry in addition.

GENERAL RULES

1) *Hun nobles.* These enjoy the same benefits as their Scythian counterparts, specifically:

    a)   Nobles may turn without any movement penalties.

    b)   Nobles may fire their bows after they move (they may not fire before movement).

2) *Hun light cavalry.* These had light spears in addition to bows. Since this added to their potency in mêlée, Hun Light Cavalry may re-roll any hand-to-hand combat dice that miss their target. However, this benefit only applies in the first round of any combat.

3) *Allies.* If an allied contingent is deployed, equal numbers of allied cavalry and allied infantry units must be fielded.

SUGGESTED DEPLOYMENT

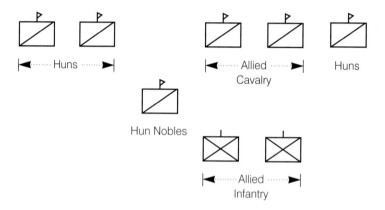

This commander has chosen to field a full complement of allies. Given the ineptitude of the infantry, they are placed in reserve, with the allied cavalry to the fore. The Huns can provide effective missile support; whereas the Hun nobles are positioned to either add their bowfire to any attack, or engage the enemy in hand-to-hand combat, as the opportunity arises.

CREATING THE ARMY IN MINIATURE

Many metal figure companies have Huns in their selection. Gothic ranges provide suitable allies. Unfortunately, plastic Hunnic figures are not yet available.

ALTERNATIVE ARMIES

The allies may serve in Gothic armies. Hun Light Cavalry were often recruited by Byzantine forces as barbarian allies, up to and including the seventh century.

PRIMARY SOURCES

Ammianus Marcellinus (c. 390). *The Later Roman Empire* (tr. Walter Hamilton), Penguin, 1986

SECONDARY SOURCES

Barker, Phil. *The Armies and Enemies of Imperial Rome*, Wargames Research Group, 1981

Hildinger, Erik. *Warriors of the Steppe*, Spellmount, 1997

Karasulas, Antony. *Mounted Archers of the Steppe 600 BC–AD 1300*, Osprey, 2004

Lambshead, John and Newsom, Leslie. *Fall of the West*, Warhammer Historical Wargames, 2000

A BRUTISH PEOPLE

The people of the Huns . . . are quite abnormally savage. From the moment of birth they make deep gashes in their children's cheeks, so that when in due course hair appears its growth is checked by the wrinkled scars; as they grow older this gives them the unlovely appearance of beardless eunuchs. They have squat bodies, strong limbs, and thick necks, and are so prodigiously ugly and bent that they might be two-legged animals. . . . Their way of life is so rough that they have no use for fire or seasoned food, but live on the roots of wild plants and the half-raw flesh of any sort of animal, which they warm a little by placing it between their thighs and the backs of their horses. They have no buildings to shelter them, but avoid anything of the kind.

Ammianus Marcellinus (c. 390), *The Later Roman Empire* (tr. Walter Hamilton), Penguin, 1986.

As was the case with the Scythians, the Huns were incapable of anything other than destruction. Following Attila's death, the Hunnic Empire disintegrated: the Huns may have been able to conquer, but had no idea how to build anything worthwhile.

ROMANO-BRITISH ARMY
(410–945)

Unit type	Number per army
Cavalry (Heavy Cavalry, medium armour, Elite)	2–4
Roman Remnants (Dark Age Infantry, medium armour, Average)	0–2
Militia (Dark Age Infantry, light armour, Levy)	2–4
Archers (Light Infantry (bow), light armour, Average)	0–2

This list covers the armies that fought to defend Roman Britain from the Saxons and Pict invaders (although it has to be said that very little of the Roman inheritance remained after the mid-sixth century, when the remaining kingdoms had reverted to a Celtic heritage). Despite the general weakness of the infantry (with the partial exception of those units which retained vestiges of their Roman training and identity), the power of the cavalry provides an intriguing contrast with the Saxon and Pictish armies. This army has the added appeal of being King Arthur's, which should be enough to inspire any wargamer with an ounce of passion.

SPECIAL RULES

1) *Roman Remnants.*

    a)   These may adopt the shieldwall tactic.
    b)   They may not be fielded after 600.

2) *Knights* (optional rule). King Arthur is believed to have led an Elite Heavy Cavalry unit. To reflect this, implement the following rules:

    a)   Reclassify one of the cavalry units as follows:

Knights (Heavy Cavalry, heavy armour, Elite).

    b)   The knights may roll one additional die per base remaining, in the first round of any hand-to-hand combat.

3) *Welsh Armies* (600–1100). Although the Welsh retained their Romano-British affiliation, the mountainous environment of their homeland resulted in a change of army composition from the seventh century onwards. Accordingly, Welsh armies use the following list:

Unit type	Number per army
Cavalry (Heavy Cavalry, medium armour, Elite)	0–2
Spearmen (Dark Age Infantry, light armour, Average)	2–4
Archers (Light Infantry (bow), light armour, Average)	2–4

a) Welsh spearmen may use the shieldwall tactic.

SUGGESTED DEPLOYMENT

Cavalry · · · Militia · · · Roman Remnants · · · Militia · · · Archers · · · Knights · · · Cavalry

This army is deployed in order to maximise the width of the force, thereby allowing the cavalry to launch outflanking moves. Note how the archers can support the assault of the knights with bowfire, thereby improving the horsemen's chances of success even more. Although the infantry is extremely weak, the Roman Remnants should provide some endurance, which is why they are positioned in the centre of the close-order foot units.

CREATING AN ARMY IN MINIATURE

Romano-British miniatures abound in all scales of metal figures. Those who use plastic armies will have to improvise: Late Romans can form Roman Remnants; Saxons become militia; and Gothic or Roman cavalry become their Romano-British equivalents. To add a touch of glamour, late Roman Cataphracts can become Arthur's knights.

ALTERNATIVE ARMIES

The wargamer who uses plastic figures can deploy his forces in their host armies. So far as metal figures are concerned, Romano-British units can often serve in the Late Roman roster.

PRIMARY SOURCES

Bede (731). *Ecclesiastical History of the English People* (tr. Leo Sherley-Price), Penguin, 1990
Gildas (*c.* 540). *The Ruin of Britain* (tr. Michael Winterbottom), Phillimore, 1978
Nennius (*c.* 800). *History of the British* (tr. John Morris), Phillimore, 1980

SECONDARY SOURCES

Ellis, Peter Berresford. *Celt and Saxon*, Constable, 1993
Heath, Ian. *Armies of the Dark Ages*, Wargames Research Group, 1980
Mersey, Daniel. *Glutter of Ravens*, Outpost Wargame Services, 1998

THE GREAT REVIVAL

When the victorious invaders had scattered and destroyed the native peoples and returned to their own dwellings, the Britons slowly began to take heart and recover their strength. . . . Their leader at this time was Ambrosius Aurelianus, a man of good character and the sole survivor of Roman race from the catastrophe. . . . Under his leadership the Britons took up arms, challenged their conquerors to battle, and with God's help, inflicted a defeat on them. Thenceforward victory swung first to one side and then to the other, until the battle of Badon Hill, when the Britons made a considerable slaughter of the invaders.

Bede (731), *Ecclesiastical History of the English People* (tr. Leo Sherley-Price), Penguin, 1990

The British revival of the late fifth century put a halt to Saxon expansion for two generations. It has been speculated that Ambrosius Aurelianus and Arthur were the same person: it may, however, be true that the latter was a warlord in the army of the former.

HISTORICAL FICTION

Readers may well encounter Geoffrey of Monmouth's *History of the Kings of Britain* (Penguin) in bookshops. This twelfth-century work is a very enjoyable piece of literature; but everyone should bear in mind that Geoffrey made up most of his history, to suit his political prejudices. Nobody should use it as a historical source.

BYZANTINE ARMY
(475–1100)

Unit type	Number per army
Kataphraktoi (Heavy Cavalry (bow), Heavy armour, Elite)	2–6
Skutatoi (Dark Age Infantry, heavy armour, Average)	1–3
Psiloi (Light Infantry (bow), light armour, Average)	1–2
Barbarians (Light Cavalry (bow), light armour, Average)	0–2

By the end of the fifth century, the East Roman Empire had revived (although I shall follow prevailing historical prejudices and refer to it as the Byzantine Empire, in order to save confusion). The new army was the most graphic example of the Byzantine renaissance; although based upon Heavy Cavalry rather than legionary infantrymen, it was nonetheless a most formidable instrument of war. It may have frequently been outnumbered by its opponents, but was seldom outclassed by them.

To add to the period flavour, I have used contemporary terms to describe the various units. This may lead to a degree of confusion, since the ordinary heavy cavalry were referred to as kataphraktoi – these are not Cataphracts (for the latter, see special rule no. 5 below). The barbarian cavalry varied in origin: Huns served up to the seventh century, whereas Pechenegs and Bulgars were recruited later.

SPECIAL RULES

1) *Massed missiles*. Kataphraktoi and skutatoi units were equipped with heavy darts, which they threw just before combat. To reflect their effect, kataphraktoi and skutatoi may re-roll any dice that miss, during the first round of any hand-to-hand combat.
2) *Shieldwall*. Skutatoi may adopt shieldwall formation.
3) *Kataphraktoi archery*. To reflect their high standards of training, kataphraktoi units may fire their bows after they move.
4) *Early armies* (475–600). Kataphraktoi and skutatoi units were not so well protected in earlier forces. Downgrade their equipment from heavy to medium armour.
5) *Later armies* (960–1100). These include the following units:

Unit type	Number per army
Klibanophoroi (Cataphracts, extra-heavy armour, Elite)	1–2
Varangian Guard (Dark Age Infantry, heavy armour, Elite)	0–1

a) *Klibanophoroi*. These may use massed missiles (see special rule no. 1).

b) *Varangian Guard*. Apply the following rules:

    i) *Shieldwall*. Varangian Guard may form shieldwall.
    ii) *Mounted infantry*. These troops rode horses on the battlefield, until they dismounted to fight. They may move up to 12cm per turn until they either charge, are charged by the enemy, or form shieldwall.
    iii) *Savagery*. The Varagians were Viking mercenaries, and seem to have retained their bloodlust. Accordingly, Varangian Guard may roll one extra die per base involved in the first round of any hand-to-hand combat.

SUGGESTED DEPLOYMENT

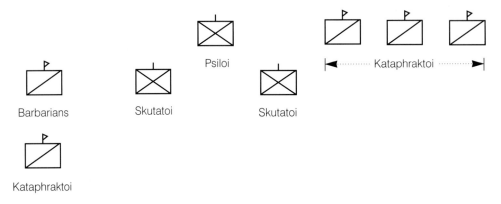

This army relies upon the performance of the massed kataphraktoi on the right flank. They are supported by the psiloi's archery. Should things go well, the skutatoi can move into the assault, supported by the barbarians and the remaining kataphraktoi unit. If events do not prove so favourable, the psiloi can retreat between the skutatoi, and the barbarians and kataphraktoi on the left, can hold that flank.

CREATING THE ARMY IN MINIATURE
Byzantine figures are available in all metal miniature scales. The same cannot unfortunately be said of plastic figures.

ALTERNATIVE ARMIES
Barbarians may serve as Huns or Danube barbarians (see following army list) as appropriate. Varangian Guards may double as Saxon nobles or Viking huscarls.

PRIMARY SOURCES
Procopius (550). *The Secret History* (tr. G.A. Williamson), Penguin, 1966
Psellus, Michael (1060–80). *Fourteen Byzantine Rulers* (tr. E.R.A. Sewter), Penguin, 1966

SECONDARY SOURCES
Baekkelund, Heine. *Byzantium – Beyond the Golden Gate*, Warhammer Historical Wargames, 2005
Heath, Ian. *Armies of the Dark Ages*, Wargames Research Group, 1980
Nicolle, David. *Romano-Byzantine Armies 4th–9th Centuries*, Osprey, 1992
Norwich, John Julius. *A Short History of Byzantium*, Penguin, 1997

THE RESOLUTE APPROACH

When all was ready, strict orders were given that no soldier should advance in front of the line or break rank under any circumstances. . . . The decisive factor in the achievement of victory was, in his [Basil II's] opinion, the massing of troops in one coherent body, and for this reason alone he believed the Roman armies to be invincible.

Psellus, Michael (1060–80), *Fourteen Byzantine Rulers* (tr. E.R.A. Sewter), Penguin, 1966, p. 47.

Basil II was a notably austere character, who became renowned for creating and commanding disciplined armies. His success against the Bulgars destroyed the threat from that people, and led to his becoming known as the 'Bulgar Basher'.

THE GREEK ROMANS

It is one of history's ironies that the Byzantines, who saw themselves as the heirs to the Roman Empire, spoke Greek rather than Latin.

DANUBE BARBARIAN ARMY (550–1018)

Unit type	Number per army
Nobles (Heavy Cavalry (bow), medium armour, Elite)	1–3
Horse Archers (Light Cavalry (bow), light armour, Average)	3–5
Slavs (Warband, light armour, Average)	2–4

This list covers the armies of the Avars, Magyars and Bulgars, all of whom fought in a similar style. The wargames general can choose the roster that best fits his or her style: any of these three troop types can play a decisive role under the appropriate circumstances – although it will take great willpower to resist the temptation of fielding three units of nobles.

SPECIAL RULE

1)   *Nobles*. These, like those of the Huns and Scythians, were distinctly mobile. They may turn without penalty, and may fire their bows after movement.

SUGGESTED DEPLOYMENT

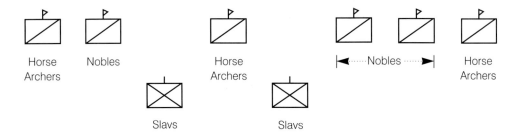

Horse Archers Nobles   Horse Archers   ◀·······Nobles·······▶   Horse Archers

Slavs   Slavs

This wargamer could not resist temptation, predictably deploying three units of nobles. Note how the horse archers are positioned to protect the nobles' flanks, and that the Slavs are ready to unleash a fearsome Warband assault as required.

CREATING THE ARMY IN MINIATURE

This is not one of the most popular wargames armies, and although (as always) metal figures are available in all scales, relatively few manufacturers provide specific ranges. There are no suitable figures in plastic. However, an army can be improvised from other forces: nobles and horse archers can be represented by Huns, and Slavs by Gothic or Saxon infantry. Readers should also be aware that Avars, Magyars and Bulgars wore similar attire and were of somewhat Hunnic appearance (since all these peoples originally came from the Russian and Central Asian steppes, this is hardly surprising); as a consequence, all three armies are interchangeable.

ALTERNATIVE ARMIES

As already stated, cavalry may serve as Huns, and infantry can potentially represent Saxons and Goths.

SECONDARY SOURCES

Heath, Ian. *Armies of the Dark Ages*, Wargames Research Group, 1980
Hildinger, Erik. *Warriors of the Steppe*, Spellmount, 1997
Karasulas, Antony. *Mounted Archers of the Steppe 600 BC–AD 1300*, Osprey, 2004

MOBILE WARFARE

They [the Avars] prefer battles fought at long range, ambushes, encircling their adversaries, simulated retreats and sudden returns, and wedge-shaped formations, that is, scattered groups. When they make their enemies take to flight . . . they do not let up at all until they have achieved the complete destruction of their enemies, and they employ every means to this end.

(Byzantine) Emperor Maurice (*c.* 570), *Strategikon*, quoted in Hildinger, Erik, *Warriors of the Steppe*, Spellmount, 1997, pp. 77–8.

Tiring the enemy out by a combination of long-range archery, feigned retreats and surprise counter-attacks was a standard tactic of the Avars and other Danubian barbarians. It was often very effective.

ARAB ARMY
(620–970)

Unit type	Number per army
Arabs (Heavy Cavalry, medium armour, Elite)	3–5
Bedouins (Light Cavalry (javelin), light armour, Average)	1–2
Spearmen (Warband, light armour, Average)	1–4
Archers (Light Infantry (bow), light armour, Average)	1–2

The Arab cavalry inevitably form the core of this army, with their mobility allowing them to pick and choose where they hit the enemy (see special rule no. 1 for details of their added potency when manoeuvring). The infantry and Bedouins should not be neglected, however: a Warband assault supported by missilry can be very effective.

Note, however, the special rule relating to Late Arab armies, in which spearmen are reclassified as Dark Age Infantry. This change reflects the situation whereby the religious zeal of the initial conquest period had receded somewhat: later armies must inevitably rely upon Arab horse to a much greater extent than those of the Prophet Muhammad and the early Caliphate.

SPECIAL RULES

1) *Arabs*. These Heavy Cavalry enjoy the following benefits:

   a) They may turn without any movement penalties.
   b) They may withdraw from combat (during the second or any subsequent rounds) with enemy Heavy Cavalry.

2) *Later armies* (800–900). Apply the following changes to the main list:

   a) Spearmen are reclassified as Dark Age Infantry.
   b) Half the bases of spearmen units are equipped with bows.
   c) It is no longer compulsory to field any archer units: 0–2 can be deployed.

SUGGESTED DEPLOYMENT

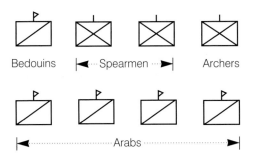

Bedouins |◄····Spearmen ····►| Archers

|◄·······················Arabs·······················►|

This general is evidently well-read, and has followed the historic Arab tactic of placing the secondary troops in the front line. This will serve to weaken any enemy assault, allowing the Arab cavalry to assail the foe at a point of their choosing.

CREATING THE ARMY IN MINIATURE

Many metal figure manufacturers supply figures for this army. Those who use plastic miniatures will have to improvise with troops from other periods, however. The Saracen Warriors produced by Italeri provide suitable infantry and cavalry, for example, and an army can be constructed using these figures.

ALTERNATIVE ARMIES

Since Arabs wore similar attire and were frequently equipped with the same weapons down the centuries, an army for this period can also be used in a Saracen force (and other Middle Eastern armies up until as late as the nineteenth century).

PRIMARY SOURCES

The Koran (644–56) (tr. N.J. Dawood), Penguin, 1999

SECONDARY SOURCES

Bloom, Jim. 'Sword of Allah' in *Command* no. 20 (January 1993), 44–62
Fletcher, Richard. *The Cross and the Crescent*, Penguin, 2003
Heath, Ian. *Armies of the Dark Ages*, Wargames Research Group, 1980
Neate, Stephen. 'The Arab Conquests up to 711: Their Speed, Scale and Success' in *Slingshot* no. 225 (January 2003), 26–28
Nicolle, David, *The Armies of Islam 7th–11th Centuries*, Osprey, 1982

THE PERILS OF RETREAT

Believers, when you encounter the infidels on the march, do not turn your backs to them in flight. If anyone on that day turns his back to them, except for tactical reasons, or to join another band, he shall incur the wrath of God and Hell shall be his home: an evil fate.

The Koran (644–56) (tr. N.J. Dawood), Penguin, 1999, p. 127.

The belief that God would take an exceptionally dim view of those Muslims who ran away from the battlefield, goes a long way to explain the fanatical determination of many Arab armies during the Islamic Conquests.

HOBSON'S CHOICE

Those who believe that medieval Islam represented a beacon of enlightenment that matches any contemporary western democracy, should be aware of the ultimatum issued to any potential opponents. They had three options: to accept Islam; to continue practising their religion under Islamic rule, but only enjoying inferior status and having to pay additional taxes for the privilege; or to fight war to the death. This may have been an effective policy; it was not, however, a particularly enlightened one.

FRANKISH ARMIES
(700–1100)

Unit type	Number per army
Nobles (Heavy Cavalry, heavy armour, Elite)	3–6
Retainers (Light Cavalry (javelin), light armour, Average)	1–3
Spearmen (Dark Age Infantry, light armour, Average)	1–4
Archers (Light Infantry (bow), light armour, Levy)	0–2

This list covers the Carolingian, Ottonian and Norman armies, all of whom fought in a similar way. These early feudal armies reflected societal values, with the nobles being at the cutting edge of the army, and the infantry only having limited potential. Fortunately for the Franks, a massed charge of Heavy Cavalry may not be the most subtle of tactics, but can nevertheless be a remarkably effective one.

SPECIAL RULES

1) *Spearmen.* Up to half the units of spearmen may be equipped with medium armour. Always round any fractions down (for example, if three units are deployed, only one may have medium armour).
2) *Norman nobles.* These were noted for the ferocity of their charge. Accordingly, they may roll an additional die for every base engaged in the first round of any hand-to-hand combat.

3) *Crossbowmen*. From 1000 onwards, one unit of archers may be equipped with crossbows instead, if the wargamer desires.

4) *Retainers* (optional rule). There has been some debate concerning the role of retainers. Although I have classified them as Light Cavalry, other writers have argued that they used shock action. If the wargamer takes the latter view, retainers can be reclassified as Heavy Cavalry.

SUGGESTED DEPLOYMENT

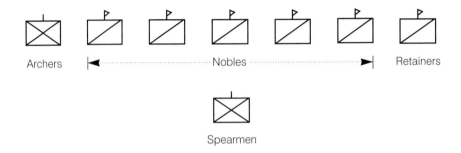

Archers |◀┄┄┄┄┄┄┄┄┄┄┄┄┄ Nobles ┄┄┄┄┄┄┄┄┄┄┄┄┄▶| Retainers

Spearmen

This army has a simple approach to warfare. The nobles will charge the enemy as soon as possible, with the retainers and archers giving whatever support they can. A Norman commander would have an even greater chance of success, given the power of their nobles, and the extra option of the crossbowmen (these missilemen could be redeployed to the centre, where their fire can assail enemy shieldwalls with great effect, given the crossbow's enhanced armour penetration ability).

CREATING THE ARMY IN MINIATURE
Carolingian, Ottonians and Normans are all available from metal figure manufacturers. Buyers should however be aware that Normans are much more widespread than the other armies. Carolingian and Norman cavalry can be found in plastic, but suitable infantry are not yet available: Saxons can serve as Carolingians; but Normans cannot really be provided for by any alternative nation (this is because the Norman soldier had a very distinctive kite-shaped shield). However, plastic Normans can occasionally be found second-hand.

ALTERNATIVE ARMIES
The Carolingian and Ottonian armies wore identical dress (since they were both Frankish kingdoms, this is hardly surprising).

PRIMARY SOURCES
Einhard (829–36) and Notker the Stammerer (884–7). *Two Lives of Charlemagne*, tr. Lewis Thorpe, Penguin, 1969

SECONDARY SOURCES

Davis, R.H.C. *A History of Medieval Europe*, Longman, 1970

Heath, Ian. *Armies of the Dark Ages*, Wargames Research Group, 1980

Nicolle, David. *The Age of Charlemagne*, Osprey, 1984

Reuter, Timothy. 'Carolingian and Ottonian Warfare' in Keen, Maurice (ed.),
  Medieval Warfare, Oxford, 1999, 13–35

A GREAT COMMANDER

> Charlemagne was by far the most able and noble-spirited of all those who ruled
> over the nations in his time. He never withdrew from an enterprise which he had
> once begun and was determined to see through to the end, simply because of
> the labour involved; and danger never deterred him.
>
> Einhard (829–36), *Life of Charlemagne*, in *Two Lives of Charlemagne* (tr. Lewis
> Thorpe), Penguin, 1969, pp. 63–64.

Charlemagne was undoubtedly a remarkable leader; however, readers should be
aware that chroniclers tended to idealise their subjects, and should not be
regarded as entirely reliable.

ETHNIC CONFUSION

The Carolingians were the only Franks who genuinely remained French – although
their dynasty was replaced by that of the Capetians by the start of the eleventh
century. The Ottonians were originally Franks, but they had become German by
the time their dynasty won the title of Holy Roman Emperor. Conversely, the
Normans were originally Viking raiders who had settled in France.

VIKING ARMY
(790–1070)

Unit type	Number per army
Huscarls (Warband, medium armour, Elite)	1–3
Bondi (Warband, light armour, Average)	3–7
Thralls (Light Infantry (javelin), light armour, Levy)	0–2

The Vikings seem to have relied upon impetuous charges rather than shieldwall
formation. Given that many of their opponents were overrun, this was evidently a
most effective approach – especially since the attacks of the Norsemen were
assisted by berserk fanatics (see special rule no. 1). However, the presence of
archers in the ranks of the bondi units allow the latter some useful defensive
capability (see special rule no. 2).

SPECIAL RULES

1) *Berserkers*. These fanatics were assigned to huscarl units, and unleashed a frenzied attack on the first available enemy unit. To simulate this effect, on the first time any huscarl units are engaged in hand-to-hand combat, they hit their foes on dice rolls of 3–6 in the first round.

2) *Bondi archers*. The bondi could deploy considerable numbers of bowmen in their ranks. Bondi units may shoot at the enemy with half their remaining bases if they remain stationary (round any fractions up), or with a single base if they move.

SUGGESTED DEPLOYMENT

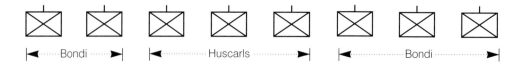

With an army as strong as the Vikings, subtlety is not required. This force has the intention of marching through the enemy lines, crushing the foe in the process. It is a very simple tactic: however, there is no reason to use finesse if it is not required – something the Vikings frequently proved.

CREATING THE ARMY IN MINIATURE
The Vikings have always been a very popular army with wargamers; accordingly, figures are readily available in metal and plastic.

ALTERNATIVE ARMIES
Vikings may serve as Saxons, and vice versa.

PRIMARY SOURCES
Sturluson, Snorri (c. 1235). *King Harald's Saga* (tr. Magnus Magnusson and Hermann Pálsson), Penguin, 1966

SECONDARY SOURCES
Clarke, H.B. 'The Vikings' in Keen, Maurice (ed.), *Medieval Warfare*, Oxford, 1999, 36–58
Heath, Ian. *Armies of the Dark Ages*, Wargames Research Group, 1980
Patten, Stephen. *Shieldwall*, Warhammer Historical Wargames, 2002
Wise, Terence. *Saxon, Viking and Norman*, Osprey, 1979

NO QUARTER

The two great war-leaders,
Shieldless, shunning armour,
Called for thrust and parry,
Armies were locked in battle.
Stones and arrows were flying,
Sword-blades were dyed crimson;
All around, doomed warriors
Fell before the onslaught.

Stein Herdisarson, quoted in Sturluson, Snorri (*c.* 1235), *King Harald's Saga*
(tr. Magnus Magnusson and Hermann Pálsson), Penguin, 1966.

This account of the Battle of the Nissa (fought between King Svein of Denmark and King Harald of Norway) doubtless uses poetic licence, but nevertheless conveys the savage aggression of Viking warfare remarkably well. Incidentally, the battle referred to was fought between two fleets of longships. However, it cannot really be seen as a naval action given that the enemy ships soon collided, and the warriors on board proceeded to engage each other in a vicious mêlée. For the record, the Norwegians won.

THE ENTREPRENEURIAL SPIRIT

Academic historians often seek to establish their reputation by challenging established shibboleths. Some writers have accordingly argued that the Vikings were not really brutal warriors, but actually traders seeking to establish new markets by taking selected territories. This rather neglects the fairly obvious fact that historical clichés tend to become entrenched precisely because they are true. In reality, the Vikings did plunder, pillage, and rape their way across Europe: trading networks came as an afterthought.

Chapter 15

Dark Age Battle Report

O
ne rather self-evident characteristic of the Dark Ages is that battles are not necessarily well documented. As a result, many wargamers prefer to confine any tabletop simulations to engagements which are recorded in some detail – such as the Battle of Hastings. However, a far more interesting experience can be derived by constructing a wargame scenario for a battle where few accounts survive. Accordingly, this chapter covers the engagement that was said to mark King Arthur's greatest victory over the Saxon invaders, the Battle of Mount Badon (c. 495).

THE BATTLE IN HISTORY

Sources for events in fifth- and sixth-century Britain are conspicuous by their absence. All are cited in the reading list at the end of this chapter, but it is important to note that the only work whose provenance is incontestably contemporary is that of Gildas, whose *The Ruin of Britain* can be dated to around 540. Nennius' *History of the British* is also useful, since its writer was more of an editor rather than an author; the text is actually a compilation of assorted works, which (although now lost) were in existence at the time Nennius was writing (c. 800). He saw his task as being to preserve old records for posterity:

> I, Nennius . . . have undertaken to write down some extracts that the stupidity of the British cast out; for the scholars of the island of Britain had no skill, and set down no record in books. I have therefore made a heap of all that I have found, both from the Annals of the Romans and from the Chronicles of the Holy Fathers, and from the writings of the Irish and English, and out of the tradition of our elders.
> Nennius (c. 800), *History of the British* (tr. John Morris), Phillimore, 1980, p. 9.

Nennius' methodology may have been somewhat indiscriminate, but the documents included in his anthology do contain some vital insights. Two other works can also be mentioned. *The Welsh Annals* (c. 960) contain a reference to the Battle of Mount Badon whose provenance may be contemporary; whereas Bede's *Ecclesiastical History of the English People* (731) draws heavily upon Gildas for his brief account of fifth-century Britain.

Gildas and Nennius both describe Britain as being riven with strife following the departure of the Romans in 410. The old elite was divided between those who wished to continue the Roman ways, and those whose loyalties were more towards the old Celtic mode of living. Nominal affiliations notwithstanding, all wanted power. As if all this chaos was not bad enough, Britain was also assailed by plundering expeditions launched by Pictish and Irish raiders, and by occasional outbreaks of plague.

One British leader, who has been named Vortigern by Nennius (and is referred to as the 'proud tyrant' in Gildas' text) saw a way to cement his power. During the first half of the fifth century, Vortigern invited a contingent of Saxon mercenaries to Britain; these were intended to crush the barbarian raiders, and in the process consolidate Vortigern's authority over his British rivals. However, the Saxons soon realised that they could easily depose Vortigern, and promptly did so, winning control of south-east England (including much of East Anglia) in the process. Moreover, they could call for reinforcements from Germany – and in a country where armies were often numbered in mere hundreds, just a thousand new arrivals could make a significant difference.

Nevertheless, the British were ready to resist Saxon expansion by the second half of the fifth century. Vortigern's attempts to create a new order divorced from the Roman tradition had ended in disaster; the newly emergent leader, Ambrosius Aurelianus, was a member of the traditional Romano-British elite. Not surprisingly, he attempted to rally the British with a call to return to the Roman ways he knew best – and which appeared to guarantee rather more security than Vortigern's shambolic efforts. During a later struggle with the Saxons, Ambrosius was able to carve out a secure base in western England.

There is, however, no reason to suppose that Ambrosius was primarily a military leader. He may well have enjoyed the assistance of an able lieutenant, who commanded the cavalry force that represented such a vital element of Romano-British armies. That subordinate may well have been the man we know today as King Arthur. He may not have been a king; but his cavalry Warband effectively kept the British kingdom in being. This explains why the precise locations of the twelve battles of Arthur, described in Nennius' account, have generally been identified over such a wide area. It is possible that his cavalry fought Saxons in Lincolnshire, and Pictish raiders in northern Britain. However, although there is protracted debate over the location of the first eleven of

Arthur's battles, most historians agree that the twelfth, Mount Badon, was fought near Bath.

The reasons for selecting Bath as the likely area stem from an identification with Badon in other chronicles. More pertinently, the city of Bath was a very sensible place for the Saxons to attack. The old Roman road network led from Saxon territory to Bath on an east–west axis, making movement easy. Moreover, the capture of the old Roman city would result in the splitting of Ambrosius' territories, with the west of England separated from the south-west region of Devon and Cornwall. Bath could also become a base for a Saxon advance upon the British kingdoms in what was to become Wales. Having therefore established that Mount Badon was a hill (possibly an old Celtic hill fort) near Bath, the surviving evidence can be quoted in full:

> From then on [the arrival of Ambrosius] victory went now to our countrymen, now to their enemies. . . . This lasted right up till the year of the siege of Badon Hill, pretty well the last defeat of the villains, and certainly not the least.
>   Gildas (c. 540), *The Ruin of Britain* (tr. Michael Winterbottom), Phillimore, 1978, p. 28.

> [Arthur's] twelfth battle was on Badon Hill and in it nine hundred and sixty men fell in one day, from a single charge of Arthur's, and no one laid them low save he alone.
>   Nennius (c. 800).

> The Battle of Badon, in which Arthur carried the Cross of our Lord Jesus Christ for three days and three nights on his shoulders and the Britons were the victors.
>   *The Welsh Annals* from *History of the British* (tr. John Morris), Phillimore, 1980, p. 45.

These accounts may be rather brief, but a narrative of the battle can be constructed from the information therein. The most plausible interpretation is that the Saxons were able to gather a substantial contingent by contemporary standards (probably about 1,500 men) and advance upon Bath. This move succeeded in surprising Ambrosius, who was only able to gather a few hundred infantry militia (no more than 700) to defend the area. These occupied the nearest hill, and prepared to hold out while Ambrosius (a political rather than a military leader) sent for Arthur's cavalry. This explains Gildas' reference to the 'siege' of Badon; it was Ambrosius' militia who were besieged, and had to face the Saxon assaults. Arthur was meanwhile busy gathering the nearby nobility under the Christian banner (*The Welsh Annals*' reference to 'Cross of our Lord' probably describes a shield design –

especially since horsemen bore their shields on their backs when not fighting; hence the reference to bearing the Cross 'on his shoulders'). This mustering must have taken some time, which may explain the 'three days and three nights' terminology. However, once Arthur's combined force of his own Elite cavalry and the local mounted nobility (this would only have been a small body of men – probably no more than 500) arrived on the battlefield, they were confronted by the spectacle of the Saxons assaulting the beleaguered British infantry. This allowed Arthur the opportunity of launching a charge upon the Germans' flanks (his reference to Arthur personally slaying 960 men can be taken as dramatic licence; this figure would represent the casualties inflicted by Arthur's combined cavalry force).

This account of Mount Badon is, to say the least, highly conjectural (for example, I would have followed those writers who see the battles as having been fought in the 490s, rather than the date of 516 stated in *The Welsh Annals*). Readers may wish to construct their own version from the evidence provided above, and from the vast range of books written by modern historians (anyone who does so should be aware that some interpretations are distinctly implausible; it is best to read several works before reaching any considered verdict). What is not in any doubt, however, is the decisive nature of the Battle of Mount Badon. It allowed the Romano-British kingdoms to survive intact for over half a century; the Saxons were only able to begin their ultimately successful attacks upon the British during the second half of the sixth century, following the weakening of the indigenous kingdom by a severe outbreak of plague, and the civil wars so roundly condemned by Gildas.

The fate of Arthur remains to be considered. The only reference to his death is in *The Welsh Annals*, which point out that Arthur and Medraut (who has become infamous in the legends as the traitor Mordred) fell at the Battle of Camlann. However, the *Anglo-Saxon Chronicles*, which diligently record Saxon victories and contain no reference to fifth- and sixth-century defeats, do not record any success at Camlann. To my mind, Arthur continued to be an enormously respected military leader, defending the British cause. Medraut, far from being a traitor, was probably his lieutenant. The disastrous Battle of Camlann was probably fought against Pict or Scot armies (no sources from the latter peoples survive to record such victories). Again, this interpretation is somewhat conjectural; Arthur and Medraut may have fallen in one of the British civil wars (and may of course have fought each other as the legends suggest). Nobody really knows; and nobody ever will. We are only left with the undoubted fact of the Battle of Mount Badon, whose wargaming re-enactment is recounted below.

RECREATING THE BATTLEFIELD
I made the assumption that the battle saw the Saxons assaulting the Romano-British infantry on Mount Badon, followed by Arthur and his cavalry putting in an appearance. Constructing such terrain is simplicity itself. Some books were placed

under part of a 4ft × 3ft table, and a green cloth draped over it. Moreover, the result looked surprisingly good; wargamers should bear in mind that expensive terrain layouts are not always essential when depicting appropriate battlefields.

ARMY COMPOSITION

Given the lack of any detailed historical information, the respective armies were improvised from the lists provided in Chapter 14. For the Saxons, a raiding force was postulated, containing three units of nobles, four of peasants, and one of archers. The maximum number of nobles was fielded in order to take account of Mount Badon's significance; a major push to secure Bath and to divide Ambrosius' realm, would undoubtedly have involved an Elite force. The archers were deployed in order to take account of Gildas' reference to the 'siege' of Mount Badon; they would have been needed for the preliminary skirmishing that represented a prelude to any concerted assault. Finally, the Saxon army used the 'Early Armies' special rule in the Anglo-Saxon list; all nobles and peasants were reclassified as Warband, and were not permitted to form shieldwalls.

As for the Romano-British, their army comprised two elements: the garrison of Mount Badon, and Arthur's relieving cavalry force. It was felt that the infantry contingent would be fairly weak, as it had been cobbled together in a hurry. Two units of militia were deployed accordingly. A single unit of archers was fielded, in order to account for the siege situation. That left one more infantry unit, and it was felt that Bath's importance to Ambrosius would have meant that some of its garrison would have retained Roman training. As a result, the Romano-British were permitted to deploy one unit of Roman Remnants.

Arthur's cavalry force was accounted for by the maximum permitted number of four units. Moreover, one of these was upgraded to knights (see special rule no. 2 in the Romano-British army list). Given the decisive role of Arthur's force, this could only be adequately represented by allowing it to be as strong as possible, both in terms of numbers and unit potency.

PLANS AND DEPLOYMENT

Since Arthur's cavalry took the Saxons completely by surprise in the historical battle, our re-enactment had to reproduce this factor. The best way of doing so was to have an umpire present, who would only give the players such information as they would have been aware of in 495. Thus it was that whereas the Romano-British player knew that Arthur's cavalry would appear at some point to be determined by the umpire, his Saxon opponent was blissfully unaware of this rather unwelcome event.

The umpire decided that the Saxon player would be told that his objective was to destroy all the Romano-British infantry by the end of turn 6. This would, the Saxon player was informed, be a test of the latter's ability to launch a rapid assault

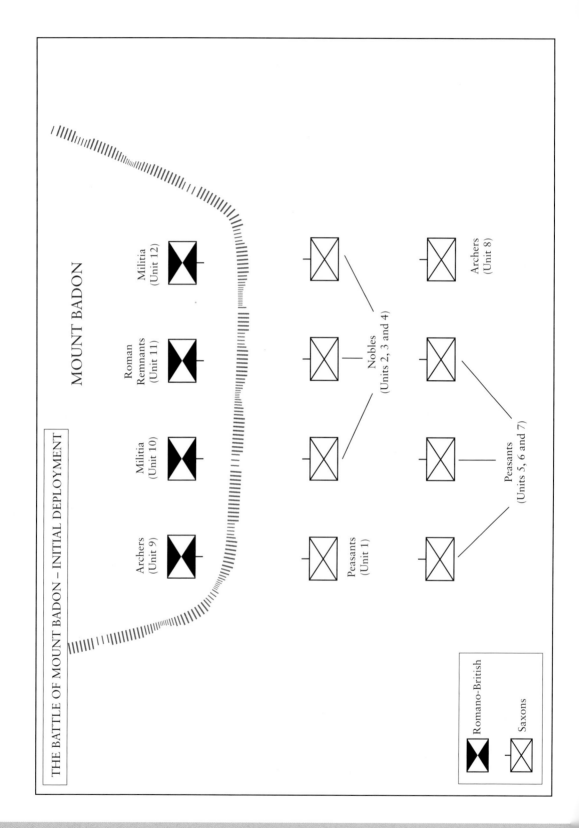

THE BATTLE OF MOUNT BADON – INITIAL DEPLOYMENT

MOUNT BADON

Archers
(Unit 9)

Militia
(Unit 10)

Roman
Remnants
(Unit 11)

Militia
(Unit 12)

Peasants
(Unit 1)

Nobles
(Units 2, 3 and 4)

Archers
(Unit 8)

Peasants
(Units 5, 6 and 7)

Romano-British

Saxons

with an overwhelming force – any delay in achieving such a simple objective would be evidence of gross incompetence. Meanwhile, the umpire decided that Arthur's cavalry would arrive on turn 5; he did not tell the Romano-British player when they would appear but (in response to entreaties from the latter) he did allow them to arrive on the left side of the battlefield, on the Saxon flank. Once Arthur's cavalry materialised, the Saxon player was to be informed that his victory conditions had changed to those of a normal battle (that is to say, reducing the enemy army to two remaining units). This combination of explanations (forcing the Saxon player to act in ignorance of any enemy reinforcements; and allowing the Romano-British general to know that Arthur's cavalry would arrive at some point, but not to tell him precisely when) was calculated to create an appropriate element of uncertainty.

The Romano-British were ordered to deploy first, since the umpire felt that the Saxons would have had ample opportunity to send scouts to reconnoitre the enemy lines. Mount Badon's garrison was deployed at the top of the slope, allowing it to take advantage of the first round combat bonus provided by hilltops. With Arthur's cavalry due to arrive on the Saxon left, it was felt that the weakest infantry unit could be deployed here (since the horsemen would relieve this point first). The archers (unit 9) were located accordingly, given that their weakness in hand-to-hand combat would militate against their prolonged survival. Next along came a contingent of militia (unit 10), then the Roman Remnants (unit 11), followed by the final militia (unit 12). The aim of this set up was to allow the Roman Remnants (who would fight in shieldwall) to form the centre of the close-order infantry line – their greater resilience would hopefully allow Mount Badon's garrison to hold out long enough for Arthur's cavalry to save the day.

With the umpire informing the Saxon player (almost as an afterthought) that his units would only be permitted to exit the battlefield from the hill itself, the Germanic invaders deployed in two lines. The intention was that the second would reinforce the main attack given that a frontal assault was essential: since the Saxon player believed that he only had six turns to fulfil his objectives, any intricate flanking manoeuvre would fail for lack of time.

When faced with the Romano-British deployment, the Saxon wargamer believed that the enemy archers would not provide any great obstacle. As a result, he placed two lines of peasants (units 1 and 5) on his left. However, the enemy close-order infantry provided a more formidable barrier. Consequently, the Saxon nobles (units 2, 3 and 4) were placed opposite these. The remaining peasants (units 6 and 7) were placed in the second line in support. The archers (unit 8) were deployed on the right-hand side of the second line; the Saxon player believed that they could shoot over the heads of the front-line nobles (unit 4) and engage the Romano-British militia (unit 12). In any event, the Saxon general reasoned, his nobles would require little assistance in dealing with an effete bunch of Romano-British townsmen.

Faced with these deployments, the umpire gave an inward smile of satisfaction. Only he knew just how important a rapid Saxon success would be; the Germanic invaders would not know what hit them when Arthur's cavalry turned up, but the Romano-British general did not know when his enemy was going to be hit. It promised to be an interesting battle.

TURN-BY-TURN ANALYSIS

The first three turns of the battle saw the Saxons advancing towards Mount Badon, punctuated only by some rather ineffective firing by their archers (unit 8), which inflicted just one casualty point upon the Romano-British militia (unit 12); they were able to fire over the heads of the nobles (unit 4) only because their victims were at a higher level. The Romano-British firing was rather more effective; their archers (unit 9) were able to indulge in two turns of shooting, and succeeded in eliminating a base from their peasant victims (unit 1).

Turns 3 and 4 saw the Saxons engage Mount Badon's defenders in hand-to-hand combat. Notwithstanding some surprisingly stiff resistance from the Romano-British archers (Unit 9), who destroyed another base of the Saxon peasants (unit 1), they were wiped out by their Germanic aggressors. The adjacent militia (unit 10) also suffered severely, losing two bases (one in combat, and one to a failed morale test). However, the Roman Remnants (unit 11) showed just how valuable a shieldwall could be in defence; providing as it did the equivalent of extra-heavy armour, the Remnants barely suffered any losses, and destroyed a base of the noble attackers (unit 3). The remaining combat saw a thoroughly bizarre result; a fight between Saxon nobles (unit 4) and Romano-British militia (unit 12) saw both sides lose a base in combat, but the resulting morale tests saw the Elite nobles fail (losing another base in the process) and the Levy militia pass.

End of Turn 4	Eliminated Units
Saxons	None
Romano-British	One unit (9)

Turn 5 saw the Saxon general with an important decision to make. With his left-most peasants (unit 1) having eliminated their opponents, they could either turn to their right and engage the Romano-British militia (unit 10) in flank; or advance straight ahead and exit the table on turn 6 – thereby eliminating two Romano-British units. With the potential victim of the flank assault looking likely to be eliminated in short order without any assistance, an advance was the obvious step. Accordingly, the peasants (unit 1) advanced towards the edge of the battlefield, with the second line peasants (unit 5) following on behind. This decision undoubtedly appeared to be the correct one, when the nobles (unit 2) destroyed their militia foes (unit 10). As soon as the Saxons exited the peasants (unit 1) from the table, the Romano-British player would be forced to eliminate his remaining forces (units 11 and 12), thereby ending the battle. The Saxon general began to congratulate himself on a job well done. As for the Romano-British commander, it was beginning to look as if Arthur's cavalry would not arrive in time.

It was at this point that the umpire took a hand in the proceedings, allowing the Romano-British general to deploy his cavalry. Arthur had arrived; the Saxon player looked on with consternation. Although the umpire informed him that he no longer had to win the battle by turn 6, now that the normal victory conditions had superceded the previous ones, this was of little comfort. For the Romano-British general was able to hit the Saxon peasants (units 1 and 5) with two units of cavalry each – moreover, the peasants were assailed in flank and rear, thereby maximising their losses (units 14 and 15 confronted unit 1; units 13 and 16 assaulted unit 5). By the end of this onslaught, the peasants only had one base remaining in each unit, and had inflicted few losses in return. The situation at this stage can be seen on the map provided.

End of Turn 5	*Eliminated Units*
Saxons	None
Romano-British	Two units (9 and 10)

With the onset of turn 6, the stunned Saxon general had more decisions to make. Having just eliminated its opponents, one of the Saxon nobles (unit 2) had three options. Firstly, it could head for the edge of the table, and exit on turn 7. This option was rejected on the basis that to do so would expose its flank to cavalry assault – the Saxon peasants (units 1 and 5) could scarcely be expected to survive another combat phase. Secondly, the nobles could turn to their right and take the enemy shieldwall (unit 11) in flank; however, that would have exposed its rear to the enemy horsemen. The remaining choice was to incline leftwards and hit the nearest enemy cavalry unit (15) in flank. Meanwhile, the peasant unit in support could advance half a move and turn to its left, thereby presenting a new obstacle for the enemy cavalry. This was the option decided upon; and some losses were duly inflicted upon the cavalry opponent (unit 15), which lost a base. However, this was not enough to save those units already under attack from Arthur's army; both peasant contingents (units 1 and 5) were eliminated. As if this was not bad enough, the Saxon right-hand unit (4) was killed in turn by their militia foes (unit 12).

The Romano-British turn saw more mounted action. The unit (15) assaulted in its flank by the Saxon nobles (unit 2) promptly turned and faced it head on. Their unengaged neighbour (unit 14) promptly attacked the Saxons (unit 2) on their right flank. Meanwhile, Arthur's knights (unit 13) attacked the nearest Saxons (unit 6)

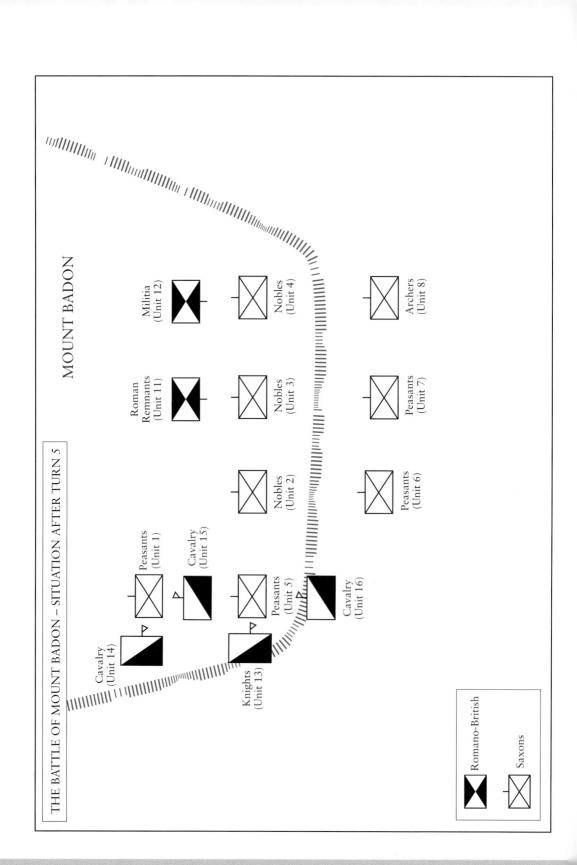

THE BATTLE OF MOUNT BADON – SITUATION AFTER TURN 5

MOUNT BADON

Peasants (Unit 1)

Cavalry (Unit 15)

Cavalry (Unit 14)

Knights (Unit 13)

Peasants (Unit 5)

Cavalry (Unit 16)

Nobles (Unit 2)

Peasants (Unit 6)

Roman Remnants (Unit 11)

Militia (Unit 12)

Nobles (Unit 3)

Nobles (Unit 4)

Peasants (Unit 7)

Archers (Unit 8)

Romano-British

Saxons

frontally, while the remaining cavalry (unit 16) formed up to the knights' right, ready to engage their foes on the following turn.

All this excitement notwithstanding, the infantry battle on the Saxon right was continuing. With no opponents to face, the Romano-British militia (unit 12) turned to their right and assailed the remaining unit of Saxon nobles (unit 3), which was engaged with the Roman Remnants (unit 11). Their combined pressure saw the nobles' elimination. The situation at this stage is illustrated on the map provided.

End of Turn 6	*Eliminated Units*
Saxons	Four units (1, 3, 4 and 5)
Romano-British	Two units (9 and 10)

The onset of turn 7 saw the Saxons still determined to achieve something. The Romano-British militia (unit 12) had exposed its flank and rear to the Saxon second line (units 7 and 8), which proceeded to attack accordingly. The results were devastating, with the militia being eliminated. Surprisingly, the Romano-British cavalry were not able to kill their victims, despite the fact that the remaining unengaged unit (16) was able to turn to its left and attack the Saxon peasants (unit 6).

End of Turn 7	*Eliminated Units*
Saxons	Four units (1, 3, 4 and 5)
Romano-British	Three units (9, 10 and 12)

Turn 8 saw the Saxons assault the Roman Remnants (unit 11), whose slowness had rendered them unable to assist their militia comrades (unit 12) on the previous turn; units in shieldwall are very formidable in defence, but cannot manoeuvre effectively. The peasants (unit 7) attacked the Remnants frontally, whereas the archers (unit 8) took them in the flank. As an aside, Light Infantry can be extremely effective if it is presented with an open flank; the lack of movement penalties for turning means that such assaults can be executed quickly. The resultant pressure saw the elimination of the Roman Remnants (unit 11), thanks to the combination of combat losses and a failed morale test. However, the Saxons had no time to celebrate destroying the last of Mount Badon's initial defenders. While his infantry attacks were going on, the Saxon left (units 2 and 6) finally succumbed to Arthur's cavalry assault. With only two units remaining, the Saxons had lost the battle, and King Arthur had once again saved British civilisation.

End of Turn 8	*Eliminated Units*
Saxons	Six units (1, 2, 3, 4, 5 and 6)
Romano-British	Four units (9, 10, 11 and 12)

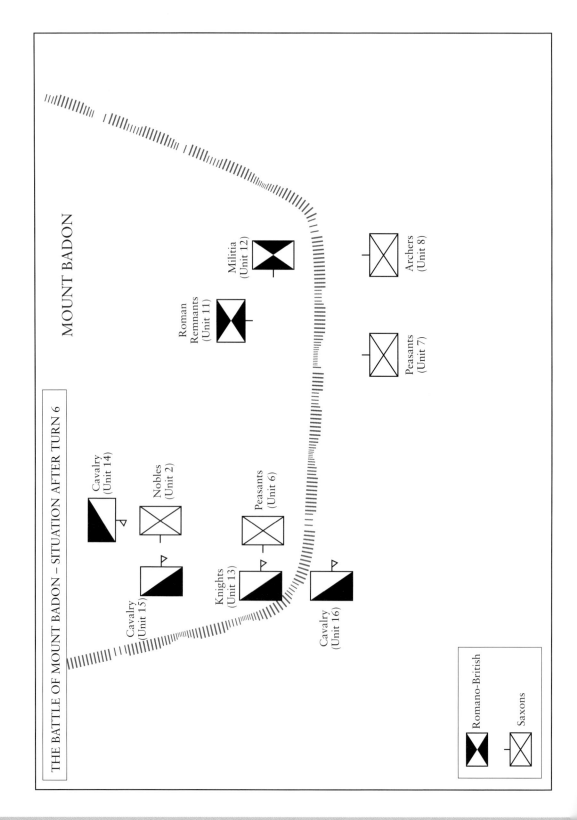

THE BATTLE OF MOUNT BADON – SITUATION AFTER TURN 6

MOUNT BADON

Cavalry
(Unit 14)

Nobles
(Unit 2)

Cavalry
(Unit 15)

Knights
(Unit 13)

Peasants
(Unit 6)

Cavalry
(Unit 16)

Roman
Remnants
(Unit 11)

Militia
(Unit 12)

Peasants
(Unit 7)

Archers
(Unit 8)

Romano–British

Saxons

CONCLUSIONS AND SUMMARY

So far as the Romano-British were concerned, Arthur's modern-day wargamer fought with great skill, deploying his cavalry with great ability. The combination of stolid infantry defence (especially from the Roman Remnants in their shieldwall), and aggressive mounted action from Arthur's horsemen, guaranteed victory.

As for the Saxons, their general bewailed the difficult situation in which he was placed when the Romano-British horsemen attacked. Although there is some justice in this, our wargames general should have been aware that whenever an umpire is involved in a tabletop engagement, there is generally a nasty surprise in store for someone. Accordingly, the Saxon player would have been advised to withdraw two of his second line units (6 and 7) and redeploy them on the left and right flanks respectively; thereby forming three lines on each flank, and only one in the centre. This would have presented a greater potential barrier to Arthur's horsemen.

The reader may still take the view that Mount Badon is a difficult battle for the Saxons to win. He or she would be right; however, it must be remembered that not all battles in history were even. Moreover, the umpire deserves great credit for devising a scenario in which fortune swung between the antagonists with such rapidity. If the game is properly constructed, it does not have to give both sides an equal chance to give each player an enthralling time.

PRIMARY SOURCES

Bede (731). *Ecclesiastical History of the English People* (tr. Leo Sherley-Price), Penguin, 1990
Gildas (*c.* 540). *The Ruin of Britain* (tr. Michael Winterbottom), Phillimore, 1978
Nennius (*c.* 800). *History of the British* (tr. John Morris), Phillimore, 1980
The Nennius volume also contains a translation of *The Welsh Annals* (*c.* 960).

SECONDARY SOURCES

Ellis, Peter Berresford. *Celt and Saxon*, Constable, 1993
Morris, John. *The Age of Arthur*, Phoenix, 1973

Chapter 16

Medieval Warfare 1100–1485

KEY EVENTS

Date	Event
1096–99	First Crusade. Christian reconquest of Holy Land culminates in capture of Jerusalem.
1169	Saladin's Ayyubid dynasty seizes control of Egypt.
1187	Battle of Hattin. Saracen armies crush crusaders and retake Jerusalem.
1189–92	Third Crusade. Richard the Lionheart leads Christian recovery, culminating in successful siege of Acre.
1219–21	Fifth Crusade results in humiliation as Christian attempt to take Egypt is repulsed.
1237–41	Mongols ravage Eastern Europe, but succession crisis in their Empire results in retreat to Mongol heartland.
1277–83	English armies under command of Edward I conquer Wales.
1291	Saracen armies recapture Acre. Crusader kingdoms destroyed.
1296–8	Edward I defeats Scots under William Wallace.
1314	Battle of Bannockburn. Robert the Bruce secures Scottish independence by routing Edwards II's English army.
1315	Battle of Mortgarten. Swiss destruction of chivalric Austrian army stuns Europe.
1337	Start of Hundred Years War between England and France.
1346	Battle of Crécy. English longbowmen prove decisive in victory over French mounted knights.
1396	Battle of Nicopolis. Hungarian and French crusader army destroyed by Ottoman Turks. Ottoman control of Bulgaria secured.
1415	Battle of Agincourt. Henry V annihilates French. English armies close to victory.

1419–34	Hussite religious reformers resist Holy Roman Empire, until internal divisions lead to defeat.
1428–9	Joan of Arc leads French revival, relieving Orléans and defeating English at Battle of Patay.
1449–53	French destroy remaining English armies, ending the Hundred Years War.
1453	Ottoman Turks besiege and take Constantinople, destroying the remnants of the Byzantine Empire. The fallen city is renamed Istanbul.
1455–71	Wars of the Roses. Dynastic struggle between English noble families ends with victory of Yorkists over Lancastrians.
1459–67	Ottoman conquest of Southern Balkans.
1475–7	Duke Charles the Bold of Burgundy engages in catastrophic campaigns against the Swiss. Following Charles' death at the Battle of Nancy, the French take advantage of Burgundy's subsequent weakness by seizing control of the Duchy.
1485	Battle of Bosworth. Henry Tudor defeats and kills King Richard III of England. House of Tudor established.

THE AGE OF CHIVALRY

By the start of the twelfth century, feudalism was no longer merely a defensive phenomenon. With the barbarian invaders either defeated or assimilated, Medieval Europe began to acquire a certain self-confidence. It also had a sense of religious mission. For Christians had been forced to endure seeing the Holy Land under Islamic rule for centuries – and in 1095, Pope Urban II preached for a crusade, to win back the territories in question.

The response was astonishing. Nobles from across Western Europe pledged to join the crusade, and served with their retinues. As a result, the First Crusade enjoyed remarkable success, culminating as it did in the capture of Jerusalem. Here was proof that Western Europe could spread the Christian faith into the heart of the Islamic world, and that Medieval civilisation had true vitality.

Unfortunately for the crusaders, their kingdoms were ultimately doomed to failure. This was due both to political and strategic factors. The former saw their expression in disunity and maladministration. In essence, the key difficulty was that several kingdoms were set up in the Holy Land, by adventurers who came to be more intent upon acquiring power and wealth, rather than by serving the cause of Christianity. Moreover, this self-centred view saw further expression in the inability of the new regimes to win the allegiance of their subjects. Brutality, rapaciousness and bigotry were all features of the crusader states, which tended to produce extreme depopulation as the indigenous Muslims and Jews fled. As has already been covered in Chapter 11, the Islamic world may not have been a beacon of liberal enlightenment, but was at least tolerant: moreover, its governments were far more efficient. In this particular clash of civilisations, Christianity could not be said to have covered itself in glory.

The inability to establish any sort of popular support had important strategic ramifications for the crusaders. Without any local recruits, they constantly had to rely upon volunteers from Western Europe. This meant that they were always at a manpower disadvantage in relation to their Islamic foes. For a time, this did not matter, since the mounted knight proved superior to the Muslim nobles, who were seldom able to withstand the impact of a crusader charge. However, crusader victories only won time, whereas a single defeat could result in catastrophe. Thus it was that the Saracen victory at Hattin in 1187 effectively sealed the crusaders' fate.

Notwithstanding their strategic failure in the Holy Land, mounted knights had shown themselves to be the rulers of the battlefield, and their supremacy in Europe was unchallenged during the twelfth century. The heavily armoured cavalryman was well protected against missiles, with the exception of the crossbow – and the latter weapon suffered from having a slow rate of fire. Moreover, the horse was also protected, firstly with cloth and later with metal, which increased the knight's powers of endurance. The offensive power of the lance-armed nobility was such that Medieval Levy infantry (often poorly motivated peasants) could not face up to horsemen, and fled before contact. It was frequently the case that the only way of confronting a mounted knight was to oppose him with another knight on horseback.

The dominance of the mounted nobility was such that their position was enshrined in society. The Medieval world became divided into three estates, each of which had a vital function. Thus it was that the clergy formed the first estate, which provided for society's spiritual and cultural needs; the knights and their armed retainers formed the second estate, which upheld justice; and the labourers formed the third estate, which provided economic support for the whole. The result of this was that the knight saw himself as the rightful secular ruler, since he protected Christian civilisation. Such a self-perception was supported by three major sources: the Matter of Britain, in the shape of the King Arthur legends; the Matter of France, as expressed in the stories relating to Charlemagne and his paladins; and the Matter of Rome the Great, relating to the history of Greece and Rome, and especially heroes such as Alexander, Caesar and the legendary figures from Homer.

With societal values and literary works supporting his position, the role of the knight became almost ritualised, as was demonstrated by the growth of the tournament. This opulent display of jousting became immensely popular from the twelfth century onwards, and the more successful participants even had their achievements celebrated in biographical works. The combination of genuine martial achievement, literary glorification, and the spectacle of the tournament duel led to the development of a code of chivalry. This was stated by the twelfth-century writer John of Salisbury as being:

to defend the Church, to assail infidelity, to venerate the priesthood, to protect the poor from injuries, to pacify the province, to pour out their blood for their brothers . . . and, if need be, to lay down their lives.

John of Salisbury, quoted in Bennett, Matthew et al., *Fighting Techniques of the Medieval World*, Spellmount, 2005, p. 109.

It therefore appeared that the position of the mounted knights was unassailable. However, one characteristic of warfare is that it has no respect for any established values: the sole measure of military excellence is the effectiveness of weapon systems, as the knights were to find out during the fourteenth century.

THE INFANTRY CHALLENGE – LONGBOW AND PIKE

As we have seen, the humble infantryman had been eclipsed somewhat by the more glamorous cavalry since the development of feudalism. However, the principles of warfare had not changed; and it would always be true that either an effective missile weapon, or especially rigid close-order drill, would threaten the dominance of cavalry. Much to the discomfiture of the mounted chivalry, English longbowmen and Swiss pikemen had precisely the qualities required.

Ironically enough, the longbow was not even an English weapon. It was first used by the Normans' Welsh opponents, and was rapidly adopted by the former in an attempt to counter the effectiveness of the latter. Moreover, the longbow was a very simple weapon – it was in essence a single piece of wood (yew, to be specific) carved into a bow shape. However, those archers who had the strength to use it found that the longbow had a long range (it was very effective up to 200m), good armour penetration, and most crucially of all a high rate of fire. This last characteristic was essential: its chief rival, the crossbow, had its bowstring drawn mechanically rather than manually – this meant that, long range and deadly armour penetration notwithstanding, the length of time taken to reload made it less effective that the longbow on the battlefield.

English archers therefore found themselves in a position to challenge mounted knights. However, like all missilemen they needed effective support – once the enemy engaged archers in hand-to-hand combat they could be very vulnerable. Accordingly, English longbowmen needed to have reliable close-order infantry on their flanks, and were also inclined to protect their frontage by emplacing a row of stakes. These were hammered into the ground at an angle of 45°; the consequent prospect of becoming impaled meant that any aggressor (especially one on horse-back) would not charge at full tilt, but would instead be forced to cross the barrier of stakes with some care. This did, of course, allow the archers to assail their aggressors with further volleys of arrows, while the stake obstacle was being crossed.

Effective as the longbow was, it could not win a battle on its own. The same drawback did not apply where the Swiss pikemen were concerned. As we have seen in the Classical period (see Chapter 6) Heavy Infantry in close-order formation could rule the battlefield, and nothing had changed in Medieval times. Men on foot in close-order formation, equipped with long spears, could threaten any cavalryman – and although Flemish and Scottish spearmen had shown themselves able to win battles, the Swiss infantry demonstrated that they could win wars.

The chief secret of the Swiss success is that they combined ferocity and discipline. These hardy men of the Alps possessed homicidal tendencies to a pronounced degree (thus it was that although defeated knights could normally expect to be captured and ransomed rather than killed, the Swiss never took prisoners – no matter how exalted their rank), but were also renowned for retaining their cohesion under the most extraordinary stress. Moreover, the Swiss soon adopted their weaponry to the conditions in which they fought. Thus it was that they originally used halberds (viciously effective two-handed cutting weapons); but largely replaced these with the much longer pike, which was more effective at repelling cavalry, by insuring that the latter would suffer serious losses in trying to get through a hedge of pikes. In essence, the Swiss recreated the Classical Heavy Infantry phalanx – and it was to prove just as effective as Alexander the Great's original model.

COMBINED ARMS

The revival of infantry created something of a crisis for the Medieval world. However, the answer was quite literally already to hand. Specifically, Medieval generals tended to be aware of the precepts contained in Vegetius' *The Military Institutions of the Romans* (*c*. 390). Over 150 manuscript copies are known to have been circulated in the Medieval world, and most other military writers drew heavily upon it (sometimes to the point of outright plagiarism). However, much of this popularity owed a great deal to the Medieval belief that the foundations of all greatness lay in Ancient Roman culture (suitably modified and enhanced by Christianity, of course). Vegetius actually had little validity during the ascendancy of the mounted knight, since the purpose of his work was to extol the virtues of the Roman legionary. However, with the rise of longbow and pike, it became apparent that Vegetius could be used as a blueprint for the development of a more balanced army. The text did, for example, suggest that cavalry was particularly useful when protecting the flanks of the infantrymen; with heavy horse on the foot soldiers' flanks, and lighter cavalry both guarding the extreme wings of the army – potentially outflanking the enemy in the process. Accordingly, a new variety of light horseman developed from the ranks of the knights' retainers. Equipped with a cuirass of chain mail with leg protection for the thighs, but with an unarmoured horse, the Light Cavalry could move fast; and armed as they were with one of a crossbow, throwing spear, or light lance, guard the flanks or provide a rearguard.

They were, however, most useful not so much on the field of war, but in the subsidiary function of scouting the enemy before the battle itself, or screening the army from the attention of enemy scouts.

However, it was apparent that the new predominance of infantry condemned the mounted knight to a subordinate role. Nevertheless, the nobility showed themselves to be willing to face up to the new realities, and many knights simply fought on foot rather than on horseback. Moreover, they made formidable infantry. Although not as effectively drilled as the Swiss, they still had a great sense of *esprit de corps*; and their heavy armour gave them great endurance. Speaking of which, it is vital that the myth of knights being unable to move in their armour, be repudiated comprehensively. For the new plate armour developed in the fourteenth and fifteenth centuries weighed between 60lb and 80lb. Although this may sound a lot, it is actually no more than the load a twentieth-century infantryman carried into battle – and it was, of course, evenly distributed. The most physically fit knights could even vault into their horses' saddles.

The dismounted knight therefore formed a vital part of many Medieval armies. His presence in the line of battle had another positive impact, specifically upon the morale of the army. For if commoners saw the previously aloof mounted knights sharing the footsloggers' burden, the morale of the former was frequently enhanced. The new combination of dismounted knights supporting commoner infantry (many of whom were equipped with longbows or crossbows), with mounted knights and lighter horse providing flank protection, produced an effective army – albeit one which was still unable successfully to counter the Swiss pike phalanx.

THE ARRIVAL OF GUNPOWDER

As we have seen, the role of the medieval knight had been modified thanks to the development of combined-arms tactics. However, the development of gunpowder weaponry was to prove even more revolutionary. Despite the drawback of a very slow reloading time, and a tendency to burst their barrels (much to the extreme discomfiture of their crews), late medieval cannon could still destroy any castle. This made any nobleman vulnerable to assault: a local power base was no longer immune from attack. Moreover, the expense of an artillery train proved so colossal, that only monarchs could afford to maintain it. This resulted in the growth of royal power in the latter half of the fifteenth century: in addition, cannon could play a role on the battlefield, albeit a limited one (the combination of a slow rate of fire and total immobility saw to that).

However, other firearms also developed. The individual foot soldier could be equipped with rudimentary handguns from the start of the fifteenth century. These were essentially tiny cannon – gunpowder was poured down the muzzle, a ball rammed down over it, and propelled outwards once the powder was ignited by a spark applied to an external hole. The guns took a long time to reload, and had a very short effective range (only in the order of 80m): this explains why some handgunners were heavily armoured, since they would have to endure immediate close combat if their volley of fire did not stop the enemy. These drawbacks notwithstanding, the armour penetration of the handgun was of a very high order, and the extreme noise of firearms could terrify an adversary: horses were especially prone to panic.

Ultimately, the ability of cannon and hand firearms to penetrate armour was to render the knight obsolete: the early sixteenth century was to see not only his extinction, but also the end of the Medieval age (a process that was greatly facilitated by the rupture of Christian unity resulting from the Reformation). Gunpowder really was revolutionary: it was to make royal power and centralised states inevitable, whereas in the Medieval era such developments were inconceivable.

PRIMARY SOURCES

Curry, Anne (ed.). *The Battle of Agincourt: Sources and Interpretations*, Boydell, 2000

Froissart, Jean (1380–1410). *Chronicles* (tr. Geoffrey Brereton), Penguin, 1978

Joinville, Jean de (1309). 'The Life of St. Louis' in *Chronicles of the Crusades* (tr. M.R.B. Shaw), Penguin, 1963

Pizan, Christine de (1410). *The Book of Deeds of Arms and of Chivalry* (tr. Sumner Willard), Penn State, 1999

Vegetius (*c.* 390). 'The Military Institutions of the Romans' in Phillips, T.R. (ed.), *Roots of Strategy*, Stackpole, 1985 (originally 1940)

SECONDARY SOURCES

Bennett, Matthew et al. *Fighting Techniques of the Medieval World*, Spellmount, 2005

Bianchi, John. *Vlad the Impaler*, Warhammer Historical Wargames, 2006

Bradbury, Jim. *The Medieval Archer*, Boydell, 1985

Burne, Lt Col Alfred H. *The Crécy War*, Wordsworth, 1999 (originally 1955)

Burne, Lt Col Alfred H. *The Agincourt War*, Wordsworth, 1999 (originally 1956)

Contamine, Phillipe. *War in the Middle Ages* (tr. Michael Jones), Blackwell, 1984

Davis, R.H.C. *A History of Medieval Europe*, Longman, 1970

Ellis, John. *Cavalry*, Pen & Sword, 1993 (originally 1978)

Fletcher, Richard. *The Cross and the Crescent*, Penguin, 2003

Fuller, J.F.C. *Decisive Battles of the Western World, Volume 1*, SPA Books, 1993 (originally 1954)

Heath, Ian. *Armies and Enemies of the Crusades 1096–1291*, Wargames Research Group, 1978

Heath, Ian. *Armies of the Middle Ages, Volume 1*, Wargames Research Group, 1982

Heath, Ian. *Armies of the Middle Ages, Volume 2*, Wargames Research Group, 1984

Hildinger, Erik. *Warriors of the Steppe*, Spellmount, 1997

Keen, Maurice (ed.) *Medieval Warfare*, Oxford, 1999

Montgomery, Field Marshal Viscount. *A Concise History of Warfare*, Wordsworth, 2000 (originally 1968)

Oman, Sir Charles. *A History of the Art of War in the Middle Ages, Volume Two: 1278–1485*, Greenhill, 1998 (originally 1924)

Payne, Robert. *The Crusades*, Wordsworth, 1998 (originally 1984)

Seymour, William. *Battles in Britain*, Wordsworth, 1997

Waley, Daniel and Denley, Peter. *Later Medieval Europe*, Longman, 2001

Wise, Terence. *Medieval European Armies*, Osprey, 1975

Wise, Terence. *Armies of the Crusades*, Osprey, 1978

JOURNAL ARTICLES

Patrick, Stephen B. 'Empires of the Middle Ages' in *Strategy and Tactics* no. 80 (May 1980), 23–32

Reeve, Paul. 'Some Thoughts on How We View 15th Century Warfare' in *Slingshot* no. 203 (May 1999), 50–2

Storer, Ian. 'The Rise of the Free Companies, and Their Relationship to the Knightly Class and its Chivalric Values' in *Slingshot* no. 202 (March 1999), 28–32

Vickers, Ralph. 'Great Medieval Battles' in *Strategy and Tactics* no. 77 (November 1979), 29–39

Chapter 17

Medieval Wargaming

Rulesets for the Medieval period must take account of the societal focus upon the primacy of the nobility. Armies of the Middle Ages were centred upon the knightly class, which is why both Foot and Mounted Knights tend to enjoy superiority over commoners, at least until the rediscovery of Heavy Infantry (in the case of the Swiss), and the development of the longbow, handgun and artillery.

So far as the longbow is concerned, many British wargames writers tend to indulge in a spot of intoxication concerning its performance – one could be forgiven for thinking the English foot were actually equipped with heavy machine guns, such is the effectiveness of longbow fire in some sets of wargames rules. Such dangers notwithstanding, the longbow does seem to have been a very accurate weapon in the right hands (which is why its practitioners score a hit on a die roll of 3–6). Moreover, it also had a better armour penetration capacity than the ordinary bow (albeit not so effective as the crossbow), which ability is accounted for by imposing a penalty of –1 on armour saving rolls for troops hit by longbowmen.

Firearms began to have a considerable effect upon warfare at the end of the Medieval period, their slow rate of fire (and short range in the case of the handgun) notwithstanding. Their chief damage was moral rather than physical: close-range handgun fire made a very loud noise, which panicked both men and horses; whereas cannonballs inflicted hideous wounds liable to demoralise all who witnessed them. This is why all units suffering casualties (irrespective of whether or not a base is removed) from firearms have to test morale.

The troop types familiar from previous sections are Heavy Infantry, Heavy Archers, Heavy Cavalry, Light Infantry and Light Cavalry. New troop classifications (and old ones operating with different effects) are covered below.

FOOT KNIGHTS

As already described, knights were (contrary to popular myth) fully prepared to dismount in order to support their infantry. There were often very good reasons for doing so. They effectively become more heavily armoured without having to worry about protecting the horse, and also presenting a smaller target for enemy archery (which is why Foot Knights tend to enjoy the benefits of a higher saving roll than their mounted comrades). Dismounting also served to improve the morale of commoner infantry, who would be greatly encouraged by seeing the nobility share their burden (which is why commoner foot enjoy a bonus on their morale scores if Foot Knights are in close proximity). These benefits often outweighed the loss of the impetuous charge enjoyed by their mounted counterparts.

MEDIEVAL INFANTRY

These are essentially Dark Age Infantry renamed, in the sense that they are less effective versions of Heavy Infantry. However, they are inferior to some of their Dark Age predecessors in so far that Medieval Infantry did not use the shieldwall tactic. Nevertheless, their fighting skills are fully the equal of Foot Knights; they simply lack the morale and armour protection of the nobility.

PEASANTS

It is a historical truism to say that being a peasant isn't at all pleasant. This was especially the case in the Middle Ages, when the average rural denizen had virtually no rights and all too many responsibilities. One of the least welcome of all duties was to turn up and fight at the whim of the local nobility. Being untrained, Peasants tended not to fight with any efficiency (which is why they are classed as the equivalent of Heavy Archers, but without the benefit of any missile weaponry), and were also prone to demoralisation (they have to test morale at the end of each round of hand-to-hand fighting, irrespective of whether or not they lose any bases).

As might be expected, most Peasants are of Levy status. However, some were religious fanatics who, limited fighting skills notwithstanding, enjoy extraordinarily high morale levels.

WARBAND

Our old friends return in these rules, with their customarily rapid movement, and combat effectiveness in wooded terrain. Unfortunately for them, the ferocious charge of their knightly opponents seems to have cooled their martial ardour somewhat. As a consequence, Warband no longer enjoy an enhanced combat capability in the first round of hand-to-hand fighting.

MOUNTED KNIGHTS

Chivalry on horseback may not enjoy the same saving rolls of their footslogging brethren, but Mounted Knights have some very real advantages. They are still well armoured compared with most troops, can move quickly, and have the benefit of an impetuous charge (allowing them to roll an extra die for every base involved in the first round of hand-to-hand combat). Mounted Knights were the traditional rulers of the Medieval battlefield; they can often emulate such achievements on the wargames table.

ARTILLERY

Although most heavy ordnance appeared only in sieges, some lighter cannon did play a growing role on the battlefield. The grievous effects of Artillery upon enemy morale has already been covered; unfortunately, gunnery has its problems. Firstly, cannon reload very slowly, and may only fire every other turn. More crucially, primitive guns were inclined to burst their barrels, with fatal consequences to their crew (which is why an artillery unit is eliminated if a '1' is scored on the die roll to hit the target). This does, of course, eliminate a unit without any enemy intervention. All these defects notwithstanding, cannon are great fun to use, and can strike terror into the hearts of any enemy wargamer.

It will be apparent that the age of chivalry has an enticing flavour for any wargamer. It is liable to prove especially attractive to any figure painter. Every individual knight can have different livery and chivalric emblems, creating a blaze of colour. Even commoners can create a striking effect, clad as they often were in the colours of the noble they served. The combination of visual spectacle and exotic troop types, not to mention new weaponry in the shape of firearms, is a singularly attractive one for any wargamer.

Chapter 18

Medieval Wargames Rules

UNITS

Each unit generally consists of four bases, each of which has dimensions of 40mm × 20mm. Each base has a variable number of figures on it, depending upon the troop type, as listed below. (Note: the standard base size is ideal for 15–20mm figures. However, 25mm miniatures may require larger dimensions: 60mm × 40mm is suitable for these larger-size figures.) As noted, units usually have four bases, which are aligned in two ranks of two bases. However, Artillery units consist of a single base.

Troop Type	Figures/models per base
Heavy Infantry, Foot Knights, Medieval Infantry, Peasants, Heavy Archers	4
Warband, Mounted Knights, Heavy Cavalry	3
Light Infantry, Light Cavalry	2
Artillery	1 artillery piece and 2–4 crew

HOW TO WIN

Victory is achieved as soon as one side is reduced to a strength of two remaining units.

a) *Exiting the map*. For every Infantry unit (other than Light Infantry) exiting the mapboard on the enemy side, the enemy immediately withdraws *two* of his units. All three count as eliminated.

SEQUENCE OF PLAY

Each side follows the sequence listed below in each of its turns:

1) Charge sequence.
2) Movement.
3) Shooting.
4) Hand-to-hand combat.
5) Morale tests.

1) The Charge Sequence

Every time a general wishes a unit to enter into hand-to-hand combat with an enemy unit, the procedure is as follows:

1a) *Charge declaration.* Declare the charge. Measure the distance between the units. If the charging unit can reach the enemy, move it into physical contact (bases touching).

1b) *Defensive fire.* If the defender is equipped with javelins, and if the attacker launched its charge from further than 8cm away, the defender may fire at its assailant.

1c) *Initiate hand-to-hand combat.* After removing any losses caused by defensive fire, the two antagonists will fight in the hand-to-hand phase.

2) Movement

2a) *Movement allowances.* In general, units move the distance listed below during each turn. They do not have to use up all their movement allowance, but may not carry over any unused movement to the next turn.

Troop Type	Movement per turn
Light Cavalry	24cm
Mounted Knights, Heavy Cavalry	20cm
Warband, Light Infantry	12cm
Heavy Infantry, Foot Knights, Medieval Infantry, Peasants, Heavy Archers	8cm
Artillery	May not move

2b) *Turning.* If a Warband, Heavy Infantry, Foot Knight, Medieval Infantry, Peasant, Heavy Archer, Mounted Knight or Heavy Cavalry unit wishes to deviate more than 30° from a straight line, it must use up half its movement allowance to do so.

i) Light Infantry and Light Cavalry may turn without penalty.

2c) *Difficult terrain.* Ancient battles generally involved no more than three types of terrain; specifically hills, rivers and woods. They affect movement in varying ways.

i) Hills have no effect on movement (they were usually gentle slopes).

ii) All units take a complete turn to cross a river.

iii) Cavalry may not enter woods.

iv) Heavy Infantry, Foot Knights, Medieval Infantry, Peasants and Heavy Archers have their movement reduced to 4cm every turn they move in a wood.

v) Light Infantry and Warbands are unaffected by woods, and may move up to their full movement allowance if desired.

2d) *Moving and firing.* Heavy troops may never move and fire. Light Infantry and Light Cavalry may do so under certain circumstances.

i) Light Infantry may move and fire if equipped with javelins. The firing may either precede or follow movement.

ii) Light Cavalry may move and fire if equipped with bows (firing must either precede or follow movement). However, Light Cavalry equipped with javelins are allowed to split-move. That is to say, they may not only move and fire, but are allowed to fire at any point during their move (if the target is in range at the time of firing). They may, for example, move half their allowance, throw their javelins, turn around, and retire their remaining half-move away from the enemy they had just shot at.

iii) No unit may ever fire if it is charging an enemy unit.

3) Shooting

3a) *Missile ranges.* When a unit wishes to shoot, it must first check to see if the enemy is in range.

Weapon	*Range*
Longbow, bow and crossbow (on foot)	24cm
Javelin	8cm
Artillery	48cm
Bow and crossbow (on horseback), handgun, sling	16cm

3b) *Rolling to hit.* Infantry and cavalry units with bows, slings, longbows, handguns, crossbows or javelins roll one die for each base currently remaining. A successful hit may possibly inflict a casualty point on the defending unit.

i) Longbowmen hit on a roll of 3–6.
ii) Bowmen, slingers and javelinmen hit on a throw of 4–6.
iii) Crossbowmen and handgunners hit on a throw of 5–6.
iv) Units in woods only suffer half the number of hits registered.

3c) *Saving rolls.* However, the defender is permitted what is known as a saving roll for each potential casualty. This is dependent upon armour thickness. For every hit scored, the defender rolls a die. If the score achieves the required saving roll, the casualty is not inflicted.

i) When assessing casualties from crossbow or handgun fire, the defender suffers a –2 dice-roll modifier on its saving roll.
ii) When assessing casualties from longbow fire, the defender suffers a –1 dice-roll modifier on its saving roll.

Type of armour	Saving roll required
Extra-heavy armour	3–6
Heavy armour	4–6
Medium armour	5–6
Light armour	6

3d) *Artillery fire.* This is resolved as follows:

i) Roll a die to determine the number of shots permitted. If a 1 is rolled, the gun explodes, killing its crew and eliminating the weapon (without inflicting any casualties on the enemy).
ii) Assuming the gun did not misfire, roll a die for every shot. A hit is inflicted for every score of 4–6. Halve the number of hits if the target is in a wood.
iii) No saving roll allowed. All hits cause a casualty point to be inflicted.
iv) Artillery may only fire every other move.

3e) *Base removal.* For every four casualty points inflicted, remove a base (denote the current number of casualties using markers).

4) Hand-to-Hand Combat

4a) *Procedure.* When units engage in hand-to-hand combat, the fight usually continues each turn until one side is eliminated (Cavalry or Light Infantry may withdraw a full move after a round of combat, but only if their movement rate exceeds that of their assailants. Note that Mounted Knights may never withdraw from combat).

4b) *Order of striking.* Blows are always struck simultaneously.

4c) *Hand-to-hand combat (open terrain).* Each base in a unit rolls a variable number of dice, depending upon the type of opponent it is engaging.

Own unit	Enemy unit			
	Heavy Infantry	Foot Knights, Medieval Infantry, Warband, Mounted Knights, Heavy Cavalry	Peasants, Heavy Archers	Light Cavalry, Light Infantry
Heavy Infantry	1	2	3	4
Foot Knights	1	1	2	3
Medieval Infantry	1	1	2	3
Warband	1	1	2	3
Mounted Knights	1	1	2	3
Heavy Cavalry	1	1	2	3
Peasants	1	1	1	2
Heavy Archers	1	1	1	2
Light Cavalry	1	1	1	1
Light Infantry	1	1	1	1

i)   Mounted Knights roll one extra die per base remaining in the first round of any combat. Note that Warband no longer receive this advantage.

ii)   Units uphill of their antagonists also roll one extra die per base remaining in the first round of any combat

iii) Units defending a river bank similarly roll one extra die per base remaining, if their assailants are crossing the river at the time. Again, this only applies during the first round.

iv)   Units attacking the flank or rear of an enemy always roll an additional die per base engaged.

v)   Units hit in their flanks may turn to face their enemy in the second or subsequent rounds of hand-to-hand combat, but only if they are not simultaneously being engaged to their front.

vi)   For every dice rolled, a 4–6 is needed to stand the chance of inflicting a casualty point loss on the enemy.

4d) *Saving roll.* As with shooting, the defending unit is entitled to a saving roll for each potential casualty. Use the same chart provided in the shooting section of these rules (see 3c above).

i)   Artillery is defenceless in hand-to-hand combat, and is automatically exterminated if engaged.

4e) *Combat in woods.* This uses a (very) different hand-to-hand combat table.

Own unit	Enemy unit	
	Warband	Non-Warband
Warband	1	2
Non-Warband	1	1

5) Morale tests

5a) *When to test morale.* Morale is tested on the following occasions:

   i)   Whenever troops suffer casualties (irrespective of whether or not a base is removed) from artillery or handgun fire.

   ii)   Whenever any unit loses a base as a result of hand-to-hand combat (one test must be taken for each base removed).

   iii) If a Peasant unit is engaged in hand-to-hand combat, it must test morale at the end of every round of fighting.

5b) *How to test morale.* A unit must roll a die on each occasion a test is mandated. If it fails to achieve the appropriate score, another base is removed.

Class of unit	Morale roll
Fanatic	2–6
Elite	3–6
Average	4–6
Levy	5–6

   i)   If a commoner infantry unit (everything other than Foot Knights) has one or more Foot Knights units within 8cm, it may add 1 to all morale die rolls. (Note that Fanatics do not receive the benefits of this rule: a die roll of 1 on any morale test is always a failure).

Chapter 19

Medieval Wargames Armies

Fourteen of the more prominent or militarily interesting armies are described in this chapter. As always, wargames forces comprise eight units. I would suggest that up to three terrain pieces be present on the battlefield: hills, woods and rivers can appear in Western Europe; but hills alone may be deployed in deserts.

CRUSADER ARMY
(1130–1300)

Unit type	Number per army
Knights Templar (Mounted Knights, heavy armour, Fanatic)	0–1
Knights Hospitaller (Mounted Knights, heavy armour, Fanatic)	0–1
Other Knights (Mounted Knights, heavy armour, Elite)	1–2
Turcopoles (Light Cavalry (bow), light armour, Average)	1–3
Infantry (Medieval Infantry, medium armour, Average)	2–6
Pilgrims (Peasants, light armour, Fanatic)	0–2

Although the Infantry and Turcopoles can provide some useful support, any successful crusader army relies upon the power of its Mounted Knights. The wargamer should always aim to engage the enemy in hand-to-hand combat, since the crusaders will never defeat the Saracens in a missile duel.

   The most notable feature of the crusader army was the presence of military orders (the Knights Templar and Knights Hospitaller). These were effectively religious orders who were devoted to defending Christendom by force of arms: their combination of piety and violence encapsulates the contradictions of Medieval Christian civilisation.

Incidentally, the classification of the pilgrims is not a misprint. They were fanatically devoted to their cause, but were also completely untrained; which is why they are classed as both having Fanatic morale, but with the fighting skills of peasants.

SPECIAL RULES

1)   *Infantry.* These units were partially equipped with crossbows. Accordingly, half the remaining bases of any unit (always round fractions up) may fire each turn (provided that the unit does not move beforehand).
2)   *Military order deployment* (optional rule). The Templars and Hospitallers may have been allies, but their rivalry led to much mutual distrust. Accordingly, units of Templars and Hospitallers may not deploy within 16cm of each other (they may move within 16cm once the game commences).

SUGGESTED DEPLOYMENT

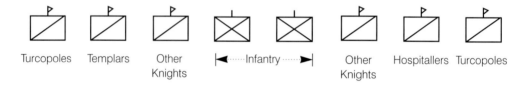

Turcopoles   Templars   Other |◄······Infantry······►| Other   Hospitallers Turcopoles
                        Knights   Knights

This army is deployed in order to enter hand-to-hand combat as soon as possible – although the Turcopoles and Infantry can provide some missile support. Note how the Templars and Hospitallers have their flanks protected, so that these vital units are able to reach the enemy lines with as little interference as possible.

CREATING THE ARMY IN MINIATURE
Coverage of this army is very comprehensive, in mediums of both metal and plastic.

ALTERNATIVE ARMIES
Although this book does not cover them, crusader figures can be used in European armies of the same time span (1130–1300).

PRIMARY SOURCES
Joinville, Jean de (1309). 'The Life of St. Louis' in *Chronicles of the Crusades* (tr. M.R.B. Shaw), Penguin, 1963

SECONDARY SOURCES
Edbury, Peter. 'Warfare in the Latin East' in Keen, Maurice (ed.) *Medieval Warfare*, Oxford, 1999, 89–112

Heath, Ian. *Armies and Enemies of the Crusades 1096–1291*, Wargames Research Group, 1978

Payne, Robert. *The Crusades*, Wordsworth, 1998 (originally 1984)

Wise, Terence. *Armies of the Crusades*, Osprey, 1978

Wise, Terence. *The Knights of Christ*, Osprey, 1984

JUST WAR

The soldiers of Christ wage the battles of their Lord in safety. They fear not the sin of killing an enemy or the peril of their own death, inasmuch as death either inflicted or borne for Christ has no taint of crime and rather merits the greater glory.

Bernard, Cistercian Abbot of Clervaux, quoted in Wise, Terence, *The Knights of Christ*, Osprey, 1984, p. 5.

Although the idea of Christianity being spread by means of homicidal violence may seem somewhat incongruous, given Jesus' own views on turning the other cheek, Abbot Bernard's ideas concerning the Christian virtue of the Knights Templar were commonplace.

WITH FRIENDS LIKE THAT . . .

When the Fourth Crusade was launched in 1204, it might have been expected that its participants would head for the Holy Land. However, the crusaders instead took the opportunity of besieging and taking Constantinople, ravaging the city in the process. It is not immediately apparent how the crusaders' cause was best served by pillaging Christendom's most venerable and cultured city. The Byzantines were able to regain control of their capital in 1261; the crusaders never recovered any moral credit.

SARACEN ARMY
(1170–1300)

Unit type	Number per army
Guards (Heavy Cavalry (bow), medium armour, Elite)	1–3
Cavalry (Heavy Cavalry (bow), medium armour, Average)	1–4
Turkomans (Light Cavalry (bow), light armour, Average)	2–4
Infantry (Heavy Archers (bow), light armour, Average)	1–4

The Saracen armies varied somewhat in their composition, and this list takes such trends into account; any of the troop types can play a major role in the final force according to the predilections of the wargamer. However, one constant factor is the stress upon missiles; the Saracens relied upon the power of archery to weaken the crusaders, before becoming engaged in hand-to-hand combat. The wargamer should do the same.

SPECIAL RULES

1) *Guards and cavalry.* Saracen Heavy Cavalry enjoy the following benefits:

    a)   They may turn without any movement penalties.
    b)   They may fire their bows after they move.
    c)   They may withdraw from combat (during the second or any subsequent rounds) with enemy Heavy Cavalry or Mounted Knights.

2) *Infantry firepots.* Saracen infantry units often contained men equipped with rudimentary hand grenades (filled with an incendiary liquid). To reflect this, Saracen infantry always inflict 1–3 additional hits (roll a die and halve the results, rounding up any fractions) in the first round of their initial hand-to-hand combat. These additional hits are automatic kills – the enemy may not attempt any saving rolls.

3) *Infantry movement.* Saracen infantry fight as Heavy Archers, but may move (and should ideally be based) as Warband.

SUGGESTED DEPLOYMENT

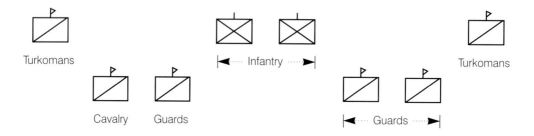

This army has positioned its Turkomans and Infantry in the front line, in order to assail the enemy with missiles. The Turkomans should always avoid hand-to-hand combat. The Guards and Cavalry are in reserve, from where they can add their archery to that of the front line, and engage a weakened enemy in hand-to-hand fighting.

CREATING THE ARMY IN MINIATURE

The wargamer is spoilt for choice with the Saracens; a wide range of figures is available, both in metal and plastic.

ALTERNATIVE ARMIES

Saracen figures can be used in Dark Age Arab armies, and can also feature in Ottoman Turk forces (and many other Middle Eastern and North African armies up to the nineteenth century).

PRIMARY SOURCES

Joinville, Jean de (1309). 'The Life of St. Louis' in *Chronicles of the Crusades* (tr. M.R.B. Shaw), Penguin, 1963

SECONDARY SOURCES

Edbury, Peter. 'Warfare in the Latin East' in Keen, Maurice (ed.) *Medieval Warfare*, Oxford, 1999, 89–112
Heath, Ian. *Armies and Enemies of the Crusades 1096–1291*, Wargames Research Group, 1978
Nicolle, David. *Saladin and the Saracens*, Osprey, 1986
Payne, Robert. *The Crusades*, Wordsworth, 1998 (originally 1984)
Wise, Terence. *Armies of the Crusades*, Osprey, 1978

A UNITED ATTACK

The enemy tackles him [the King of Sicily] in the way that men play chess, for first of all they sent their footmen forward to attack him, and these hurled Greek fire at his troops. Then all the Saracens, both mounted and unmounted, pressed so hard on our people that the King of Sicily, who was on foot amongst his knights, was quite overpowered.

Joinville, Jean de (1309), 'The Life of St. Louis' in *Chronicles of the Crusades* (tr. M.R.B. Shaw), Penguin, 1963.

This account of the French King (subsequently Saint) Louis's campaign in Egypt in 1250 shows how adept the Saracens were at combined infantry and cavalry assaults. Incidentally, 'Greek Fire' was a Byzantine weapon, of which the Arab firepots were an inferior copy (the Byzantines used Greek fire projectors as flamethrowers in naval battles, with devastating effect).

A CHIVALROUS FOE

It was rather ironic that one of the most noble and humane men of the Middle Ages was the Saracen leader Saladin, who was renowned for his chivalrous conduct towards his enemies. This did not alter the fact that he was a fanatical

Muslim, with an implacable hatred of all that the crusades stood for (although given the brutality of many of the Christian invaders, it could be argued that Saladin's views were understandable).

MONGOL ARMY

Unit type	Number per army
Guards (Heavy Cavalry (bow), medium armour, Elite)	0–1
Cavalry (Heavy Cavalry (bow), light armour, Elite)	1–3
Horse Archers (Light Cavalry (bow), light armour, Elite)	4–7

The Mongols were able to combine great mobility, massed archery, and effectiveness in hand-to-hand combat. Accordingly, they were able to defeat most foes they faced, before the customary lack of political stability (in keeping with other steppe nomads such as the Scythians and the Huns) forced a retreat to their heartland. Saracen armies (to be specific, the Iranian Khwarismians) were among their victims, as were the states of Eastern Europe. To reflect the latter, the Crusader army list may be used as a basis, although the pilgrims should be deleted. This gives a reasonable reflection of an Eastern European army, although some of the troop types differ (thus the Templars and Hospitallers become the Teutonic order, and Turcopoles are actually Lithuanians).

SPECIAL RULES

1) *Guards and Cavalry*. These enjoy the same benefits as their Saracen equivalents (see Saracen special rule no. 1).

SUGGESTED DEPLOYMENT

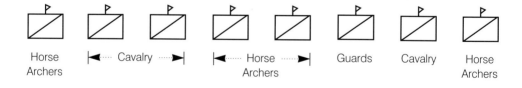

| Horse Archers | ◄···· Cavalry ····► | ◄····· Horse ·····► Archers | Guards | Cavalry | Horse Archers |

This general has decided to deploy the army in order to maximise the amount of archery, by placing all units in the front line. However, the manoeuvrability of the Mongols is such that the army can easily divide into two wings (in order to outflank the enemy), or send the horse archers forward (thereby allowing the shock cavalry to become a reserve force).

CREATING THE ARMY IN MINIATURE

Mongols are readily available in metal and plastic miniatures.

ALTERNATIVE ARMIES

Strictly speaking, Mongols should not serve as other troops. However, for wargamers who are not too fussy about precise accuracy, Mongols bear a slight resemblance to Huns.

SECONDARY SOURCES

Davis, R.H.C. *A History of Medieval Europe*, Longman, 1970
Hildinger, Erik. *Warriors of the Steppe*, Spellmount, 1997
Karasulas, Antony. *Mounted Archers of the Steppe 600 BC–AD 1300*, Osprey, 2004
Turnbull, Stephen. *The Mongols*, Osprey, 1980

CATCH US IF YOU CAN

And ye shall understand that it is a great dread for to pursue the Tartars if they flee in battle . . . for in fleeing they shoot behind them and slay both men and horses. And when they will fight they will shock them together in a plump.

Sir John Mandeville, quoted in Turnbull, Stephen, *The Mongols*, Osprey, 1980, p. 24.

The feigned retreat was a devastatingly effective Mongol tactic. If the enemy swallowed the bait, his headlong pursuit would lead to disorder in the ranks – suitably augmented by archery from the supposedly routing Mongols. Once the pursuers had become both hopelessly disorganised and bereft of friendly support, the Mongols would engage them in hand-to-hand combat with overwhelming numerical superiority (the phrase 'shock them together in a plump' can be loosely translated as 'charge en masse').

SCOTTISH ARMY
(1250–1485)

Unit type	Number per army
Knights (Mounted Knights, heavy armour, Average)	1–2
Yeomen (Medieval Infantry, light armour, Average)	5–7
Highlanders (Warband, light armour, Average)	0–2
Archers (Light Infantry (bow), light armour, Levy)	0–2

The Scots relied upon the endurance of their yeomen, when deployed in schiltron formation (see special rules below). The wargamer would be advised to do the same, notwithstanding the formation's very slow movement rate. Historically, the other troops had their uses, but the Scottish armies were only victorious when their yeomen performed well. However, any wargamer leading a Scots army should be extremely concerned about the effects of the English longbow.

SPECIAL RULES

1) *Schiltron formation*. Yeomen may deploy in this formation at the start of the game (all units must form schiltron, if the wargamer chooses this option). The schiltron has the following effects:

   a)   The yeomen are reclassified as Heavy Infantry.
   b)   They are treated as having medium armour.
   c)   They move at half their normal speed.
   d)   If any units choose to leave the schiltron, they revert to their original classification, and may never enter the schiltron formation again.

2) *Knight morale* (optional). Scottish knights often had divided loyalties; torn as they were between the desire for independence, and the bribes offered by the English Crown. Such internal divisions tended to become more pronounced in proportion to the number of knights deployed on the battlefield (if only a few nobles turned up, these were more likely to be dedicated nationalists prepared to risk all; conversely, if a larger number were effectively press-ganged, their dedication was somewhat limited). There was often no way of knowing how the knights would perform until they went into action. To reflect this rather interesting situation, apply the following rules:

   a)   Scottish knights are no longer automatically classed as having Average morale.
   b)   Whenever a Scottish knight unit has to test morale for the first time in the game, it must assess its morale level prior to taking the test. Roll a die:

Die Roll	Morale Level
1–2	Levy
3–4	Average
5–6	Elite

(The unit retains its classification for the remainder of the game.)

   i)   If only one unit of knights is fielded, add 2 to the die roll.
   ii)   If two units of knights are fielded, subtract 2 from the die roll.

SUGGESTED DEPLOYMENT

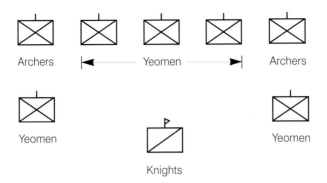

This army has a reinforced centre, with the archers providing support fire for the yeomen (who should adopt schiltron formation). The yeomen to the rear of the archers provide additional flank protection, and the single unit of knights (only one is fielded, in order to maximise its morale potential; see special rule no. 2) is intended to respond to any enemy threat, rather than be at the forefront of the assault. Scottish commanders should remember that it is the infantry who will win the battle; knights only provide support.

CREATING THE ARMY IN MINIATURE
Suitable figures are available in all metal scales. Infantry are now provided by one plastic manufacturer (Strelets); knights can be fielded from any other European nation of the relevant period, since they tended to look similar.

ALTERNATIVE ARMIES
Scottish foot were fairly distinctive, and cannot be fielded in other armies. Knights may serve in most other European forces.

PRIMARY SOURCES
Froissart, Jean (1380–1410). *Chronicles* (tr. Geoffrey Brereton), Penguin, 1978

SECONDARY SOURCES
Heath, Ian. *Armies of the Middle Ages, Volume 1*, Wargames Research Group, 1982
Oman, Sir Charles. *A History of the Art of War in the Middle Ages, Volume 2: 1278–1485*, Greenhill, 1998 (originally 1924)
Seymour, William. *Battles in Britain*, Wordsworth (1997 reprint)

DOUGHTY FIGHTERS
It should be repeated that the English and Scots, when they meet in battle, fight hard and show great staying power. They do not spare themselves, but go on to

the limits of endurance. . . . They stand their ground in the battle, dauntlessly wielding axes and other weapons for as long as their breath lasts.

Froissart, Jean (1380–1410), *Chronicles* (tr. Geoffrey Brereton), Penguin, 1978, p. 345.

The Scots were renowned for their endurance, both in the Anglo-Scots wars and the Hundred Years War, when they fought on the French side.

THE PERILS OF TECHNOLOGY

King James II was a great believer in the power of artillery. When besieging Roxburgh Castle in 1460, James personally inspected the firing of one of his cannon. Unfortunately for the King, the gun misfired, bursting its barrel and killing him instantly.

HUNDRED YEARS WAR ENGLISH ARMY (1290–1455)

Unit type	Number per army
Men-at-Arms (Foot Knights, extra-heavy armour, Elite)	2–4
Archers (Heavy Archers (longbow), light armour, Average)	3–6
Billmen (Medieval Infantry, medium armour, Average)	0–2
Hobilars (Heavy Cavalry, light armour, Average)	0–2

Many English readers will be familiar with this army, even if only through the distorting prism of nationalistic myths. The longbow is, as may be suspected, a fundamental and very effective part of this army; however, archers cannot win the battle single-handed. The men-at-arms are likely to be the truly decisive component; it will be up to them to defeat the enemy in hand-to-hand combat.

SPECIAL RULES

1) *Stakes*. Archer units may deploy these to their front at the start of the game. They have the following effects:

   a) Enemy units take a full move to cross the stake barrier.
   b) Enemy mounted units must take a morale test when crossing the stakes (horses were frequently very unwilling to traverse the obstacle).
   c) Archer units defending the stakes roll one extra die per base engaged in the first round of any hand-to-hand combat.

d)   Once archer units move across the stake barrier (which they may do without suffering any movement penalties), they may not deploy behind it again; the stakes are removed from the battlefield.

2)   *Army deployment.* Remarkable as it may seem, English armies seem to have been able to advance in the face of the enemy before the archers emplaced their stakes. To take account of this, apply the following rules:

a)   English armies always deploy after their opponents.
b)   English armies may deploy within longbow range (24cm) of their opponents, if desired.
c)   English armies may take the first turn in the battle, if they so desire. If they choose this option, they may not move their units; their archers may, however, fire at the enemy.

3)   *Early armies* (1290–1320). English forces from this period fought with mounted men-at-arms. Accordingly, early men-at-arms are reclassified as follows:

Men-at-Arms (Mounted Knights, heavy armour, Elite)

SUGGESTED DEPLOYMENT

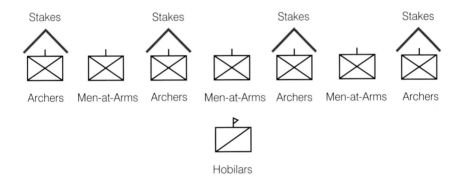

This wargamer is using the historical tactic of combining archers and men-at-arms in a mutually supportive deployment. Given its success on most battlefields, there is much wisdom in following history. The single unit of hobilars is deployed in reserve, ready to counter any enemy flanking attack.

CREATING THE ARMY IN MINIATURE

There is a wide selection of suitable figures available in all scales, both in metal and plastic. For those who enjoy wargaming in a truly massive format, Italeri and Accurate produce appropriate figures in 54mm/1:32 scale.

ALTERNATIVE ARMIES

Those European armies who employed English longbowmen (such as the Burgundians) can use figures from this army. The men-at-arms figures may serve in most contemporary European forces (including the French), since one knight looked much the same as the next.

PRIMARY SOURCES

Curry, Anne (ed.). *The Battle of Agincourt: Sources and Interpretations*, Boydell, 2000

Froissart, Jean (1380–1410). *Chronicles* (tr. Geoffrey Brereton), Penguin, 1978

SECONDARY SOURCES

Burne, Lt Col Alfred H. *The Crécy War*, Wordsworth, 1999 (originally 1955)

Burne, Lt Col Alfred H. *The Agincourt War*, Wordsworth, 1999 (originally 1956)

Curry, Anne and Hughes, Michael (eds). *Arms, Armies and Fortifications in the Hundred Years War*, Boydell, 1994

Heath, Ian. *Armies of the Middle Ages, Volume 1*, Wargames Research Group, 1982

THE POWER OF THE LONGBOW

And then, when the enemy were nearly ready to attack, the French cavalry posted on our flanks made charges against those of our archers who were on both sides of our army. But soon, by God's will, they were forced to fall back under showers of arrows and to flee to their rearguard.

'The Deeds of Henry V' (c. 1417) in Curry, Anne (ed.), *The Battle of Agincourt: Sources and Interpretations*, Boydell, 2000, p. 35.

Although this account of the Battle of Agincourt goes on to point out that the emplaced stakes also played a vital role in blocking the French cavalry assault it does illustrate how deadly the longbow could be.

ROBIN HOOD

Although the most popular renditions of the Robin Hood stories are set in the reign of King Richard the Lionheart, they were originally spread in the fifteenth and sixteenth centuries. The legends were a distinctly subversive attempt to show that common men could possess more real virtue and chivalry than medieval knights. The notion that a band of outlaws could withstand the assaults of the Sheriff of Nottingham and Sir Guy of Gisborne, stemmed from the power and status conferred upon the common soldiers by the longbow – which had proven its ability to kill large numbers of nobles in battle.

SWISS ARMY
(1300–1485)

Unit type	Number per army
Infantry (Heavy Infantry, medium armour, Fanatic)	4–7
Crossbowmen (Heavy Archers (crossbow), light armour, Elite)	1–2
Allied Knights (Mounted Knights, heavy armour, Elite)	0–1
Allied Foot (Medieval Infantry, light armour, Levy)	0–1

Advancing straight through the opposition lines may not have been the most subtle approach to warfare, but finesse was hardly necessary for a Swiss army that had the finest infantry in Europe. Massed infantry columns are likely to have a devastating effect on the wargames table (see special rule no. 1); however, the Swiss were also adept at forcing the enemy to give battle in unfavourable terrain (see special rule no. 2).

SPECIAL RULES

1) *Combined units*. Swiss infantry may deploy in deep columns. To reflect this, the infantry units are grouped in twos, forming up in four ranks (on a frontage of two bases). This has the following effects:

   a) The combined unit moves and fights as a single unit; that is to say, up to eight bases (if the combined unit is at full strength) may engage the enemy in hand-to-hand combat.
   b) If the combined unit is eliminated, the enemy counts this success as killing two units.
   c) If a combined unit is withdrawn after an enemy infantry unit exits the map on the Swiss baseline, this counts as two units being eliminated.
   d) If a combined unit exits the map on the enemy baseline, four enemy units must be eliminated (two Swiss units count as being destroyed).

2) *Rocky terrain*. The Swiss were very adept at using the mountainous areas of their homeland to good effect. If a battle is deemed to be fought in Switzerland, up to two pieces of impassable terrain may be deployed anywhere on the battlefield.

3) *Homicidal intent*. Swiss infantry units must advance at their full movement rate, and attempt to engage the enemy in hand-to-hand combat. Swiss crossbowmen and allied troops are not affected by this rule.

4) *Crossbowmen*. These units may deploy as Light Infantry if desired (the wargamer must decide which formation they are to adopt before the game commences; units may never change formation during the wargame itself).

5) *Handgunners*. For battles fought after 1400, one unit of crossbowmen may be reclassified as follows, if the wargamer desires (special rule no. 4 also applies to the handgunners):

   Handgunners (Heavy Archers (handgun), medium armour, Elite).

6) *Allies*. If the allied units are deployed, both must be fielded. In essence, if the wargamer wants knights in a Swiss army, he or she is also stuck with a distinctly indifferent foot unit.

SUGGESTED DEPLOYMENT

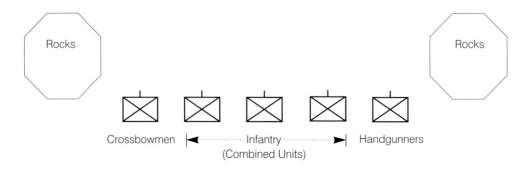

This fifteenth-century army has fielded a unit of handgunners. With the rocks effectively screening the army from flank assaults, both crossbowmen and handgunners are deployed as Heavy Archers, thereby maximising their potential in hand-to-hand fighting. However, the decisive element of this force is the central block of combined units. The enemy will find them very difficult to stop.

CREATING THE ARMY IN MINIATURE
Swiss armies are widely available in all metal scales. The plastic figure gamer will have to improvise somewhat; Renaissance landsknecht (which are effectively German copies of Swiss pikemen) figures are produced by Orion, and can be used as Swiss.

ALTERNATIVE ARMIES
Swiss infantry, crossbowmen and handgunner figures can serve as pikemen in Condottieri armies; or mercenaries in Wars of the Roses English forces. As usual, knights may serve in any European army.

SECONDARY SOURCES
Heath, Ian. *Armies of the Middle Ages, Volume 1*, Wargames Research Group, 1982

McCormack, John. *One Million Mercenaries*, Leo Cooper, 1993

Oman, Sir Charles. *A History of the Art of War in the Middle Ages, Volume 2: 1278–1485*, Greenhill, 1998 (originally 1924)

Wise, Terence. *Medieval European Armies*, Osprey, 1975

THE HORRIFYING HALBERD

The Swiss were armed with a lethal kind of battleaxe which is called 'Halberd' in the vernacular; with this terrifying weapon they could cut up even well-armoured opponents as though with a razor, slicing them in pieces.

John of Winterthur, quoted in Waley, Daniel and Denley, Peter, *Later Medieval Europe*, Longman, 2001, p. 84.

This account of the Battle of Mortgarten (1315) shows just how lethal the halberd was, in close-quarter fighting. It was the staple armament of most Swiss infantry until the fifteenth century, when pikes were adopted in order to keep cavalry at a greater distance than was possible with the shorter halberd.

MISAPPLIED PSYCHOLOGY

When Charles the Bold of Burgundy captured the Swiss town of Grandson in 1476, he executed its erstwhile garrison in an attempt to intimidate the approaching Swiss army. His action proved to be a spectacular miscalculation; far from being cowed, the Swiss were motivated by a desire for revenge, and became even more homicidally inclined than usual. The ensuing battle saw the rout of the Burgundians.

IMPERIAL GERMAN ARMY
(1310–1485)

Unit type	Number per army
Nobles (Mounted Knights, heavy armour, Elite)	2–3
Mercenaries (Mounted Knights, heavy armour, Average)	1–3
Militia Infantry (Medieval Infantry, light armour, Levy)	1–3
Militia Archers (Heavy Archers (crossbow), light armour, Levy)	1–2

Thanks to the prolonged struggle for control of Italy between the Papacy and Emperor Frederick II (r. 1220–50), resulting in a Papal victory, the Holy Roman Empire was somewhat weakened. Indeed, the Emperors found themselves wielding little authority, even over the German imperial heartlands. Accordingly, the Holy Roman Empire was rather weak, relying as it did upon a small core of nobles, and having an indifferent infantry element. It has been included here primarily as an opponent for the Swiss and Hussite armies (although given the central location of Germany within Europe, it makes a good potential adversary for almost any force covered in this chapter).

SPECIAL RULE

1) *Later armies* (1420–1485). For armies from this period, add the following troops to the list:

Unit type	Number per army
Handgunners (Heavy Archers (handgun), medium armour, Average)	1–2
Artillery	0–1
Pikemen (Heavy Infantry, light armour, Average)	0–2

SUGGESTED DEPLOYMENT

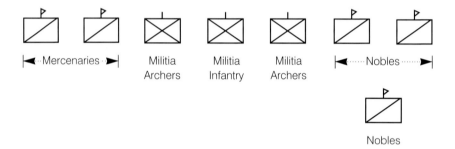

This early Imperial army has concentrated its nobles on the right flank, with one unit placed in reserve as a reinforcement. The mercenaries provide some attacking potential on the left, while the archers can assail the enemy lines with crossbow fire.

CREATING THE ARMY IN MINIATURE

Although specific figures are not always easy to track down, most manufacturers produce ideal generic types, both in metal and in plastic. Those who game in the latter medium can comfortably purchase Hundred Years War French or English figures, Teutonic knights or even crusaders; all will give a reasonable match.

ALTERNATIVE ARMIES

As has just been implied, Imperial German troops can easily serve in other Western European armies.

SECONDARY SOURCES

Heath, Ian. *Armies of the Middle Ages, Volume 1*, Wargames Research Group, 1984

Waley, Daniel and Denley, Peter. *Later Medieval Europe*, Longman, 2001

Wise, Terence. *Medieval European Armies*, Osprey, 1975

VOLTAIRE'S VERDICT

The French eighteenth-century writer Voltaire evidently regarded the Holy Roman Empire as an oxymoron, describing it as being 'neither Holy, Roman, nor an Empire'. Although this was a little harsh (the Imperial regime's piety was not in any doubt), the late Medieval Empire was unquestionably an enfeebled rump that had little control over Germany, and held even less sway over Europe as a whole.

ITALIAN CONDOTTIERI ARMY
(1320–1485)

Unit type	Number per army
Condottieri Lancers (Mounted Knights, heavy armour, Average)	2–6
Militia (Medieval Infantry, medium armour, Levy)	1–2
Crossbowmen (Heavy Archers (crossbow), light armour, Levy)	1–3
Mounted Crossbowmen (Light Cavalry (crossbow), light armour, Average)	0–2

Warfare in Italy became the preserve of mercenary specialists, who became known as condottieri. They acquired a reputation for great tactical finesse (see special rule no. 3), but were also famous for spurning infantry and relying upon traditional Mounted Knights. Since this decision did not seem to have impaired their efficiency, the wargamer would be advised to follow their example.

SPECIAL RULES

1) *Early armies* (1320–1400). English longbowmen formed an important part of some condottieri forces at this time. Add the following items to the army list:

Unit type	Number per army
English Archers (Heavy Archers (longbow), medium armour, Elite)	0–2
English Men-at-Arms (Foot Knights, extra-heavy armour, Elite)	0–2

2) *Later armies* (1400–85). Fifteenth-century Italian forces often used firearms, and also developed a specialist body of infantry swordsmen. Apply the following rules:

a) Some or all units of crossbowmen may be replaced by the following, if the wargamer desires:

Handgunners (Heavy Archers (handgun), medium armour, Levy)

b) Add the following to the army list:

Unit type	Number per army
Swordsmen (Warband, medium armour, Levy)	0–2
Artillery	0–2

3) *Tactical finesse*. 1–3 units (roll a die and halve the result, rounding up any fractions) may benefit from their general's tactical skills. Roll another die to determine which attribute applies.

Die Roll	Effect
1–3	Entrenchments (infantry units only). All units defending these count as having extra-heavy armour. However, this benefit does not apply against attacking swordsmen (who were trained to assault entrenchments).
3–4	Redeploy (cavalry units only). Units may be repositioned after the opponent has deployed his or her army.
5–6	Outflank (cavalry units only). Units may be removed from the battlefield, and may re-enter on any table edge from the second turn onwards.

SUGGESTED DEPLOYMENT

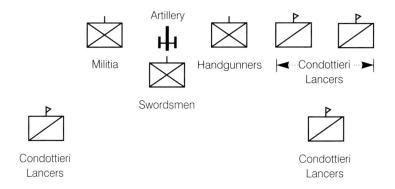

This later army has concentrated the strike-force on the right flank, with the Artillery and handgunners providing some missile support. The left flank is protected by the remaining unit of lancers; while the swordsmen are poised to reinforce the infantry, or sally forth and assault any enemy entrenchments.

CREATING THE ARMY IN MINIATURE

As with the Imperial German army, suitable generic types can be obtained in metal and in plastic.

ALTERNATIVE ARMIES

Units from a Condottieri force may serve in most other Western European armies.

PRIMARY SOURCE

Machiavelli, Niccolo (1514). *The Prince* (tr. George Bull), Penguin, 1981

SECONDARY SOURCES

Heath, Ian. *Armies of the Middle Ages, Volume 1*, Wargames Research Group, 1982

Nicolle, David. *Italian Medieval Armies: 1300–1500*, Osprey, 1983

Oman, Sir Charles. *A History of the Art of War in the Middle Ages, Volume 2: 1278–1485*, Greenhill, 1998 (originally 1924)

THE DANGERS OF MERCENARIES

Mercenaries . . . are useless and dangerous. If a prince bases the defence of his state on mercenaries he will never achieve stability or security. For mercenaries are disunited, thirsty for power, undisciplined, and disloyal; they are brave among their friends and cowards before the enemy. . . . They are only too ready to serve in your army when you are not at war; but when war comes they either desert or disperse.

Machiavelli, Niccolo (1514), *The Prince* (tr. George Bull), Penguin, 1981, pp. 77–8.

This decidedly uncharitable view of the condottieri has become somewhat entrenched among historians. Machiavelli's opinions were undoubtedly affected by his advocacy of a citizen militia, and by the failure of the condottieri to repel the French and Spanish invaders during the Italian Wars (1494–1525). In reality the mercenaries were effective soldiers.

THE ENGLISH CONDOTTIERE

One of the most effective of the fourteenth-century condottieri was the Englishman Sir John Hawkwood. His White Company of men-at-arms and longbowmen acquired an almost legendary reputation.

HUNDRED YEARS WAR FRENCH ARMY
(1330–1455)

Unit type	Number per army
Mounted Men-at-Arms (Mounted Knights, heavy armour, Elite)	1–2
Dismounted Men-at-Arms (Foot Knights, extra-heavy armour, Elite)	2–4
Crossbowmen (Heavy Archers (crossbow), light armour, Average)	1–2
Commoners (Medieval Infantry, medium armour, Levy)	2–4

The French army was in many ways a model European force, relying as it did upon the power of its knights. However, encounters with the English led to the realisation that mounted chivalry could come unstuck against the longbow. Accordingly, most knights operated on foot after the Battle of Crécy (1346); but it still took the French a very long time to find a winning formula. The real difficulty stemmed from lack of effective missile support, given that the French crossbowmen were always outnumbered by the English archers. However, the French were eventually able to win; this was due to a considerable increase in the competence of its commoner infantry, and the introduction of artillery on the battlefield.

SPECIAL RULES

1) *Early armies* (1330–55). These forces were noted for fielding large numbers of rather impetuous mounted nobles. Apply the following rules:

   a) Dismounted men-at-arms may not be deployed.
   b) The number of mounted men-at-arms units is increased to 3–5.
   c) If a unit of mounted men-at-arms is positioned behind a unit of commoners or crossbowmen, it must test to see if it retains its discipline. Roll a die for each unit every turn: on a roll of 1–2, it refuses to accept the indignity of being deployed behind its social inferiors, and advances its full move distance. It must ride through its unfortunate compatriots if necessary; the mounted men-at-arms inflict casualties at a level of one die per base engaged.

2) *Peasant horde*. Units of commoners may be replaced by Peasants if desired:

   a) Peasants are classified as follows:

   Peasants (Peasants, light armour, Levy)

    b)   Units comprise 8 bases: they deploy in 2 ranks.

    c)   Every time a morale test is failed, the Peasants remove 2 bases.

3)   *Later armies* (1435–55). The existing list is modified as follows:

    a)   Commoners are upgraded to Average morale.

    b)   The Peasants may not be fielded.

    c)   1–2 units of Artillery must be deployed.

SUGGESTED DEPLOYMENT

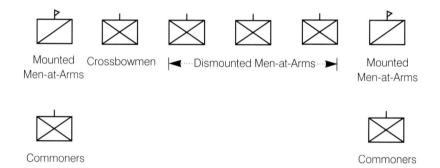

Mounted Men-at-Arms   Crossbowmen   ◄····Dismounted Men-at-Arms····►   Mounted Men-at-Arms

Commoners   Commoners

Although the crossbowmen provide some support for the mounted men-at-arms on the left flank, the army is largely dependent upon the dismounted men-at-arms. If these can reach the enemy intact, they can wreck havoc. Their assault can be assisted by the mounted men-at-arms, who are not only assigned to protect the army's flanks, but can also assail the enemy lines (the commoners can provide some useful support to any cavalry attack).

CREATING THE ARMY IN MINIATURE

A wide range of figures is available both in metal and plastic (even in 54mm/1:32 scale).

ALTERNATIVE ARMIES

Since the French represented the model for many Western European armies, Condottiere and Imperial German forces may quite legitimately deploy French troops. The dismounted men-at-arms may also serve in English armies.

SOURCES

The book-list for the Hundred Years War English army also applies to the French army of this period.

STANDING AND FIGHTING

> But it must be said that the Battle of Poitiers was much better than Crécy. . . .
> [The King of France] had shown his determination never to retreat when he
> commanded his men to fight on foot and, having made them dismount, he did
> the same and stood in the forefront of them with a battle-axe in his hands.
>
> Froissart, Jean (1380–1410), *Chronicles* (tr. Geoffrey Brereton), Penguin,
> 1978, p. 138.

Following the shambolic display of the French mounted chivalry at the Battle of
Crécy (1346), King Jean II of France adopted a dismounted approach at Poitiers
(1356). Although the French still lost, their evident determination to engage in a
prolonged fight went a long way towards restoring their confidence. It also
demonstrated the increased effectiveness of infantry compared to cavalry.

THE MAID OF ORLÉANS

According to legend, the inspirational presence of the teenage Joan of Arc saved
France in her darkest hour. The legend is absolutely true. Joan's proclamation of
the need for an aggressive strategy saved Orléans and restored French morale.
Although she was eventually captured and executed by the English (following a
trial of notably dubious legality), Joan of Arc remains the quintessential French
heroine to this day.

OTTOMAN TURK ARMY
(1340–1485)

Unit type	Number per army
Sipahis (Heavy Cavalry (bow), medium armour, Elite)	1–4
Akinjis (Light Cavalry (bow), light armour, Levy)	1–4
Janissaries (Warband (bow), light armour, Fanatic)	1–2
Azabs (Light Infantry (bow), light armour, Levy)	2–4

The Turks have an intriguing combination of Elite troops and unenthusiastic Levy.
Their original commanders tended to use inferior men as cannon fodder,
absorbing the enemy assault before launching a counter-attack with the sipahis
and janissaries. Since this invariably proved victorious, the wargamer could do a
lot worse than follow the historical approach. Note that the army is liberally
provided with field fortifications, to protect its infantry (see special rules nos 2 and
3). For this reason, any Ottoman wargamer worth his or her salt would be well
advised to provoke an enemy attack.

SPECIAL RULES

1) *Sipahis.* These enjoy the same benefits as Saracen guards and cavalry (see Saracen army special rule no. 1 for details).
2) *Stakes.* Azab units were protected by stakes. These have exactly the same effect as those used by English archers (see Hundred Years War English army special rule no. 1 for details).
3) *Entrenchments.* The janissary units were protected by sophisticated field entrenchments. These have all the advantages of stakes, and also have the following qualities:

    a)   Defending units are treated as having extra-heavy armour.
    b)   Attacking units only ever roll one die per remaining base.

4) *Later armies* (1420–85). Modify the existing list as follows:

    a)   One unit of janissaries may be equipped with handguns.
    b)   1–3 Artillery units are fielded.

SUGGESTED DEPLOYMENT

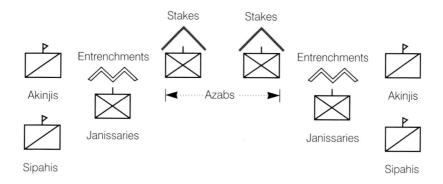

This wargamer has adopted the historical Ottoman tactic of defence in depth. The Akinjis have the crucial task of provoking an enemy assault upon the Ottoman entrenchments. By the time the opponents reach the janissaries and sipahis, they will be badly affected by missilry. Should the enemy not be so obliging as to attack, a combination of janissaries and sipahis will be forced to assault the enemy lines, with Akinjis and Azabs providing support from their archery.

CREATING THE ARMY IN MINIATURE

Ottoman forces are readily available in all metal scales. A plastic army can be created by using the janissaries produced by Orion, together with the Saracens made by Italeri.

ALTERNATIVE ARMIES

Sipahis, Akinjis and Azabs can frequently serve in other Islamic armies, from the days of the Arab conquests to the nineteenth century.

SECONDARY SOURCES

Bianchi, John. *Vlad the Impaler*, Warhammer Historical Wargames, 2006

Goodwin, Godfrey. *The Janissaries*, Saqi, 1997

Heath, Ian. *Armies of the Middle Ages, Volume 2*, Wargames Research Group, 1984

Kinross, Lord. *The Ottoman Centuries*, Morrow, 1977

Nicolle, David. *Armies of the Ottoman Turks, 1300–1774*, Osprey, 1983

Oman, Sir Charles. *A History of the Art of War in the Middle Ages, Volume 2: 1278–1485*, Greenhill, 1998 (originally 1924)

ABSTINENCE MAKES THE ARMY STRONGER

The Islamic injunction against alcohol tended to make Ottoman army camps well-ordered and hygienic. This resulted in an absence of disease, giving the Turks a huge advantage over their somewhat disorderly Christian foes.

HUNGARIAN ARMY
(1350–1485)

Unit type	Number per army
Nobles (Mounted Knights, heavy armour, Elite)	1–2
Szekelers (Light Cavalry (bow), light armour, Elite)	1–3
Hussars (Light Cavalry (bow), light armour, Average)	2–4
Skirmishers (Light Infantry (bow), light armour, Levy)	0–3

The Hungarians possessed one of the few European armies that could fight a truly mobile battle. The szekelers and hussars frequently wore down the enemy with archery, before the nobles launched a decisive charge. The wargamer would be advised to follow a similar approach; those who prefer a more defensive style can select a later Hungarian army (see special rule no. 3), which adopted the Wagon Forts first used by the Hussites.

SPECIAL RULES

1) *Szekelers*. These light horsemen were equipped with lances, and could prove very effective in a mêlée. Accordingly, szekelers roll one extra die per base engaged in the first round of any hand-to-hand combat.

2) *Crusaders*. Western Europeans occasionally allied themselves to the Hungarian army, in attempts to repel the Ottomans (most notably in the disastrous Nicopolis campaign of 1396). To reflect such armies, apply the following rules:

   a)   Add the following item to the army list:

Unit type	Number per army
Crusaders (Mounted Knights, heavy armour, Fanatic)	1–2

   b)   Crusader units are impetuous. They must move their full distance towards an enemy unit each turn, and attempt to engage in hand-to-hand combat if possible.

3) *Later armies* (1440–85). The Hungarians had developed reliable infantry by the mid-fifteenth century. To field such an army, apply these rules:

   a)   Add the following items to the army list:

Unit type	Number per army
Handgunners (Heavy Archers (handgun), medium armour, Average)	1–2
Armati (Medieval Infantry, medium armour, Average)	0–2

   b)   *Wagon forts*. The handgunner units may be placed in war wagons. The following rules apply for these forts:

   i)   The handgunners are regarded as having extra-heavy armour.
   ii)   The handgunners roll an additional die for every base engaged, in the first round of any hand-to-hand combat.
   iii)   Enemy units take an entire turn to cross the wagon barrier.
   iv)   Enemy units only ever roll one die per base engaged in hand-to-hand combat, with the defenders of a Wagon Fort.
   v)   Enemy cavalry units must test morale, for every turn they engage in hand-to-hand combat with a Wagon Fort.
   vi)   If the handgunners ever leave the Wagon Fort, they may never return.

vii) The wagons may move 6cm per turn until their occupants fire for the first time, from which moment they may not move (they are assumed to have formed a circle, and chained themselves together).

SUGGESTED DEPLOYMENT

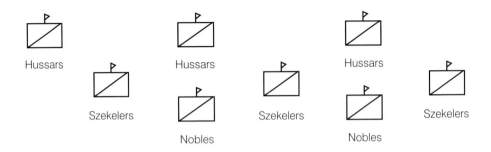

The deployment in depth allows for tactical flexibility. A delaying approach can be adopted, with the hussars falling back behind the szekelers after preliminary skirmishing. Alternatively, the szekelers can provide direct support to the hussars, in a bid to engulf the enemy with archery. Either way, the nobles are placed in reserve to deliver the *coup de grâce*.

CREATING THE ARMY IN MINIATURE
The Hungarians are not one of the more popular wargames armies, although some metal manufacturers do supply comprehensive ranges. The same cannot be said of plastic figure companies.

ALTERNATIVE ARMIES
The Hungarian nobles resemble other European knights, and may be fielded in other armies accordingly. The remaining units wore rather distinctive attire, and cannot serve in other forces.

SECONDARY SOURCES
Bianchi, John. *Vlad the Impaler*, Warhammer Historical Wargames, 2006
Heath, Ian. *Armies of the Middle Ages, Volume 2*, Wargames Research Group, 1984
Oman, Sir Charles. *A History of the Art of War in the Middle Ages, Volume 2: 1278–1485*, Greenhill, 1998 (originally 1924)

THE HUNGARIAN ROCK
We regard the heavy infantry as an immovable wall that, if necessary, would fight and die to the last man where they stood. When the opportunity presents itself

the light infantry make forays, but, if their attack loses its impetus or if they are hard-pressed, they fall back behind the heavy infantry.

King Matthias Corvinus (1480), quoted in Heath, Ian, *Armies of the Middle Ages, Volume 2*. Wargames Research Group, 1984, p. 80.

King Matthias realised that the advent of reliable infantry allowed for effective defensive tactics. It is also interesting to note that, for all their reliance upon cavalry, the Hungarians saw nothing dishonourable in letting the enemy attack them.

RASH ALLIES

Fanatical determination notwithstanding, the crusaders were often a hindrance rather than a help. This was particularly evident during the Battle of Nicopolis (1396). Here, the crusaders refused to let the hussars and szekelers undermine the Turks with preliminary skirmishing, preferring instead to launch a headlong charge. The battle ended in a catastrophic crusader defeat.

HUSSITE ARMY
(1415–40)

Unit type	Number per army
Skirmishers (Heavy Archers (Crossbow or Handgun), light armour, Elite)	1–3
Artillery	1–3
Flailmen (Medieval Infantry, light armour, Elite)	2–4
Gentry (Heavy Cavalry, light armour, Elite)	0–2

The Hussites took their name from Jan Hus, a Bohemian religious reformer who was appalled at the moral laxity of the Catholic Church. Such protests against the established order had obvious revolutionary implications, and Hus was duly burned at the stake in 1415 (having rather ill-advisedly accepted a solemn pledge of safe-conduct from King Sigismund of Hungary, to what Hus thought would be a theological debate; this was not the first or last occasion on which a Christian secular ruler's word of honour proved somewhat less than binding). However, Hus' followers promptly took to arms, and were moreover led by a military genius in the person of Jan Zizka. Under his leadership, the Hussites pioneered the use of the Wagon Fort which, bristling as it was with Artillery and skirmishers, wrought havoc among the Hussites' Imperial German foes. Sadly for the Hussites, the death of Zizka in 1424, combined with theological divisions, served to weaken their resistance and result in their neutralisation (although Hussite ideas survived long enough to form a branch of the Protestant Reformation of the sixteenth century).

SPECIAL RULES

1) *Skirmisher weapons.* Skirmisher units are equipped with either crossbows or handguns (at least one unit must choose crossbows).
2) *Wagon Forts.* Skirmisher and Artillery units are deployed in Wagon Forts (each fort must contain one unit of each troop type). Apply the following rules:

    a)   See Hungarian special rule no. 3b. Rules (i)–(vii) all apply.
    b)   Artillery units in a Wagon Fort may never be engaged in hand-to-hand combat until the accompanying skirmisher unit is eliminated.

SUGGESTED DEPLOYMENT

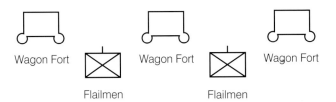

Wagon Fort   Flailmen   Wagon Fort   Flailmen   Wagon Fort

This wargamer is relying almost entirely upon the power of the Wagon Fort. One of the flanking forts should have skirmishers equipped with crossbows (whose long range provides an effective means of sabotaging an enemy outflanking move), with the other two using handguns (whose effect upon morale can wreak havoc). The flailmen are positioned in reserve, ready to attack any units surviving the massed Artillery, handgun and crossbow fire.

CREATING THE ARMY IN MINIATURE
As always, coverage in metal is adequate. There are not yet any suitable plastic miniatures available.

ALTERNATIVE ARMIES
Hussite troops can serve as Peasants in the Hundred Years War French army (or any other force using Peasant levies). The Wagon Forts may be used by the Hungarian army.

SECONDARY SOURCES

Heath, Ian. *Armies of the Middle Ages, Volume 2*, Wargames Research Group, 1984

Oman, Sir Charles. *A History of the Art of War in the Middle Ages, Volume 2: 1278–1485*, Greenhill, 1998 (originally 1924)

Turnbull, Stephen. *The Hussite Wars 1419–36*, Osprey, 2004

THE WAGON TRAP

[The Wagon Forts] become a hopeless labyrinth for the enemy, from which he could find no exit and in which he was caught as in a net. When the enemies were broken up, cut off and isolated in this manner, the foot troops easily completed their full defeat with their swords and flails, or the enemy was overcome by the marksmen standing on their wagons. Zizka's army was like a many headed-monster which unexpectedly and quickly seizes its prey, squeezes it to death and swallows up its pieces.

Aeneas Silvanus Piccolomini (later Pope Pius II), quoted in Turnbull, Stephen, *The Hussite Wars 1419–36*, Osprey, 2004, pp. 39–40.

Piccolomini's account shows how the Hussite wagons could easily ensnare any attacking army, leaving it hopelessly disordered.

A UNIQUE COMMANDER

Jan Zizka was blind in one eye from an early age. In 1521 he lost his other eye on the battlefield. Incredibly, total blindness had absolutely no effect upon his leadership; he remained the most formidable European general of his time.

WARS OF THE ROSES ENGLISH ARMY
(1455–85)

Unit type	Number per army
Men-at-Arms (Foot Knights, extra-heavy armour, Elite)	1–2
Archers (Heavy Archers (Longbow), light armour, Average)	3–5
Billmen (Medieval Infantry, medium armour, Average)	2–4
Currours (Heavy Cavalry, light armour, Average)	0–1
Artillery	0–1
Mercenaries (see special rule no. 2)	0–2

The stability of fifteenth-century England was gravely undermined by King Henry VI (who reigned from 1422 until 1461), who ascended to the throne as an infant.

Although he was considered old enough to rule by himself in 1437, he never showed any interest in government; his sole interests lay in religion and the planning of educational foundations (which included Eton College). This resulted in a savage power struggle between the competing factions of Lancaster and York, in which the latter proved victorious until Henry Tudor's army defeated and killed Richard III at the Battle of Bosworth (1485). Militarily, the conflict was actually rather uninteresting; old-style armies of the Hundred Years War pattern tended to cancel each other out, with most battles taking the form of longbow duels followed by a savage mêlée. The latter bore more resemblance to a rugby scrum than a planned engagement. The encounters only really became interesting when political intrigue provided scope for treachery on the battlefield (see special rule no. 3).

SPECIAL RULES

1) *Stakes*. See Hundred Years War English army special rule no. 1 for details.
2) *Mercenaries*. Both sides may field mercenary units if desired. Although two units may be chosen, only one of each type may be selected.

    a) *Lancastrian mercenaries*. The House of Lancaster may select from the following:

Irish Bonnachts (Warband, light armour, Average)
Irish Kern (Light Infantry (javelin), light armour, Average)

    b) *Yorkist mercenaries*. The House of York may choose one or both of the units listed below:

Burgundian Pikemen (Heavy Infantry, light armour, Average).
Burgundian Handgunners (Heavy Archers (handgun), medium armour, Average).

3) *Political intrigue*. Rapid shifts in allegiance could have a decisive effect on the battlefield. Its possibility is taken account of as follows:

    a) Both sides roll a die. If one rolls a score of two or more higher than his or her opponent, the victorious player follows the procedures outlined below (if the scores are within one point of each other, then political intrigue does not occur).

    b) The victorious player rolls another die and applies the result listed below:

Die Roll Effect

1–2	No effect. Political intrigue does not bear fruit.
3–4	Extra faction. Another noble family joins in on the victorious player's side. 1–3 eliminated units (roll a die and halve the result) re-enter the battle on the friendly base line at any time. If eliminated a second time, they are removed permanently.
5–6	Treachery. One of the enemy nobles has been successfully bribed. 1–3 units can be affected: whenever the successful intriguer moves a unit within charge distance he or she rolls a die. On a roll of 4–6 the enemy unit deserts: it is now treated as a friendly unit and may move and fight accordingly.

4) *Yorkist pretenders*. Henry VII had to deal with Yorkist conspiracies during the first few years of his reign, which occasionally led to military conflict (most notably at the Battle of Stoke in 1487). The Pretender armies were slightly different from the norm, in that their lack of widespread English support led to the deployment of Irish and German mercenaries (the latter of whom have the same fighting classification as the Burgundians covered in special rule no. 2b). Accordingly, a Yorkist Pretender army uses the following roster (all troop classifications are identical to the main list):

Unit type	*Number per army*
Men-at-Arms	0–1
Archers	1–2
Billmen	1–2
Currours	0–1
Artillery	0–1
Mercenaries (see rule (a) below)	2–4

a) *Mercenaries*. All types from special rule no. 2 may be chosen (both Lancastrian and Yorkist). However, only one of each type can be selected.

SUGGESTED DEPLOYMENT

Any Wars of the Roses army has a very simple tactical plan. The archers must assail the enemy lines with bowfire, and the close combat specialists provide support as necessary. Note how the billmen are covering the flanks of the men-at-arms, so that these deadly troops are protected from an enemy pincer movement.

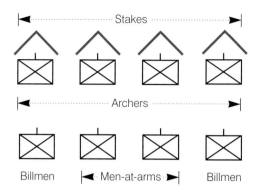

Stakes

Archers

Billmen   Men-at-arms   Billmen

CREATING THE ARMY IN MINIATURE

Metal manufacturers have extensive ranges of suitable figures. Plastic miniatures covering the Wars of the Roses are not available, but Hundred Years War figures can suffice for men-at-arms, archers and billmen. Mercenaries are not easily found, but the Orion landsknechts can masquerade as Burgundian pikemen and handgunners (and do provide an exact match for the Yorkist Pretender army's German troops).

ALTERNATIVE ARMIES

Most troops may serve in a Hundred Years War army; the men-at-arms can operate as Foot Knights in most medieval forces.

SECONDARY SOURCES

Haigh, Philip A. *The Military Campaigns of the Wars of the Roses*, Sutton, 1995
Heath, Ian. *Armies of the Middle Ages, Volume 1*, Wargames Research Group, 1982
Ross, Charles. *The Wars of the Roses*, Thames and Hudson, 1976
Seymour, William. *Battles in Britain*, Wordsworth, 1977
Wise, Terence. *The Wars of the Roses*, Osprey, 1983

AN ENLIGHTENED APPROACH

It is the custom of the English that, once they have gained a battle, they do no more killing, especially killing of common people; for each side seeks to please the commons. . . . King Edward [IV] told me that in all the battles he had won, the moment he came to victory he mounted a horse and shouted that the commons were to be spared and the nobles slain. And of the latter, few or none escaped.

Phillipe de Commynes, quoted in Wise, Terence, *The Wars of the Roses*, Osprey, 1983, p. 5.

The tendency to avoid plundering civilians, and to butcher enemy nobles, marked a reversal of contemporary European practice. Continental wars saw the people and countryside ravaged, and enemy knights taken prisoner for a subsequent ransom. However, a civil war had radically different dynamics; enemy nobles were a mortal threat, and had to be slaughtered; whereas the resources of the countryside and the loyalty of the general population were vital if one was to gain political power.

THE POWER OF THE PEN

Following Henry Tudor's victory at Bosworth, his regime had to legitimise itself by denigrating the new king's predecessor. Accordingly, the Tudors launched a vitriolic propaganda campaign against Richard III, the most notable manifestation of which was Shakespeare's famous play. Richard's reputation has never really recovered, although there is great debate over whether he was responsible for many of the foul deeds attributed to him (most notably the murder of his nephews in the Tower of London).

BURGUNDIAN ARMY
(1470–80)

Unit type	Number per army
Gendarmes (Mounted Knights, heavy armour, Elite)	1–3
Coustilliers (Heavy Cavalry, light armour, Average)	0–2
Archers (Heavy Archers (Longbow), light armour, Average)	1–3
Pikemen (Medieval Infantry, medium armour, Average)	1–3
Shot (see special rule no. 1)	1–3
Artillery	1–3

Duke Charles the Bold of Burgundy took the view that his existing army needed reform, and published a series of ordinances to that effect. The result was probably the first truly organised regular army in Medieval Europe. It offers the wargamer great potential, in that an effective combined-arms force can be deployed if desired (the options also allow armies with concentrations of either cavalry, infantry or artillery).

SPECIAL RULES

1)   *Shot*. Either or both of the following options can be selected for these units:

   Crossbowmen (Heavy Archers (crossbow), light armour, Average)
   Handgunners (Heavy Archers (handgun), medium armour, Average)

2) *Stakes.* Archers may deploy stakes. See the Hundred Years War English army special rule no. 1 for details.
3) *Mounted archers* (optional rule). The archers rode horses to the battlefield, but dismounted to fight. To simulate this, the Burgundian player may choose to do either of the following on the first turn of the game:

   a) Archers may move 16cm and emplace their stakes.
   b) Archers may move 8cm, emplace their stakes, and fire.

4) *Pikemen* (optional rule). I have classified pikemen as Medieval Infantry to reflect their poor performance against the Swiss. If the wargamer believes this is rather harsh, pikemen may be reclassified as Heavy Infantry.
5) *Infantry morale* (optional rule). Some historians believe that the Burgundian failure against the Swiss was due to the spinelessness of the former, rather than the excellence of the latter. If the wargamer is in a similarly uncharitable mood, pikemen and shot are reclassified as having Levy morale. If this option is exercised, then pikemen must remain as Medieval Infantry (special rule no. 4 may not be used).

SUGGESTED DEPLOYMENT

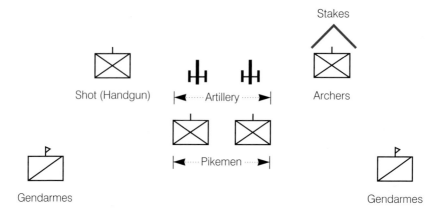

This general has placed great emphasis upon missile units, in the hope that the Artillery can wreak execution upon the enemy centre; the pikemen are then deployed to take advantage. The gendarmes are placed in reserve on the flanks, either to defend the centre against enemy attack; or to take advantage of any mayhem inflicted by Burgundian missilry, and support any attack launched by the pikemen.

CREATING THE ARMY IN MINIATURE

The multiplicity of specialised troop types means that a Burgundian force can only adequately be created using the ranges provided (in all scales), by metal figure manufactures.

ALTERNATIVE ARMIES

Owing to their distinctive blue and white livery, Burgundian figures should not really serve in other armies.

SECONDARY SOURCES

Heath, Ian. *Armies of the Middle Ages, Volume 1*, Wargames Research Group, 1982

Michael, Nicholas. *Armies of Medieval Burgundy 1364–1477*, Osprey, 1983

Oman, Sir Charles. *A History of the Art of War in the Middle Ages, Volume 2: 1278–1485*, Greenhill, 1998 (originally 1924)

Waley, Daniel and Denley, Peter. *Later Medieval Europe*, Longman, 2001

THE ARMY IN CAMP

It was the most splendid sight in the world, and so well organised. . . . It looked like a great city, with rows of tents forming long streets and crossroads, large squares for assemblies, and markets. . . . The walls were made from wagons so well fortified and equipped and full of armed defenders that no-one would have dared come near.

The chronicler Chastellain, quoted in Michael, Nicholas, *Armies of Medieval Burgundy 1364–1477*, Osprey, 1983, pp. 21–2.

This description of the Burgundian camp at Eclusier Vaux in 1468, shows just how formidable their logistical operation was. It graphically demonstrates the potential of the Burgundian army.

WHAT'S IN A NAME?

Burgundy's last duke is commonly known as Charles the Bold. However, given that he chose to pick a fight with the Swiss (notoriously the deadliest army in Europe), the alternative sobriquet of Charles the Rash is probably more appropriate – given that his choice of enemy led to the loss of his life, and the disintegration of his duchy.

Chapter 20

Medieval Battle Report

Although the Medieval period saw many interesting battles, the one that has most resonance for English-speaking readers is the Battle of Agincourt (1415), the re-enactment of which is covered below. However, it should always be remembered that the English may have won many battles, but they lost the Hundred Years War.

THE BATTLE IN HISTORY

The campaign of 1415 saw its origins in the desire of the young English King, Henry V, to assert his authority and in so doing revive his family's claim to the French throne. However, the English army only set sail for France in August, and the siege of Harfleur in Normandy was not brought to a successful conclusion until 23 September. This allowed very little time for campaigning before winter would have brought the fighting season to a close. Consequently, Henry decided upon a march from Harfleur to Calais, devastating the countryside as he went. This approach, known as a chevauchée, was common English practice during the Hundred Years War; its object was to give the French a choice of seeing their countryside despoiled and thereby lose prestige by not doing anything to stop it, or to fight a battle with the English and risk a massive defeat. However, the French advance guard under Constable d'Albret held up the English passage over the River Somme. By the time Henry's army eventually crossed, a sizeable French host had gathered outside the village of Agincourt, where the outnumbered English were forced to give battle. Henry's army of approximately 6,000 faced a French force whose strength has been hotly debated from the fifteenth century until today, but whose total was in the order of 25,000 men.

However, all was not lost. Henry had ordered a rapid advance to a position between two woods which could not be outflanked, which to a large extent negated the French numerical superiority. The English army deployed according to its traditional and battle-winning formula, with bodies of longbowmen interspersed with dismounted men-at-arms. The combination of deadly archery and steadfast knights was calculated to cause extreme discomfort to any foe; as was usual, the archers emplaced stakes to their front. These were designed to greatly impede the movement of any attacking troops, channelling them away from the archers and towards the men-at-arms.

As for the French, their front line comprised the flower of chivalry, with bodies of mounted knights on the flanks, and a majority deployed on foot in the centre. More dismounted men-at-arms were placed in a second line. Some crossbowmen were positioned behind the cavalry, and a large contingent of commoners placed in reserve. Despite the fact that the movement of this host was somewhat circumscribed by the woods that flanked the English lines, and was slowed further by the muddy condition of the battlefield, they had every reason to be confident. They planned to launch a cavalry attack on the English archers on the flanks, before launching the men-at-arms, supported by crossbow fire, to deliver the *coup de grâce* on the English centre. Unfortunately for the French, this reasonable plan was sabotaged by a less than effective chain of command. For the architects of the plan, Marshal Boucicault and Constable d'Albret, may have had much proven military experience but were outranked by the brave, if hopelessly incompetent, Dukes of Orleans, Bourbon and Alençon. For these three men honour was far more important than tactical brilliance, and their chief objective was to achieve personal glory by reaching the English line first. Accordingly, deployment of the French host was disorderly in the extreme. Most of the French nobles demanded to be in the front rank of the dismounted men-at-arms, who were to be given the role of assaulting their English equivalents. It is interesting to note that this task had far more prestige than that of the mounted knights, who were given the job of attacking the English archers: fighting on horseback per se was less important than confronting enemy chivalry, even if that meant moving on foot.

All this was to have a detrimental effect upon the cavalry assault, since the reduced numbers meant that the English longbowmen were able to deal with most of their assailants. However, some cavalrymen still reached their English lines, archery notwithstanding; the stake barrier managed to slow the advance of this gallant minority enough to ensure that the archers were able to win the mêlée that ensued.

The failure of the French cavalry attack was to have some distinctly unfortunate consequences, when the horsemen retreated in great disorder. For in trying to reach the safety of their rear, many horsemen must have attempted to pass through their own lines. This must have had the effect of delaying the advance of the French centre, thereby exposing the dismounted men-at-arms to a nagging fire from the longbows as they lumbered through the mud towards their English counterparts. However, it is most likely that the routing French mounted men-at-arms headed to the rear by means of the line of least resistance, which would have been on the French flanks, passing around and through their own crossbowmen.

All this served further to unravel what remained of the French plan. For the rout of the French horse delayed the advance of the crossbowmen, which meant that the men-at-arms attacked with very limited missile support.

The failure of the French cavalry charge did not simply have a detrimental effect upon their crossbowmen's effectiveness. For the English longbowmen on the flanks could add their fire to that of their compatriots in the centre between the three bodies of dismounted English men-at-arms. As a consequence of the close-range archery and doubtless the disruptive effect of the stakes (which would have broken up the formation of the advancing French as they would have engaged the archers) the men-at-arms engaged their English counterparts. This was not only because of the glory attached to fighting fellow nobles, but also because capturing the English battle standards in the midst of the three bodies of English men-at-arms would most likely have led to the demoralisation and consequent rout of Henry V's army.

Accordingly, the French dismounted chivalry assaulted their English counterparts, and were able to drive them backwards. Notwithstanding their rather chaotic advance, the French plan appeared to be reaping dividends.

This was the crisis point of the battle. The French vanguard had penetrated the English lines, albeit that they seem to have been impeded by the second line which, with more valour than sense, supported their attack. The effect of this was to press the French men-at-arms together to such an extent that using their weapons effectively proved very difficult. Moreover, the English longbowmen, who were now able to engage the flanks of the enemy vanguard who had ignored them to attack Henry's men-at-arms, played a decisive part in the battle.

In normal circumstances, there was no way that archers could have enjoyed any success against armoured nobility. Needless to say, the situation at Agincourt was not normal. Not only were the French men-at-arms outflanked, but their being engaged in prolonged close combat had caused them to lose both their impetus and their cohesion. In such a mêlée the English archers, unimpaired by a suffocating close-order formation, were able to pass through their own stakes with deadly effect. Moreover, many were equipped with heavy war hammers whose concussive effect could be far greater than a sword when directed against a man in full armour.

The flank assault from the longbowmen was enough to rout the French men-at-arms. However, the French rearguard, composed of three bodies of horse, was still intact and not in too much disorder, since its routing compatriots could pass through the gaps between the units. Moreover, there was a simultaneous attack on the English baggage camp to the rear of Henry V's lines by armed peasant militia led by a local squire, Isembart of Agincourt. This potential twin thrust led to Henry's infamous order to kill the French noble prisoners (of whom many in fact survived unharmed to be ransomed later). However, the French rearguard, composed as we have seen of largely inferior men, retreated without any significant engagement. The battle was over, and it was a decisive English victory; casualty estimates vary wildly, but the most plausible indicate that the English lost 100 dead, whereas the French had 6,000 killed and 1,000 more taken prisoner.

RECREATING THE BATTLEFIELD

With the field of Agincourt consisting of a flat plain bordered by woods, this was a very easy game to construct. A green cloth was draped over a 4ft × 3ft table, with the woods being depicted by some ready-made trees bought from S & A Scenics.

ARMY COMPOSITION

The army lists from Chapter 19 provided an excellent basis for the respective wargaming forces. So far as the English army was concerned, the deployment of interspersed units of archers and men-at-arms had to be possible, in order to replicate the historical deployment (assuming our wargaming Henry V so desired). Accordingly, four units of archers and three of men-at-arms were selected. The remaining unit represented the commoner elements equipped with close combat weaponry; as a result, billmen were chosen.

As for the French, the cavalry presence was accounted for by the maximum two units of mounted men-at-arms permitted. Our wargaming Constable d'Albret, the French commander, hoped that those would have more effect than in the historical battle. The lower orders were represented by the minimum allocation of one unit of crossbowmen and two of commoners; this would reflect the limited effect of both troop types in the real battle. That left three units, which comprised dismounted men-at-arms. Our wargaming d'Albret would like to have deployed the maximum listed allocation of four; unfortunately, a re-enactment does not always allow for the most effective troop types to be deployed at full strength – something a wargames general must account for in his or her plans.

PLANS AND DEPLOYMENT

Two special rules had to be devised to depict the Agincourt scenario. The first of these related to the weather, specifically mud. This was held to prevent any movement in woods (thereby preventing any unhistorical outflanking attacks from the French), and would reduce movement rates of all troops in open terrain by 25 per cent.

The second rule had to take account of the French nobility's insistence that they be in the forefront of the battle. Accordingly, it was decided that the front rank of

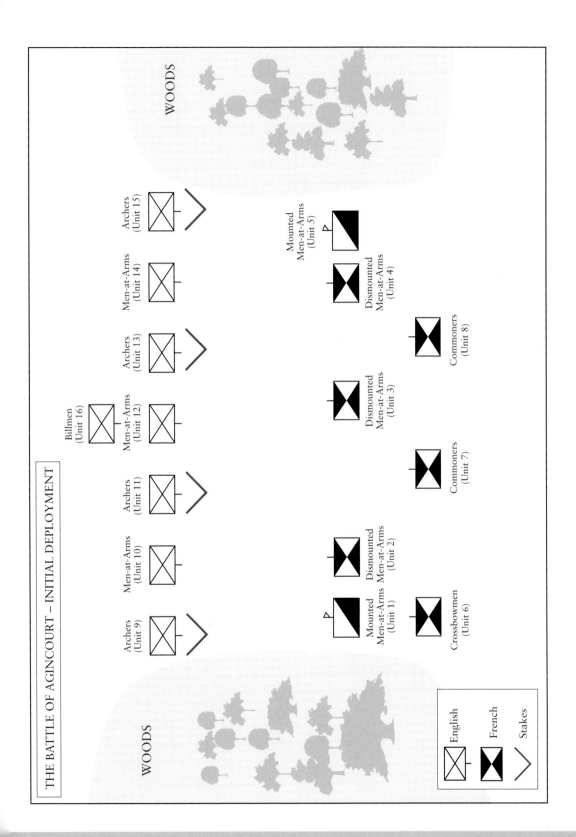

THE BATTLE OF AGINCOURT – INITIAL DEPLOYMENT

WOODS

WOODS

Archers
(Unit 15)

Men-at-Arms
(Unit 14)

Archers
(Unit 13)

Billmen
(Unit 16)

Men-at-Arms
(Unit 12)

Archers
(Unit 11)

Men-at-Arms
(Unit 10)

Archers
(Unit 9)

Mounted
Men-at-Arms
(Unit 5)

Dismounted
Men-at-Arms
(Unit 4)

Commoners
(Unit 8)

Dismounted
Men-at-Arms
(Unit 3)

Commoners
(Unit 7)

Dismounted
Men-at-Arms
(Unit 2)

Mounted
Men-at-Arms
(Unit 1)

Crossbowmen
(Unit 6)

English

French

Stakes

units could only consist of the aristocracy (mounted and dismounted men-at-arms), and that all units of nobility had to deploy in the vanguard. The second line had therefore to comprise commoners and crossbowmen.

Faced with these rules, our wargaming d'Albret (who had to deploy first, thanks to the parameters of the English army list special rule no. 2) was somewhat circumscribed. He placed his mounted men-at-arms on the flanks, ready to charge the expected archer opposition (the English invariably deployed archers on their wings). His dismounted men-at-arms were placed at intervals, allowing gaps for the units of commoners or crossbowmen in the front line, but was forced to make the best of a bad job. The commoners would at best be able to reinforce the front line reasonably quickly.

Our wargaming Frenchman's positioning of the crossbowmen was more contentious. D'Albret placed these on the left wing, behind the mounted men-at-arms. Their field of fire would inevitably be blocked by the two units of nobles (nos 1 and 2) in front of them, but d'Albret hoped that their fire would have an effect if the initial flanking attack failed.

The English deployment was straightforward. As d'Albret had guessed, our wargaming Henry V decided to replicate the historical deployment already illustrated in the English army list in Chapter 19. Archers and men-at-arms were interspersed, with the bowmen on the flanks. Stakes were naturally employed in front of the archer units, increasing their protection from attack. The only difference from the model deployment from Chapter 19 lay in the obvious fact that billmen (rather than hobilars) were in reserve, in the centre of the English line.

The English array looked distinctly formidable: our wargaming Henry V had clearly done his homework. Still, d'Albret reflected, however strong the English army was, his miniature Frenchmen could hardly be expected to do worse than their historical counterparts. Both sides therefore looked forward to the battle with some eagerness; the Englishman wanted to repeat history, while the Frenchman wished to change it.

TURN-BY-TURN ANALYSIS

The first three turns of this battle saw d'Albret order a general advance towards Henry V's lines, with the mounted men-at-arms (units 1 and 5) naturally to the fore. However, our wargaming Henry was well aware of the threat a rapid mounted assault could pose to Heavy Archers (especially with the first round combat bonus enjoyed by Mounted Knights). Accordingly, each French mounted unit was engaged by two English archers (units 9 and 11 targeted unit 1; 13 and 15 assailed unit 5). The result of this concentrated fire, and a disastrous attempt by the French to cross the stakes in front of units 9 and 15 (both units of mounted men-at-arms failed their morale tests), led to catastrophic results. Unit 1 was eliminated before engaging its foes; whereas unit 5 was reduced to a single base.

End of Turn 3

French

English

Eliminated Units

One unit (1)

None

However, the slaughter inflicted upon the mounted men-at-arms had meant that the English archers had been unable to concentrate upon their brethren on foot. Accordingly, the French dismounted men-at-arms (units 2, 3 and 4) were able to attack their English counterparts on turn 4. A protracted struggle ensued, with a conflict of almost epic proportions occurring: this was due to the endurance displayed by troops in extra-heavy armour – Foot Knight units tend to achieve their armour saving rolls. This contrasts with their mounted equivalents, who lacked similar staying power (deflecting hits on rolls of 3–6 compared with 4–6 may not sound a huge difference; but when one realises that it is in reality more effective by 17 per cent, one can appreciate just so many Medieval knights fought on foot).

While all this was going on d'Albret had not forgotten his commoners (units 7 and 8). These advanced upon two of the archer units (11 and 13), preventing them turning to engage the dismounted men-at-arms in flank. As for the crossbowmen (unit 6), these engaged in a missile duel with the archers (unit 9) on the French left flank. This distraction served to prevent the English from engaging the nearest French dismounted men-at-arms (unit 2) in their flank, but it must be said that the crossbowmen suffered grievously. This is principally because the crossbow, with its low rate of fire, is chiefly useful against armoured troops. This is due to the fact that the saving roll of the latter tends to be negated by the crossbow's penetrating power – a factor that other weapons do not possess to such a marked extent (with the exception of firearms). When engaging lightly armoured troops, however, penetration is not essential; rapid fire is. As a consequence, the crossbowmen (whose bases only hit their targets on dice rolls of 5–6) suffered compared with longbowmen (whose arrows register on rolls of 3–6).

Most of the hand-to-hand combat during turn 5 saw few meaningful results. There was one exception. This turn saw the final elimination of the remaining unit of mounted men-at-arms (unit 5); although it managed to fight with some effect, eliminating two bases from its archer opponents (unit 15).

End of Turn 5

French

English

Eliminated Units

Two units (1 and 5)

None

By turn 7 all French units save the crossbowmen (unit 6) were engaged in hand-to-hand combat. One unit of commoners (7) had, however, suffered grievous losses from archery while crossing the stakes in front of their target unit (11). This resulted in its elimination.

End of Turn 7	Eliminated Units
French	Three units (1, 5 and 7)
English	None

By turn 8, the English archers had begun to emulate their forebears by attacking the flanks of French units engaged in hand-to-hand combat. Thus it was that unit 15 attacked the right flank of unit 4 (and had already been doing so from turn 6), and unit 11 turned to its left to engage another body of dismounted men-at-arms (unit 3).

However, our wargaming Henry V was not having things all his own way. D'Albret's remaining unit of commoners (unit 8) had succeeded in eliminating their archer opponents (unit 13) in mêlée (the limited defensive ability of light armour had proved significant here).Following this victory, d'Albret ordered the commoners to turn to their right and engage the nearest English men-at-arms (unit 14) on their flank. Our French general could have ordered a left turn instead (attacking unit 12 in flank); but this made little sense, given that such a move would have exposed the commoners to a flanking attack from the English billmen (unit 16) in turn. The situation at the end of turn 8 is illustrated on the map provided.

End of Turn 8	Eliminated Units
French	Three units (1, 5 and 7)
English	One unit (13)

For the first time in the battle, King Henry had cause for concern. His left flank was beginning to look weak, so he ordered his billmen (unit 16) to turn 45° to their left and advance towards the beleaguered sector. This move would also serve to protect the English centre from any outflanking moves. The prudence of this step soon became evident: the men-at-arms on the left (unit 14) were unable to withstand the combined pressure to their front and flank, and were wiped out. This allowed the French commoners (unit 8) to turn and face the advancing billmen (unit 16), while the victorious dismounted men-at-arms (unit 4) turned to their right and engaged the English archers (unit 15) in hand-to-hand combat.

End of Turn 9	Eliminated Units
French	Three units (1, 5 and 7)
English	Two units (13 and 14)

Turn 10 saw the billmen (unit 16) engage the commoners (unit 8): a protracted and indecisive duel ensued (due chiefly to some unfeasibly lucky armour saving rolls and morale test successes achieved by the French). By turn 11, our wargaming

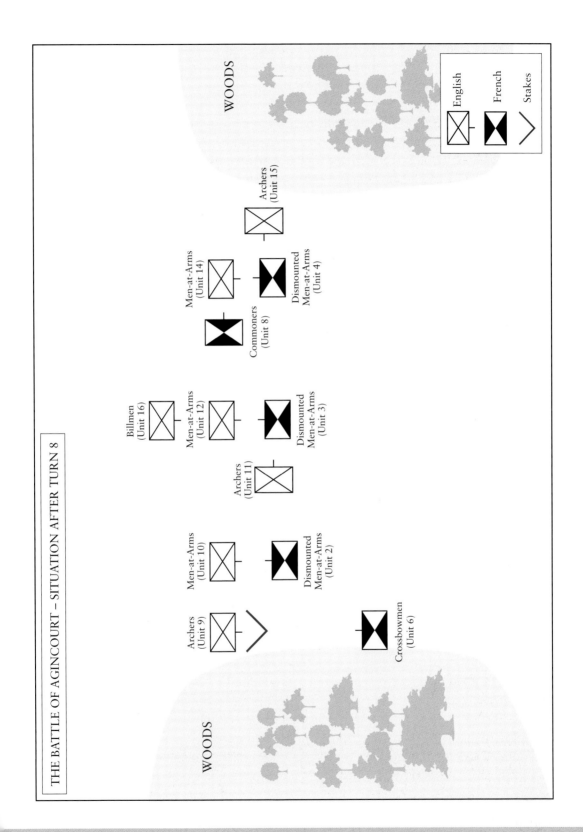

THE BATTLE OF AGINCOURT – SITUATION AFTER TURN 8

WOODS

WOODS

Archers (Unit 15)

Men-at-Arms (Unit 14)

Dismounted Men-at-Arms (Unit 4)

Commoners (Unit 8)

Billmen (Unit 16)

Men-at-Arms (Unit 12)

Dismounted Men-at-Arms (Unit 3)

Archers (Unit 11)

Men-at-Arms (Unit 10)

Dismounted Men-at-Arms (Unit 2)

Archers (Unit 9)

Crossbowmen (Unit 6)

English
French
Stakes

Henry decided that all units should be engaged in mêlée, since it was obvious that the French were putting up a rather effective display (as was to be demonstrated later in the turn when the dismounted men-at-arms (unit 4) eliminated the English archers (unit 15)). Accordingly, the remaining archers (unit 9) were ordered to cease shooting at the French crossbowmen (unit 6), cross their stakes, and engage the nearest enemy dismounted men-at-arms (unit 2) in flank. Although this did expose the archers to a flanking assault from the crossbowmen, the latter had been reduced to just one base thanks to the effect of the English longbow fire (the French crossbows had only been able to destroy a single English base in return). As a consequence, any attack from the crossbowmen (unit 6) would only have a limited impact.

End of Turn 11	Eliminated Units
French	Three units (1, 5 and 7)
English	Three units (13, 14 and 15)

Turn 12 saw the combined frontal and flanking English attacks have a serious effect upon their French victims (units 2 and 3). However, the latter bodies of dismounted men-at-arms were still in the battle (albeit being reduced to one remaining base in each case). The remaining contingent of French dismounted men-at-arms (unit 4) was ordered to advance towards the English billmen (unit 16), thereby assisting the beleaguered commoners (unit 8). They would, however, not arrive until turn 15, thanks to the effects of the mud. Meanwhile, the French crossbowmen (unit 6) engaged the English archers (unit 9) in their flank. The situation at this stage of the battle is illustrated on the map provided.

Turns 13 and 14 saw the culmination of brutal hand-to-hand fighting in the centre. It ended with the elimination of the French dismounted men-at-arms (units 2 and 3). Notwithstanding the fact that their brethren (unit 4) were advancing upon the English billmen with evil intent, the writing was now on the wall for d'Albret.

End of Turn 14	Eliminated Units
French	Five units (1, 2, 3, 5 and 7)
English	Three units (13, 14 and 15)

On turn 15, our wargaming Henry V was able to target the crossbowmen (unit 6). The English archers (unit 9) were now able to turn to their front and thereby avoid being taken in flank; meanwhile, Henry's men-at-arms (unit 10) could hit the crossbowmen's flanks. The combined effect of this assault eliminated their victim; and with the French reduced to two units, the battle had ended in an English victory.

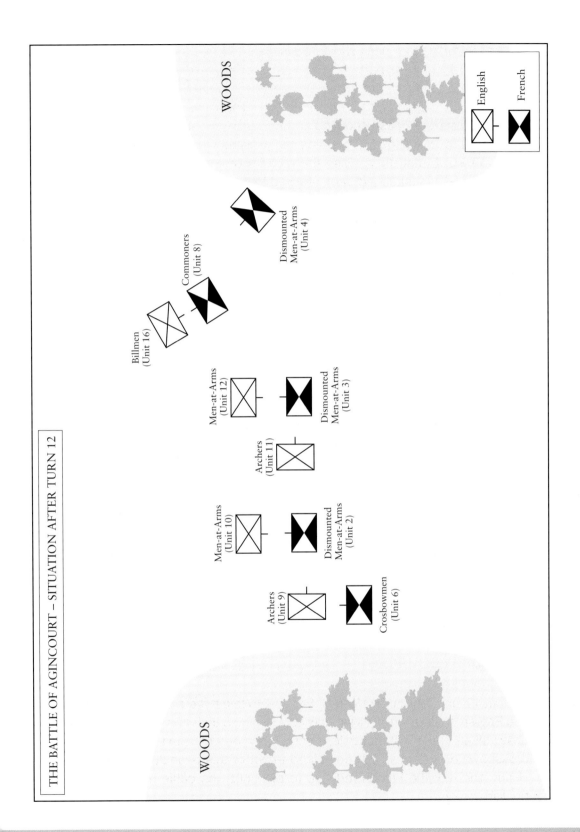

THE BATTLE OF AGINCOURT – SITUATION AFTER TURN 12

WOODS

WOODS

English

French

Dismounted
Men-at-Arms
(Unit 4)

Commoners
(Unit 8)

Billmen
(Unit 16)

Men-at-Arms
(Unit 12)

Dismounted
Men-at-Arms
(Unit 3)

Archers
(Unit 11)

Men-at-Arms
(Unit 10)

Dismounted
Men-at-Arms
(Unit 2)

Archers
(Unit 9)

Crosbowmen
(Unit 6)

End of Turn 15	**Eliminated Units**
French	Six units (1, 2, 3, 5, 6 and 7)
English	Three units (13, 14 and 15)

CONCLUSIONS AND SUMMARY

Although the French lost the battle, our wargaming d'Albret put in a good performance that markedly improved upon their historical display (uncharitable critics could point out that this would not be difficult); although the original d'Albret had actually formulated a decent plan – only to be sabotaged by the interference of the French nobility. In particular, the decision to launch the dismounted men-at-arms at the same time as their mounted comrades, meant that the latter would attract most of the English archery; as a result, the nobles on foot could reach the enemy lines with relatively little disruption from longbow fire. Similarly, using the commoners to engage the archers in the centre made good sense, since the latter could not turn to their flanks and engage the French dismounted men-at-arms if they had to fight the commoners. It is true that the crossbowmen had little effect, but this was as much due to the special rules forcing d'Albret to deploy them in the second rank, as anything else.

Unfortunately for the French wargamer, his English counterpart was on equally good form. Our modern-day Henry V adopted historical tactics, and seized all opportunities well. His willingness to use the English archers to attack the flanks of enemy units was particularly noteworthy, and showed the lessons of history had been thoroughly absorbed. Moreover, using billmen to avert the crisis on the English left also showed sound tactical acumen.

In essence, this contest featured two players at the very top of their game. On such occasions, victory will inevitably go to the player with the superior army – and in an Agincourt scenario, with muddy terrain and a position that cannot be outflanked, that meant that Henry V won again.

PRIMARY SOURCES

Curry, Anne (ed.). *The Battle of Agincourt: Sources and Interpretations*, Boydell, 2000

SECONDARY SOURCES

Bennett, Matthew. *Agincourt 1415*, Osprey, 1991
Burne, Lt Col Alfred H. *The Agincourt War*, Wordsworth, 1999 (originally 1956)
Keegan, John. *The Face of Battle*, Penguin, 1976

Appendix I

Figure Sizes, Scales and Prices

Although the major figure sizes are 25mm, 20mm (for plastic figures), 15mm and 6mm, a vast range is now available. They are listed below, together with a description of their advantages and defects for wargaming purposes. I have also provided a guide to how much an average army is likely to cost. This can obviously be seen as a very rough estimate, since prices inevitably change: they are only accurate at the time of writing. Nevertheless, the reader should have some idea how much he or she will have to pay for a general wargames army (of approximately 80 infantry and 24 cavalry figures).

1)   54mm/1:32 scale. These figures were used by H.G. Wells in his book *Little Wars*, which started the wargaming hobby. For today's wargamers, metal figures in this scale are rather expensive (especially if the ready-painted toy soldiers are purchased). Plastic miniatures are much cheaper, however, making wargaming in this scale a financially viable proposition.

The wargamer should be aware that while these figures look superb, they will need a very large table to deploy upon. A minimum of 8ft × 5ft is advisable – or alternatively a back garden.

Current price per army: painted metal figures = £1,300; unpainted metal figures = £400; unpainted plastic figures = £50

2)   42mm. Metal figures of this size are produced by Irregular Miniatures. They provide a cheaper option of gaming with large-scale metal figures than is possible with 54mm armies. However, as is the case with their larger brethren, they do require a big wargames table.

Current price per army = £130

3) 25/28mm. This is the original metal wargaming size, and these figures look absolutely splendid when painted. Readers should, however, be aware that many manufacturers produce ranges of these miniatures, and that many vary in size. The more expensive figures in particular tend to be larger than their cheaper fellows (this increase in size allows designers to include fine detail in their miniatures). These large versions tend to be listed as 28mm rather than the more traditional 25mm – a broad convention that has been followed here. These larger figures may need to have bases bigger than those suggested in the rules; in any event, all 25mm and 28mm armies fight best on larger tables: at least 5ft × 4ft is suggested.

Current price per army: 28mm = £130; 25mm = £80

(Readers should be warned that this price guide is even more approximate than the others listed: some 28mm figures will be cheaper, and 25mm products can conversely be rather more expensive.)

4) 20mm/1:72 scale plastic figures. Although 1:72 scale actually measures at 25mm, it is a wargamer's convention to define plastic products (and a few metal miniatures of this size) as 20mm. This is in order to distinguish between 1:72 plastic and those metal figures listed as 25mm. Plastic figures have the advantage of being remarkably cheap and very lightweight (this is a big factor when transporting one's army to a friend's house or flat for a wargame). Battles can be fought on a table as small as 4ft × 3ft.

Current price per army = £20

5) 15mm. As outlined in *Wargaming: An Introduction*, these metal figures became necessary when huge wargames (of over 200 miniatures per army) were in fashion. They allow for fine detail to be painted on each figure, and do take up much less space than 25mm miniatures. They will never look quite as impressive as armies consisting of larger figures, but only need a table of 4ft × 3ft for a viable game.

Current price per army = £30

6) 10mm. This new scale of metal miniatures has been popularised by Games Workshop's *Warmaster* fantasy game. I would suggest using the same bases as for 15mm figures, but deploying double the number of 10mm miniatures on each (as an alternative, use the standard number of figures on bases of 20mm × 20mm). These miniatures are beginning to make their mark on the hobby, owing to the fact that they have enough detail to look impressive when painted, without having so much as to be difficult to paint. A 4ft × 3ft table is appropriate for bases of 40mm × 20mm; 3ft × 2ft will suffice for the smaller 20mm × 20mm bases.

Current price per army: 40mm × 30mm bases = £30; 20mm × 20mm bases = £15

7) 6mm. These tiny figures were originally developed for Second World War wargames, in order to fit huge forces of tanks on small tables. Their use inevitably spread to other periods. Detailed painting is clearly impossible with such minute miniatures, but the main areas of the figures can be covered; and the armies do look very good en masse. I would suggest that the best option is to buy those figures that come ready based, as this saves time gluing miniatures to separate bases. 6mm battles can easily be fought on a table measuring 3ft × 2ft.

Current price per army = £10

8) 2mm. Unbelievable as it may seem, one company (Irregular Miniatures) really does produce figures of this size. Although mass battles can be fought using these miniatures, it is inevitably impossible to have any detailed painting on figures that are one step up from cardboard counters. I would suggest fielding approximately four of the ready made 2mm bases on a 40mm × 20mm base. However, the largest battles of the Ancient and Medieval world can be fought on a 3ft × 2ft table. If the wargamer wishes to buy these figures, I would suggest purchasing the ready-made armies supplied by the relevant manufacturer.

Current price per army = £9

The reader will have observed that I have suggested different base and table sizes, depending on which scale of figure he or she prefers. This variation is so that the figures look right; squeezing 54mm armies on a 4ft × 3ft battlefield creates a somewhat farcical impression, for example. Similar aesthetic considerations apply to movement rules and firing ranges: battles with 25mm figures may benefit from using inches rather than centimetres; and 54mm miniatures could not only make a similar switch, but could also double all measurements (so that a Heavy Infantry unit would move 16in rather than 8cm per turn).

Appendix II

Useful Addresses

The following addresses, telephone numbers and website details (where applicable) will give the wargamer an idea of where to start collecting. Any enquiries by post should always be accompanied by a fairly large (A4-size) stamped addressed envelope (two first-class stamps). This may seem pricey, but any catalogues (and sample figures) can weigh a fair amount, and therefore cost more than a standard letter to post. Do bear in mind that addresses and other contact details are liable to change. Also, note that many manufacturers are unable to receive personal callers, so do not on any account turn up on their doorstep!

1) MAGAZINES

These should be the first port of call for any wargamer. Both the journals listed below should be available over the counter in most branches of W.H. Smith, and can in any case be ordered through any local newsagent. Subscription enquiries should be made to the following addresses:

Miniature Wargames®, Pireme Publishing Ltd, Suite 13, Wessex House, St Leonards Road, Bournemouth, BH8 8QS. Tel: 01202 297 344. Web: www.miniwargames.com.

Wargames Illustrated, Stratagem, PO Box 6712, Newark, Nottinghamshire, NG24 1GY. Web: www.wargamesillustrated.net.

Both magazines are monthly publications. They contain excellent articles and are required reading for all wargamers. Moreover, all significant figure manufacturers advertise their latest releases in these journals, which provides another reason for buying them.

The following magazines are not yet available from W.H. Smith. They are, however, first-class publications that every wargamer should read. Copies and subscriptions can be obtained from the addresses listed below.

Battlegames, Battlegames Ltd, 17 Granville Road, Hove, East Sussex, BN3 1TG. Web: www.battlegames.co.uk.

Wargames Journal, web: www.wargamesjournal.com.

Wargames Soldiers & Strategy, Revistas Profesionales S.L., c/o Valentin Beato, 42–3a Madrid 28077, Spain. Web: www.revistasprofesionales.com.

2)   MILITARY BOOK SUPPLIERS

Caliver Books and Hersants offer a huge range of military history books and wargames rules. Tabletop Games supply a large selection of new rulesets.

Caliver Books, 816–18 London Road, Leigh-on-Sea, Essex, SS9 3NH. Tel: 01702 473986. Web: www.caliverbooks.com.

Hersants Military Books, 4 Delamere Drive, Swindon, SN3 4XE. Tel: 01793 821124. Web: www.hersantsbooks.com.

Tabletop Games, Reading Enterprise Hub, The University of Reading, Earley Gate, Reading, RE6 6AU. Tel: 0118 9357369. Web: www.tabletopgames.com.

Wargames Research Group, The Keep, Le Marchant Barracks, London Road, Devizes, Wiltshire, SN10 2GR. Tel: 0138 0724 558. The Wargames Research Group pioneered Ancient wargaming, and are at the cutting edge of developments to this day. Their books and rulesets are well worth purchasing.

3)   MODEL FIGURE MANUFACTURERS

It should be noted that there are some excellent wargames figure companies arising all the time. It must not be assumed that I am listing all possible manufacturers in the list below. The companies in question are, however, some of the more prominent.

Essex Miniatures, Unit 1, Shannon Centre, Shannon Square, Thames Estuary Industrial Estate, Canvey Island, Essex, SS8 0PE. Tel: 01268 682309. Web: www.essexminiatures.co.uk. Essex supply a large range of 15mm and 25mm figures from all periods, together with a variety of wargaming accessories, including terrain. They also have an in-house figure painting service.

Foundry Miniatures Ltd., 24–34 St Mark's Street, Nottingham, NG3 1DE. Tel: 0115 841 3000. Web: www.wargamesfoundry.com. Probably the largest figure company in the business, Foundry only produce 28mm miniatures. They do, however, have a very wide range, and the quality is outstanding. Unfortunately, they are more expensive than other manufacturers.

Front Rank Figurines, The Granary, Banbury Road, Lower Boddington, Daventry, Northamptonshire, NN11 6XY. Tel: 01327 262720. Web: www.frontrank.com. Another 28mm specialist, Front Rank produce a range of figures for the Hundred Years War and the Wars of the Roses. For gamers interested in these periods, the quality of these miniatures is second to none.

Games Workshop, Willow Road, Lenton, Nottingham, NG7 2WS. Tel: 0115 91 40000. Web: www.games-workshop.co.uk. Although Games Workshop are probably the world's most successful fantasy wargaming manufacturer, some of their 'Warhammer' figure ranges are suitable for historical wargaming. The 'Bretonnia' and 'Empire' miniatures are especially useful, since these can fill the ranks of many Medieval armies in 28mm scale. The reader would benefit greatly from visiting his or her nearest Games Workshop store (incidentally, the Warhammer fantasy game is an excellent product, for those who wish to sample this variety of wargaming).

Gripping Beast, 3 Shor Street, Evesham, WR11 3AT. Tel: 01386 761751. Web: grippingbeast@btconnect.com. Yet another 28mm specialist, Gripping Beast are famous for their wide range of Dark Ages figures.

Irregular Miniatures, 3 Apollo Street, Heslington Road, York, YO10 5AP. Tel: 01904 671101. Web: www.irregularminiatures.co.uk. Irregular are in many ways a unique company, in that they produce a huge selection in every single available size of figure. All ranges are moreover remarkably cheap, and their mail-order service is probably the most efficient in the hobby.

Miniature Figurines Ltd., 1-5 Graham Road, Southampton, Hampshire, SO14 0AX. Tel: 023 8022 0855. Web: www.miniaturefigurines.co.uk. The grandfather of all wargames firms still produces a huge range of 25mm figures – although it would be fair to say that these are no longer state of the art. Minifigs does, however, sell an excellent selection of high-quality 15mm miniatures.

Peter Pig, 36 Knightsdale Road, Weymouth, Dorset, DT4 OHS. Tel: 01305 760384. Web: www.peterpig.co.uk. These 15mm specialists manufacture a wide range of

Wars of the Roses figures, and a smaller selection of miniatures from other periods. They also produce sets of wargames rules that are among the most interesting in the hobby.

Old Glory Corporation, Institute House, New Kyo, Stanley, County Durham, DH9 7TJ. Tel: 01207 283 332. Web: www.oldgloryuk.com. Old Glory do produce a wide range of 15mm and 25mm figures, but are most famous for manufacturing the largest selection of 10mm miniatures currently available.

Warrior Miniatures, 14 Tiverton Avenue, Glasgow, G32 9NX. Tel: 0141 778 3426. Website: www.warriorminiatures.com. All Warrior's figures are remarkably good value, but they are renowned for their 25mm army deals. These work out at just £30 for 100 miniatures. Do, however, be aware of the cautionary point I made in *Wargaming: An Introduction*; only buy a large number of figures in one go if you are absolutely sure you want that particular army (thereby avoiding a drop in enthusiasm upon seeing a horde of miniatures needing painting). Should you feel inclined to take the plunge, however, no manufacturer offers better army deals than Warrior Miniatures.

4) PLASTIC FIGURE STOCKISTS
Harfields Military Figure Specialists, 32 St Winifreds Road, Biggin Hill, Westerham, Kent, TN16 3HP. Tel: 01959 576269. Web: www.harfields.com. Although the local toy or (if the reader is lucky enough to have access to one) model shop will always supply plastic figures, Harfields are guaranteed to fill in any gaps. A range of sale items, and out of production second-hand figures (some of which are in mint condition), is also available.

5) WARGAMES TERRAIN MANUFACTURERS
S & A Scenics, 44 King Drive, Carnforth, Lancashire, LA5 9AG. Tel: 01524 733344. Web: www.scenics.co.uk. This company produces a comprehensive range of functional terrain at a reasonable price.

6) MILITARY HISTORY SOCIETIES
The following organisations provide an outstanding forum for enthusiasts in the relevant periods of history. As such, they are well worth joining, especially as they produce regular journals that are excellent. To make an initial contact, simply send a standard-sized SAE with a first- or second-class stamp, or consult the relevant website.

The Society of Ancients, Membership Secretary, Andrew Nicoll, 39 Kempton Grove, Cheltenham, Gloucestershire, GL51 0JX. Web: www.soa.org.uk. This society covers the entire period from 3000 BC to AD 1485. Every wargamer should join.

The Lance and Longbow Society, 9 Willow Close, Ruskington, Sleaford, Lincolnshire, NG34 9GD. Web: www.lanceandlongbow.com. This society covers the epoch from 1040 to 1526, with the most popular periods being the Hundred Years War and the Wars of the Roses. Any enthusiast for Medieval warfare should join.

7) FIGURE PAINTERS

Readers who wish to avail themselves of the services provided by the master figure painters whose work adorns this book should contact the following addresses:

Brush Strokes, 38 Southland Crescent, Eltham, London, SE9 2SB. Tel: 020 8850 9385. Web: www.paulbaker.org.uk.

GJM Figurines, 74 Crofton Road, Orpington, Kent, BR6 8HY. Tel: 01689 828474. Web: www.gjmfigurines.co.uk.

Kevin Dallimore used to run the renowned Special Forces painting service in conjunction with Graham Green. Kevin no longer paints figures commercially, but many examples of his work can be seen on his website at www.kevindallimore.co.uk. Those who want to learn how to paint their own figures to the highest standards are advised to buy Kevin's excellent book, *Foundry Miniatures Painting and Modelling Guide* (Foundry Books).

Index